Library of
Davidson College

BRODSKY'S POETICS AND AESTHETICS

Also by Lev Loseff
ON THE BENEFICENCE OF CENSORSHIP: Aesopian Language in Modern Russian Literature

Also by Valentina Polukhina
JOSEPH BRODSKY: A Poet for Our Time

Joseph Brodsky (c. 1978)
(*from the personal collection of Valentina Polukhina*)

Brodsky's Poetics and Aesthetics

Edited by
Lev Loseff
Professor of Russian Literature at Dartmouth College
and
Valentina Polukhina
*Lecturer in Russian Literature
University of Keele*

St. Martin's Press   New York

© The Macmillan Press Ltd., 1990
Selection and editorial matter © Lev Loseff and Valentina Polukhina, 1990

All rights reserved. For information, write:
Scholarly and Reference Division,
St. Martin's Press, Inc., 175 Fifth Avenue,
New York, N.Y. 10010

First published in the United States of America in 1990

Printed in Hong Kong

ISBN 0–312–04511–5

Library of Congress Cataloging-in-Publication Data
Brodsky's poetics and aesthetics/edited by Lev Loseff and Valentina Polukhina.
p. cm.
ISBN 0–312–04511–5
1. Brodsky, Joseph, 1940– —Criticism and interpretation.
I. Loseff, Lev, 1937– . II. Polukhina, V. A. (Valeriĭ Anatol'evich)
PG3479.4.R64Z59   1990
891.71'44—dc20   89–70322
                                                            CIP

Contents

Foreword vii

Acknowledgement ix

Abbreviations x

Notes on the Contributors xi

1 Nobel Lecture, 1987   1
  Joseph Brodsky

2 The Complicity of the Real: Affinities in the Poetics of Brodsky and Mandelstam   12
  Leon Burnett

3 Politics/Poetics   34
  Lev Loseff

4 Variations on the Theme of Exile   56
  George L. Kline

5 The Ironic Journey into Antiquity   89
  Georges Nivat

6 Notes on the Sonnets to Mary Queen of Scots   98
  Peter France

7 'Polden'v komnate'   124
  Gerald S. Smith

8 A Journey from Petersburg to Istanbul   135
  Tomas Venclova

9 Similarity in Disparity   152
  Valentina Polukhina

10	Beginning at the End: Rhyme and Enjambment in Brodsky's Poetry *Barry P. Scherr*	180
11	An Interview with Bella Akhmadulina *Valentina Polukhina*	198

Index   205

Foreword

> Indeed we wouldn't know,
> Whether Pushkin was great or not,
> Without their doctoral dissertations
> Which shed light on everything[,]

wrote Pasternak in his 'Four Fragments About Blok'. Joseph Brodsky, who has been a Russian poet for thirty years, is no more in need of scholastic glorification than his predecessors – Pushkin, Blok and Pasternak. It is not the task of literary scholars to create the reputation of a living poet, and they should be cautious when approaching modern-day literature.

Of course the definition of 'modern-day' varies. The distinguished academician V.N. Peretz (1870–1935) considered it foolish and childish to study anything written after 1700. Boris Gasparov, a contemporary scholar, believes that nobody should attempt to investigate works which appeared after the year of his or her birth.

Leaving these, rather ritualistic, niceties aside, we believe that research in the realm of current literature has its own cognitive value: both as exegesis and as poetic analysis.

Exegetical commentary involves the reader in what Gershenzon called 'slow reading', i.e. re-reading and reading with a broad intertextual perspective in mind; while applying the analytical methods of poetics to contemporary works (may the ghost of Pasternak forgive us!) indeed sheds new light on the whole corpus of a national literature.

The authors of this collection do not share any theoretical or methodological platform; the only factor uniting them is a common interest in the work of this outstanding poet, as well as in Russian poetry and poetics in general.

The essays by Peter France, G.S. Smith and Tomas Venclova are primarily focused on individual works of Brodsky while Leon Burnett, George Kline, Georges Nivat and Lev Loseff investigate certain recurrent motifs in the poet's oeuvre. Valentina Polukhina and Barry Scherr approach Brodsky's poetry from the point of view of general poetics: they discuss problems of simile and rhyme respectively. Valentina Polukhina's conversation with Bella Akhmadulina provides exciting glimpses into the perception of Brodsky by another famous poet, who belongs to a different school of poetry – and who is a woman.

Some of the authors in the collection contributed to *Poetika Brodskogo*, published in Russian in 1986 by Hermitage. The present volume continues the free critical discussion begun there, or rather continues the *beginning* of a discussion which, in our view, promises to be productive.

LEV LOSEFF
VALENTINA POLUKHINA

NOTE

The variety of approaches adopted by the authors in this collection precludes total uniformity in such technical matters as the arrangement of references, footnoting, etc. Translations of quotations in the text were done by the authors (if not acknowledged otherwise).

L.L, V.P.

Acknowledgement

Acknowledgement is made to the Nobel Foundation for permission to include Brodsky's Nobel lecture (© Nobel Foundation 1987) in this collection of articles.

Abbreviations

The following abbreviations are used for those works of Brodsky's repeatedly cited in Russian and in English:

- S. *Stikhotvoreniya i poemy* (Short and Long Poems)
- O. *Ostanovka v pustyne* (A Halt in the Wilderness)
- K. *Konets prekrasnoi epokhi* (The End of a Beautiful Epoch)
- C. *Chast' rechi* (A Part of Speech)
- N. *Novye stansy k Avguste* (New Stanzas to Augusta)
- U. *Uraniya* (Urania)
- L. *Less Than One: Selected Essays*
- SP. *Selected Poems*
- PS. *A Part of Speech*

Notes on the Contributors

Bella Akhmadulina is a poet and has published several collections of poems, including *Taina* (Moscow, 1983) and *Sad* (Moscow, 1987).

Leon Burnett is Lecturer in Russian Literature, University of Essex, Colchester, and has written essays on Mandelstam, Keats and Pushkin, has contributed to and edited *F.M. Dostoevsky (1821–1881). A Centenary Collection* (1981).

Peter France is Professor of French at the University of Edinburgh, is the author of *Poets of Modern Russia* (1982), and has translated poems of Blok, Pasternak, Gennady Aygi, Oleg Chukhontsev and Brodsky.

George L. Kline is Professor of Philosophy at Bryn Mawr College (Pennsylvania, USA), and is the author of *Spinoza in Soviet Philosophy* (1952, 1981) and several articles on Brodsky's poetry; he is the translator of *Boris Pasternak: Seven Poems* (1969, 1972) and *Joseph Brodsky: Selected Poems* (1973, 1974); has contributed translations to Brodsky's *A Part of Speech* (1980) and *To Urania* (1988).

Lev Loseff is a poet and Professor of Russian Literature at Dartmouth College (New Hampshire), and has published collections of poems *Chudesnyi desant* (1985) and *Tainyi sovetnik* (1987), *On the Beneficence of Censorship: Aesopian Language in Modern Russian Literature* (1984) and edited *Poetika Brodskogo* (1986).

Georges Nivat is Professor of Russian Literature at the University of Geneva (Switzerland), and is the author of *Sur Soljénitsyne* (1974), *Soljénitsyne* (1980) and *Vers la fin du mythe russe* (1983, 1988); co-editor of *Histoire de la Littérature russe* in seven volumes (1989), and translator into French of Bely, Gogol, Siniavsky, Solzhenitsyn and Brodsky.

Barry P. Scherr is Professor and Chairman, Department of Russian at Dartmouth College (New Hampshire), and has written an article on Brodsky (*Poetika Brodkogo*), *Russian Poetry: Meter, Rhythm, and Rhyme* (1986) and *Maxim Gorky* (1988).

Gerald S. Smith is Professor of Russian Literature, New College, Oxford, and is the author of *Song to Seven Strings; Russian Guitar Poetry and Soviet Mass Song* (1984) and editor of D.S. Mirsky's *Uncollected Writings on Russian Literature* (1989).

Valentina Polukhina is Lecturer in Russian Literature, Department of Modern Languages, University of Keele, Staffordshire, and has written *Joseph Brodsky: A Poet for Our Time* (1989), and essays on Khlebnikov, Pasternak, Akmatova, Tsvetaeva and Brodsky.

Tomas Venclova is a poet and Assistant Professor, Department of Slavic Languages and Literatures, Yale University, and has published *Unstable Equilibrium: Eight Russian Poetic Texts* (1986).

1
Nobel Lecture, 1987
Joseph Brodsky

I

For someone rather private, for someone who all his life has preferred his private condition to any role of social significance, and who went in this preference rather far – far from his motherland to say the least, for it is better to be a total failure in democracy than a martyr or *crème de la crème* in tyranny – for such a person to find himself all of a sudden on this rostrum is a somewhat uncomfortable and trying experience.

This sensation is aggravated not so much by the thought of those who stood here before me as by the memory of those who have been bypassed by this honour, who were not given this chance to address *urbi et orbi*, as they say, from this rostrum and whose cumulative silence is sort of searching, to no avail, for release through this speaker.

The only thing that can reconcile one to this sort of situation is the simple realisation that – for stylistic reasons, in the first place – one writer cannot speak for another writer, one poet for another poet especially; that had Osip Mandelstam, or Marina Tsvetaeva, or Robert Frost, or Anna Akhmatova, or Wystan Auden stood here, they could not have helped but speak precisely for themselves, and they, too, might have felt somewhat uncomfortable.

These shades disturb me constantly, they are disturbing me today as well. In any case, they do not spur one to eloquence. In my better moments, I deem myself their sum total, though invariably inferior to any one of them individually. For it is not possible to better them on the page; nor is it possible to better them in actual life. And it is precisely their lives, no matter how tragic or bitter they were, that often moves me – more often perhaps than the case should be – to regret the passage of time. If the next life exists – and I can no more deny them the possibility of eternal life than I can forget their existence in this one – if the next world does exist, they will, I hope, forgive me and the quality of what I am about to utter: after all, it is not one's conduct on the podium which dignity in our profession is measured by.

I have mentioned only five of them – those whose deeds and whose lot matter so much to me – if only because if it were not for them, I, both as a man and a writer, would amount to much less: in any case, I would not be standing here today. There were more of them, those shades, better still, sources of light – lamps? stars? – more, of course, than just five. And each one is capable of rendering me absolutely mute. The number of those is substantial in the life of any conscious man of letters; in my case, it's doubling, thanks to the two cultures to which fate has willed me to belong. Matters are not made easier by thoughts about contemporaries and fellow writers in both cultures, poets and fiction writers whose gifts I rank above my own and who, had they found themselves on this rostrum, would have already come to the point long ago, for surely they have more to tell the world than I do.

Therefore, I will allow myself to make a number of remarks here – disjointed, perhaps stumbling, and perhaps even perplexing in their randomness. However, the amount of time allotted to me to collect my thoughts, as well as my very occupation, will or may, I hope, shield me, at least partially, against charges of being chaotic. A man of my occupation seldom claims a systematic mode of thinking; at worst, he claims to having a system, but even that in his case is borrowing from a milieu, a social order, or from the pursuit of philosophy at a tender age. Nothing convinces an artist more of the arbitrariness of the means he resorts to to attain a goal – however permanent it may be – than the creative process itself, than the process of composition. Verse really does, in Akhmatova's words, grow from rubbish; the roots of prose are no more honourable.

II

If art teaches anything (to the artist, in the first place), it is the privateness of the human condition. Being the most ancient as well as the most literal form of private enterprise, it fosters in a man, knowingly or unwittingly, a sense of uniqueness, of individuality, of separateness – thus turning him from a social animal into a perceptible 'I'. Lots of things can be shared: a bed, a piece of bread, convictions, a mistress, but not a poem by, say, Rainer Maria Rilke. A work of art, of literature especially, and a poem, in particular, addresses a man *tête-à-tête*, entering with him into direct – free of any go-betweens – relations. It is for this reason that art in general, literature especially, and poetry in particular, is not exactly favoured by the champions of the common good, masters of the masses, heralds of historical necessity. For there, where art has stepped, where a poem has been read, they discover, in place of anticipated consent and unanimity, indifference and polyphony; in place of the resolve to act, inattention and fastidiousness. In other words, into the little zeros with which the champions of the common good and the rulers of the masses tend to operate, art introduces a 'period, period, comma, and a minus', transforming each zero into a tiny human, albeit not always pretty, face.

The great Baratynsky, speaking of his Muse, characterised her as possessing an 'uncommon visage'. It's in acquiring this 'uncommon visage' that the meaning of human existence seems to lie, since it is for this uncommonness that we are, as it were, prepared genetically. Regardless of whether one is a writer or a reader, his task consists first of all in mastering a life that is his own, not one imposed or prescribed from without, no matter how noble its appearance may be. For each of us is issued with but one life, and we know full well how it all ends. It would be regrettable to squander this one chance on someone else's appearance, someone else's experience, on a tautology – regrettable all the more because the heralds of historical necessity, at whose urging, a man may be prepared to agree to this tautology, will not go to the grave with him or give him so much as a thank-you.

Language and, presumably, literature are things that are more ancient and inevitable, more durable than any form of social organisation. The revulsion, irony, or indifference often expressed by literature towards the state is essentially the reaction of the permanent – better yet, the infinite – against the temporary, against the finite. To say the least, as long as the state permits itself to interfere with the affairs of literature, literature has the right to interfere with the affairs of the state. A political system, a form of social organisation, as any system in general, is by definition a form of the past tense that aspires to impose itself upon the present (and often on the future as well), and a man whose profession is language is the last one who can afford to forget this. The real danger for a writer is not so much the possibility (and often the certainty) of persecution on the part of the state, as it is the possibility of finding oneself mesmerised by the state's features; be they monstrous or undergoing changes for the better, they are always temporary.

The philosophy of the state, its ethics – not to mention its aesthetics – are always 'yesterday'; language, literature are always 'today', and often – particularly in the case where a political system is orthodox – they may even constitute 'tomorrow'. One of literature's merits is precisely that it helps a person to make the time of his existence more specific, to distinguish himself from the crowd of his predecessors as well as his like numbers, to avoid tautology – that is, the fate otherwise known by the honorific term, 'victim of history'. What makes art in general and literature in particular remarkable, what distinguishes them from life, is precisely that they abhor repetition. In everyday life you can tell the same joke three times and, having elicited laughter each time, become the life of the party. In art, though, this sort of conduct is called 'cliché'. Art is an unrecoiling weapon, and its development is determined not by the individuality of the artist but by the dynamics and the logic of the material itself, by the previous fate of the means that each time demand (or suggest) a qualitatively new aesthetic solution. Possessing its own genealogy, dynamics, logic, and future, art is not synonymous with, but, at best, parallel to history; and the manner by which it exists continually reinvents aesthetic reality. That is why it is often found 'ahead of progress', ahead of history whose main instrument is – should we not, once more, improve upon Marx – precisely the cliché.

Nowadays, there exists a rather widely held assertion, postulating that in his work a writer, in particular a poet, should make use of the language of the street, the language of the crowd. For all its democratic appearance, and its palpable advantages for a writer, this assertion is quite absurd and represents an attempt to subordinate art, in this case, literature, to history. It is only if we have resolved that it is time for Homo sapiens to come to a halt in his development that literature should speak the language of the people. Otherwise, it is the people who should speak the language of literature. On the whole, every new aesthetic reality makes man's ethical reality more precise. For aesthetics is the mother of ethics; the categories of 'good' and 'bad' are, first and foremost, aesthetic ones, at least etymologically preceding the categories of 'good' and 'evil'. If in ethics not 'all is permitted', it is precisely because not 'all is permitted' in aesthetics, because the number of colours in the spectrum is limited. The tender babe who cries and rejects the stranger or who, on the contrary, reaches out to him, does so instinctively, making an aesthetic choice, not a moral one.

Aesthetic choice is a highly individual matter and aesthetic experience is always a private one. Every new aesthetic reality makes one's experience even more private, and this kind of privacy, assuming at times the guise of literary (or some other) taste, can in itself turn out to be, if not a guarantee, then a form of defence against enslavement. For, a man with taste, particularly literary taste, is less susceptible to the refrains and rhythmical incantations peculiar to any version of political demagogy. The point is not so much that virtue does not constitute a guarantee for producing a masterpiece, as that evil, especially political evil, is always a bad stylist. The more substantial an individual's aesthetic experience is, the sounder his taste, the sharper his moral focus, the freer – though not necessarily the happier – he is.

It is certainly in this applied, rather than Platonic, sense that we should understand Dostoevsky's remark that beauty will save the world, or Matthew Arnold's belief that we shall be saved by poetry. It is probably too late for the world, but for the individual man, there always remains a chance. An aesthetic instinct develops in man rather rapidly, for, even without fully realising who he is and what he actually requires, a person instinctively knows what he does not like and what does not suit him. In an anthropological respect, let me reiterate, a human being is an aesthetic creature before he is an ethical one. Therefore, it is not the art – particularly literature – is a by-product of our species' development, but just the reverse. If what distinguishes us from other members of the animal kingdom is speech, then literature – and poetry in particular, being the highest form of locution – is, to put it bluntly, the goal of our species.

I am far from suggesting the idea of compulsory training in verse composition; nevertheless, the subdivision of society into intelligentsia and all the rest seems to me unacceptable. In moral terms, this situation is comparable to the subdivision of society into the poor and the rich; but if for the existence of social inequality it is still possible to find some purely physical or material grounds, for intellectual inequality these are inconceivable. Unlike anything else, in this respect equality has been guaranteed to us by nature. I am speaking not of education, but of the education in speech, the slightest imprecision in which may trigger the intrusion of false choice into one's life. The existence of literature prefigures existence on literature's plane of regard – and not only in the moral sense, but lexically as well. If a piece of music still allows a person the possibility or choosing between the passive role of a listener and the active one of performer, a work of literature – of the art which is, to use Montale's phrase, hopelessly semantic – enlists him in the role of performer only.

In this role, it would seem to me, a person should appear more often than in any other. Moreover, it seems to me that, as a result of the population explosion and the attendant, ever-increasing atomisation of society (i.e., the ever-increasing isolation of the individual), this role becomes more and more inevitable for a person. I do not suppose that I know more about living than anyone of my age, but it seems to me that, in the capacity of an interlocutor, a book is more reliable than a friend or a beloved. A novel or a poem is not a monologue, but the conversation of a writer with a reader, a conversation, I repeat, which is very private, excluding all others, if you will, mutually misanthropic. And in the moment of this conversation a writer is equal to a reader, as well as the other way around, regardless of whether this writer is a great one or not. This equality is the equality of consciousnesses, and it remains with a person for the rest of his life in the form of memory, foggy or distinct, and, sooner or later, appropriately or not, it conditions a person's conduct. It's precisely this that I have in mind, in speaking of the role of the performer, all the more natural for one because a novel or a poem is the product of mutual loneliness – of a writer or a reader.

In the history of our species, in the history of Homo sapiens, the book is anthropological development, similar essentially to the invention of the wheel. Having emerged in order to give us some idea, not so much of our origins as of what this sapien is capable of, a book constitutes a means of transportation through the space of experience, at the speed of a turning page. This movement, like every movement, becomes a flight from the common denominator, from an attempt to elevate this denominator's line, previously never reaching higher than the groin, to our heart, our consciousness, our imagination. This flight is the flight in the direction of 'uncommon visage', in the direction of the numerator, in the direction of individuality, in the direction of privacy. Regardless of whose image we are created in, we already number five billion, and there is no other future for a human being save that outlined by art. Otherwise, what lies ahead is the past – the political one, first of all, with all its mass police entertainments.

In any event, the condition of society in which art in general, and literature in particular, are the prerogative of a minority appears to me unhealthy and dangerous. I do not appeal for the replacement of the state with a library – although this thought has been visited upon me frequently – but there is no doubt in my mind that, should we have been choosing our leaders on the basis of their reading experience and not their political programmes, there would be much less grief on earth. It seems to me that a potential master of our fates should be asked first of all, not about how he imagines the course of his foreign policy, but about his attitude toward Stendhal, Dickens, Dostoevsky. If only because the lock and stock of literature is indeed human diversity and perversity, it turns out to be a reliable antidote for any attempt – whether familiar or yet to be invented – toward a total mass solution to the problems of human existence. As a form of moral insurance, at least, literature is much more dependable than a system of beliefs or a philosophical doctrine.

Since no laws can protect us from ourselves, no criminal code is capable of preventing a true crime against literature: though we can condemn the material suppression of literature – the persecution of writers, acts of censorship, the burning of books – we are powerless when it comes to its worst violation, that of not reading the books. For that crime, a person pays with his whole life; if the offender is a nation, it pays with its history. Living in the country I live in, I would be the first prepared to believe that there is a set dependency between a person's material well-being and his literary ignorance; what keeps me from doing so is the history of that country in which I was born and grew up. For, reduced to a cause-and-effect minimum, to a crude formula, the Russian tragedy is precisely the tragedy of a society in which literature turned out to be the prerogative of the minority: of the celebrated Russian intelligentsia.

I have no wish to enlarge upon the subject, no wish to darken this evening with thoughts of the tens of millions of human lives destroyed by other millions, since what occurred in Russia in the first half of the twentieth century occurred before the introduction of automatic small weapons – in the name of the triumph of a political doctrine whose unsoundness is already manifested in the fact that it requires human sacrifice for its realisation. I will just say that I believe – not empirically, alas, but only theoretically – that, for someone who has read a lot of Dickens, to shoot his like in the name of some idea is more problematic than for someone who has read no Dickens. And I am speaking precisely about reading Dickens, Sterne, Stendhal, Dostoevsky, Flaubert, Balzac, Melville, Proust, Musil, and so forth; that is, about literature, not literacy or education. A literate, educated person, to be sure, is fully capable, after reading this or that political treatise or tract, of killing his like, and even of experiencing, at that, a rapture of conviction. Lenin was literate, Stalin was literate, so was Hitler; as for Mao Tse-tung – he even wrote verse. What all these men had in common, though, was that their hit list was longer than their reading list.

However, before I move on to poetry, I would like to add that it would make sense to regard the Russian experience as a warning, if for no other reason than that the social structure of the West up till now is, on the whole, analogous to what existed in Russia prior to 1917. (This, by the way, is what explains the popularity in the West of the nineteenth-century Russian psychological novel, and the relative lack of success of contemporary Russian prose. The social relations that emerged in Russia in the twentieth century apparently seem no less exotic to the reader than do the names of the characters, which prevent him from identifying with them.) For example, the number of political parties alone, on the eve of the October coup in 1917, was in no way fewer than we find today in the United States or Britain. In other words, a dispassionate observer might remark that, in a certain sense, the nineteenth century is still going on in the West, while in Russia it came to an end; and if I say, it ended in tragedy, this is, in the first place, because of the course of that social – or chronological – change. For in a real tragedy, it is not the hero who perishes; it is the chorus.

III

Although, for a man whose mother tongue is Russian, to speak about political evil is as natural as digestion, I would like to change the subject now. What's wrong with discourses about the obvious is that they corrupt conscience with their easiness, with their quickness, with which they provide one with moral comfort, with the sensation of being right. Herein lies their temptation, similar in its nature to the temptation of a social reformer, who begets this evil. The realisation or, rather, comprehension of this temptation and rejection of it are, perhaps, responsible to a certain extent for the destinies of many of my contemporaries, responsible for the literature that emerged from under their pens. It, that literature, was neither a flight from history nor the muffling of memory, as it may seem from the outside. 'How can one write music after Auschwitz?' inquires Adorno, and one familiar with Russian history can repeat the same question by merely changing the name of the camp – and repeat it perhaps with even greater justification, since the number of people who perished in Stalin's camps surpasses by far the number of German prison-camp victims. 'And how can you eat lunch?' the American poet Mark Strand once retorted. In any case, the generation to which I belong has proven capable of writing that music.

That generation – the generation born precisely at the time when the Auschwitz crematoria were working full blast, when Stalin was at the zenith of his God-like, absolute power, which seemed sponsored by Mother Nature herself – that generation came into the world, it appears, in order to continue what, theoretically, was supposed to be interrupted in those crematoria, and in the anonymous common graves of Stalin's archipelago. The fact that not everything got interrupted, at least not in Russia, can in no small degree be credited to my generation, and I am no less proud of belonging to it than I am of standing here today. And the fact that I am standing here is a recognition of the services that generation has rendered to culture; recalling a phrase from Mandelstam, I would add, to world culture. Looking back, I can say again that we were beginning in an empty – indeed, a terrifyingly wasted – place, and that rather intuitively than consciously, we aspired precisely to the recreation of the effect of culture's continuity, to the reconstruction of its forms and tropes, toward filling its few surviving, and often totally compromised, forms, with our own new, or appearing to us as such, contemporary content.

There presumably existed another path: the path of further deformation, the poetics of ruins and debris, of minimalism, of choked breath. If we rejected it, it was not at all because we thought that it was the path of self-dramatisation, or because we were extremely animated by the idea of preserving the hereditary nobility of the forms of culture we knew, the forms that were equivalent, in our consciousness, to forms of human dignity. We rejected it because in reality the choice was not actually ours, but that of culture it seems – and this choice, again, was not moral but rather aesthetic. To be sure, it is natural for a person to perceive himself not as an instrument of culture, but, on the contrary, as its creator and custodian. But if today I assert the opposite, it is not because toward the close of the twentieth century there is a certain charm in paraphrasing Plotinus, Lord Shaftesbury, Schelling, or Novalis, but because, unlike anyone else, a poet always knows that what in the vernacular is called the voice of the Muse is, in reality, the dictate of the language; that it's not that the language happens to be his instrument, but that he is the means of language toward the continuation of its existence. Language, however, even if one imagines it as a certain animate creature (which would only be just), is not capable of ethical choice.

A person sets out to write a poem for a variety of reasons: to win the heart of his beloved; to express his attitude toward the reality surrounding him, be it a landscape or a state; to capture his state of mind at a given instant; to leave – as he thinks at that moment – a trace on the earth. He resorts to this form – the poem – most likely for unconsciously mimetic reasons: the black vertical clot of words amidst the white sheet of paper presumably reminds him of his own situation in the world, of the balance between space and his body. But regardless of the reasons for which he takes up the pen, and regardless of the effect produced by what emerges from beneath that pen on his audience – however great or small it may be – the immediate consequence of this enterprise is the sensation of coming into direct contact with language or, more precisely, the sensation of immediately falling into dependence on it, on everything that has already been uttered, written, and accomplished in it.

This dependence is absolute, despotic; but it unshackles as well. For, while always older than the writer, language still possesses the colossal centrifugal energy imparted to it by its temporal potential – that is by all time lying ahead. And this potential is determined not so much by the quantitative body of the nation that speaks it (though by that, too), as by the quality of the poem written in it. It will suffice to recall Dante. And that which is being created today in Russian or in English, for instance, secures the existence of these languages in the course of the next millennium also. The poet, I wish to repeat, is language's means for existence –

or, as my beloved Auden said, he is the one by whom it lives. I who write these lines will cease to be, as will you who read them. But the language in which they are written and in which you read them will remain not merely because language is more lasting than man, but because it is more capable of mutation.

One who writes a poem, however, writes it not because he courts fame with posterity, although often he hopes that a poem will outlive him, at least briefly. One who writes a poem writes it because the language prompts, or simply dictates, the next line. Beginning a poem, the poet as a rule does not know the way it's going to end, and at times he is very suprised by the way it turns out, since often it turns out better than he expected, often his thought carries further than he reckoned. And that is the moment when the future of language invades its present. There are, as we know, three modes of cognition: analytical, intuitive, and the mode that was known to the Biblical prophets, revelation. The distinction of poetry from other forms of literature lies in that it uses all three of them at once (gravitating primarily toward the second and the third). For all three of them are given in the language; and there are times when, by means of a single word, a single rhyme, the writer of a poem manages to find himself where no one has ever been before him, further, perhaps, than he himself would have wished for. The one who writes a poem writes it above all because verse writing is an extraordinary accelerator of conscience, of thinking, of comprehending the universe. Having experienced this acceleration once, one is no longer capable of abandoning the chance to repeat this experience; one falls into dependency on this process, the way others fall into dependence on drugs or on alcohol. One who finds himself in this sort of dependency on language is, I guess, what they call a poet.

Translated by Barry Rubin

2
The Complicity of the Real: Affinities in the Poetics of Brodsky and Mandelstam
Leon Burnett

> Poetry is, first of all, an art of references, allusions, linguistic and figurative parallels.
>
> Brodsky (on Mandelstam)

BRODSKY AND 'METAPHYSICAL' POETRY

Joseph Brodsky's poetry has a strong metaphysical tendency, and his work has often been discussed in relation to the achievement of the English Metaphysical poets. The recognition of this kinship, initially at least, is attributable, on thematic and historical grounds, to the presence of such names as John Donne and Mary Stuart in the titles of his major poetic compositions. Brodsky's interest in Donne (and the historical period of the Metaphysicals), of course, is far deeper than any superficial link afforded by the title of an elegy or a sonnet sequence. The substance and dialectical movement of Brodsky's thought is reminiscent of pervasive preoccupations in the meditative verse of his English Metaphysical predecessors.

Indeed, so close is the link between the treatment of such central themes as *mortality* and *time* in Brodsky's work and in that of Donne and his contemporaries that the relation of Brodsky to the 'metaphysical' strain in his own native Russian literature is in danger of being neglected. The intention of the present essay is to redress the balance by considering a basic affinity between the poetic imagery, and the underlying metaphysic, of Brodsky and that of an earlier poet in the 'Petersburg' tradition, Osip Mandelstam.

BRODSKY/MANDELSTAM: THE NATURE OF AFFINITY

By adopting the word 'affinity', I mean to indicate a relationship that falls somewhere between what has come to be called a 'subtext'[1] and what Brodsky himself has referred to as 'the presence of an echo' (L: 132), in this case an echo originating in the nostalgic concern that the two poets have felt for world culture, and which makes the 'acoustics' of their poetry equally suitable to serve as a 'great cupola' for Classical literature as for Russian, an echo that resonates with Persephone as well as with Pushkin. Affinity is at once something less specific than an accumulation of 'cicada-like citations' and yet something more definite than 'spiritual hunger'.[2] It is a bond pledged by Brodsky's penetrative commentary in 'The Child of Civilization' (L: 123–44),[3] and redeemed by his own poetic practice.

The affinity is one that arises from the fact that the poetry of Brodsky, like Mandelstam's, is situated in the mainstream of Modernism in its intense engagement with the things of this earth, with the vital connection between the past and the present, and with poetry itself. In other words, it is an affinity that addresses itself to the themes already mentioned as being central to the English Metaphysicals: mortality and time.

TESSERA

The problems attendant upon an individual poet's awareness of the achievement of his precursors have been the subject of recent studies by Harold Bloom. In *The Anxiety of Influence*, Bloom defined six types of 'intra-poetic relationships' that could be construed as indexes of affinity. It is helpful, therefore, to repeat some remarks of his that appertain to my idea of 'affinity'. The relationship that Bloom describes is a revisionary one that exists between what he calls the 'precursor' and the 'ephebe'.[4] According to Bloom, the precursor's implicit charge to the ephebe is the paradoxical: 'Be me but not me'.[5]

Of the six types of influence that he has defined, the closest to the kind that I explore here is *tessera*. In the *tessera* (or Completion and Antithesis), Bloom comments, 'the later poet provides what his imagination tells him would complete the otherwise 'truncated' precursor poem and poet . . . a poet's stance, his Word, his imaginative identity, his whole being, *must* be unique to him, and remain unique, or he will perish, as a poet'.[6] The 'antithetical completion' that I shall discuss in this essay concerns the differing stances of Mandelstam and Brodsky to the poet's Word.

Ichnographically, it would be possible to map an ontological hierarchy common to the two poets on three levels that correspond to what I have described above as their shared Modernist concern with 'the things of this earth, the vital connection between the past and the present, and poetry itself'. Spatial objects (the 'things and people' in Brodsky's poem 'Natiurmort') occupy the lowest level of the hierarchy; on the intermediate level ideas are located along a temporal continuum; and alone on the highest level – the apex (or acme) – there exists the Word.

MORTALITY, TIME AND ACMEIST POETICS

Since time is transitive, the intermediate, or temporal, level operates in Mandelstam's Acmeist poetics as an axis of mortality, thereby ensuring that the dimensionless reality of the Word is not sealed off from man's material foundation in three-dimensional reality.[7]

In 'The Child of Civilization', Brodsky discusses in detail 'the presence of time . . . both as an entity and as a theme' (L: 125) in Mandelstam's poetry. For Brodsky, time is associated with death, which

> even as a word – is about as definite as a . . . poem, the main feature of which is its last line . . . So when we read a poet, we participate in his or his works' death. In the case of Mandelstam, we participate in both. (L: 123)

This is the credo of an ephebe, who must necessarily terminate (or 'truncate') his precursor. More importantly, it indicates the link that Brodsky forges between language and death. Conversely, for Mandelstam, the language of the poet offers the precursor the possibility of communication – and communion – with the future: the poem is expansive, forward-looking. As he states in the essay 'On the Addressee' [O sobesednike'], it is addressed to 'the reader in posterity', and the poet 'is bound only to his providential addressee'.[8] This accounts for the fact that, as Brodsky has observed, Mandelstam 'seldom looks backward in a poem . . . The past, whether personal or historical, has been taken care of by the words' own etymology' (L: 125).

Brodsky has denied the resurrection of the Word in which Mandelstam believed.[9] As a consequence of this denial of the poem as a communion through time (between the poet and the 'distant, unknown addressee'), Brodsky's attitude both to the value of 'recollection' and to people is often negative, and, for this reason, the sense of the poet's loneliness is a major theme in his work. His negative stance is in evidence in the opening sentences of the first, and title, essay, in *Less than One*:

As failures go, attempting to recall the past is like trying to grasp the meaning of existence. Both make one feel like a baby clutching at a basketball: one's palms keep sliding off. (L: 3)

It is this attitude that has on occasion recommended to Brodsky the mood and the vocabulary of Mandelstam's first phase, which is dependent upon a reiteration of the motif of emptiness that results from the sense of an oppressive, metaphysical absence.[10] The Mandelstamian *leitmotiv* is recaptured and elaborated (but, it should be said, without a great deal of reworking) in Brodsky's poem 'Sad' ('The Garden'). The poem begins:

О, как ты пуст и нем!
                     В осенней полумгле
сколь призрачно царит прозрачность сада,
где листья приближаются к земле
великим тяготением распада. (S: 64)

(How empty and silent you are!
                    In the autumnal gloom
the garden's transparence rules so spectrally,
where the leaves draw near to the ground
with the mighty weight of decay.)

The impressionistic imagery of these lines runs through the remaining five stanzas of the poem: the sound of bells ('gul kolokolov') in the second stanza, the twilight in the third, the 'sad soul' and the reality of emptiness in the fourth, the epithets conveying magnitude in the fifth and the silent, dolorous departure taken by the lyrical persona in the final stanza, all of this is Mandelstamian and the similarity is enhanced by verbal play (between, characteristically, 'prizrachnyi' ('spectral') and 'prozrachnyi' ('transparent') and a respect for heaviness ('tiagotenie') that acquires a mystical quality. It is a stance of survival in an alien world, a world where the poet finds himself within those 'great amphitheatres of solitude' to which Brodsky refers elsewhere (S: 68).

Notwithstanding his identification of language with death, Brodsky shares with Mandelstam a rich sense of the *formal immediacy of objects*, mediated by an obliqueness of vision that often makes the textual explication of the verse of both poets a challenging and contentious affair. It is this perception, almost of terror (certainly of awe and intensity) at the imminent coming into being of the image-object, a truly dynamic *experience of threat or menace*, that Brodsky appears to have inherited directly from his precursor.

The poem with which the early Brodsky rode into prominence – 'Byl chernyi nebosvod . . .' ('The black night sky . . .')[11] – functions as a powerful example of the sustained invocation of a *blackness* that is at once physical and metaphysical, for the experience involves both a dominant physical image (of the horse) and a dominant abstract condition (of its colour). In this poem of 1961, Brodsky displays an intensity of focus that was later to become an essential aspect of his 'idiostyle'. Indeed, Brodsky's imagery often begs for the epithet that he has used to describe Mandelstam's poetry: it is 'oversaturated'.[12]

In section IV of his essay, 'The Morning of Acmeism' ('Utro akmeizma'), Mandelstam wrote:

> There is no equality, no competition, there is the complicity of the real in the conspiracy against emptiness and non-being.
>
> Love the existence of the thing more than the thing itself and your being more than yourself, – this is the highest commandment of Acmeism.[13]

This Acmeist credo runs through the works of Brodsky. He has, for example, one of the two characters in his recent play *Marbles* utter a similar sentiment:

It's always the principle that counts. The idea that lies behind the thing, not the thing itself.[14]

In 'Posviashchaetsia Ialte' ('Dedicated to Yalta'), Brodsky modernises the locution, substituting contemporary terminology for Mandelstam's traditional lexicon of 'existence' ('sushchestvovanie') and 'being' ('bytie'), when he states that, in an 'atomic age', it is not things that excite people so much as 'the structure of things':

> В атомный век людей волнуют больше
> не вещи, а строение вещей. (К: 37)

What Mandelstam calls *bytie* and Brodsky *stroenie* is the very same sense of the 'formal immediacy' of the *realia* to which I have alluded earlier, the antithesis of the Symbolists' *realiora* or transcendent evaluation of things. Metaphysical as Brodsky's verse may be, it is firmly grounded in the poetics of Acmeism.

'NATIURMORT' (AND MORTALITY)

In terms of Mandelstam's poetic development, a redemptive value entered his drained cosmos, when from 1916 to 1921 he came to accept Persephone as his Muse,[15] for whereas Brodsky has (so far) remained wedded to the belief that 'in an atomic age' there is no resurrection of the word, that death and language are inseparable, Mandelstam, as it were, took the fight into the enemy camp, and in his poetry performed the Demeter-like task of partial retrieval and regenerative bestowal. The Stone Age of the later *Kamen'* poems (with their stress on spatial structures and voids) yielded primacy of place to the celebration of the temporal transitions poetry could accomplish between being and non-being. The 'conspiracy against emptiness and non-being', which is communicated by way of myth and metaphor, is to be encountered in *Tristia*.[16]

In order to exemplify the observations I have made on some aspects of Brodsky's poetry and its relation to the poetry of Mandelstam, I shall turn to the neo-Acmeist treatment of the theme of *mortality*, as it is developed in 'Natiurmort' (1971), and of *time*, as it is developed in 'Babochka' (1972). My intention is not to offer detailed readings of these two poems – this has been performed adequately elsewhere[17] – but to dwell on certain facets where the affinity of 'precursor' and 'ephebe' is particularly in evidence.

'Natiurmort' is a long, lyric poem in ten sections, each section consisting of three four-line stanzas. The basic stanza pattern is that of alternately rhyming, iambic trimeter lines. Although the rhyme scheme is constant, the length of line is readily extended to allow variations from a basic measure (a measure that is rhythmic rather than semantic). Variability in line-length is accompanied by frequent selection, as in other poems by Brodsky, of 'non-standard' syntactical units (prepositions, pronouns, particles, even on one occasion a prefix) for rhyme-words. The effect is to draw attention to a 'softening-up' process that is being applied to line-boundaries (as a lexical equivalent to the thematic loosening of the absolute division between life and death). The opening stanza is representative of Brodsky's technical attention to detail, while at the same time being indicative of his thematic concerns at large. It is worth examining some of the salient features of this stanza in order to understand Brodsky's approach to matters of 'structure':

Вещи и люди нас
окружают. И те,
и эти *терзают* глаз.
Лучше жить в *темноте*. (К: 108)

(Things and people
surround us. Both
of them *torment* the eye.
Better living in *darkness*.)

The series of four nouns (things, people, eye, darkness), moving away from the two nominatives through the accusative (but not yet accusatory) 'eye' to the outer (prepositional) 'darkness', establishes a matrix on which the poem is to develop. In this series, 'things' and 'people' form the primary opposition (as they do in the poem as a whole), but 'eye' and 'darkness' also operate derivatively as an antithesis, by which the spatially determined categories of 'things' and 'people' are measured. If 'things' and 'people' are firmly located within the three dimensions of the (primary) spatial world, then the 'eye' and the 'darkness' are able to transcend it, are able to enter the (intermediate) *temporal*, or ideational, dimension of Brodsky's poetic universe. In accordance with an Acmeist tenet, the eye does not simply 'behold' beauty; it also *crafts* it, as the reference in Mandelstam's poem 'Admiralteistvo' to *glazomer* (literally, a measurement estimated by the eye) acknowledges:

> . . . красота — не прихоть полубога,
> А хищный глазомер простого столяра.
>
> (. . . beauty is not a demigod's whim,
> But the predatory eye of a simple joiner.)

It is here that the 'meta-reality' of abstractions (life, death; existence, non-existence) supersists.[18] The 'eye' is metonymically related to existence just as much as darkness is to non-existence. It operates in the same temporal dimension, but because it is linked 'vertically' to 'people' as part of the mutable universe (just as darkness' is linked to immutable 'things'), it suffers. One notices that, structurally, the pair 'people/eye' is confined within the all-embracing boundary of the stanza's 'things-darkness' continuum. This formal arrangement is accentuated by the fact that the only line that does not contain a noun – the second – is dominated by a verb ('okruzhaiut') that simultaneously completes the opening sentence by insisting upon the physical constraint of the perceiving persona, and also initiates a further series, (of the stanza's trisyllabic words, underlined in the text – 'okruzhaiut/ terzaiut/temnote' – bound together by an acoustic effect), which, as a graphic device, puts a diagonal slash through the stanza as if to communicate the sense of threat that culminates in the concluding 'darkness'.

Yet however threatening, however life-denying this force, the poet puts his trust in it. As the last line of the first stanza declares: 'Luchshe zhit' v temnote.' Here we confront a *leitmotiv* common to Brodsky and to Mandelstam: the attraction to chaos, to non-being, whether it be a world of shadow (*ten'*), as it often is in *Tristia*, or, as it is in this instance, of darkness.[19] The corollary to this is the 'ephebe's' bluntly stated preference for things as against people, marked by the ironic *povtor* of 'Ia ne *liubliu liudei*' ('I don't love people') in the third section of 'Natiurmort', where the constitution of the poet – here more *meta*bolic than *sym*bolic – is consistent with the thematic import of *nature morte*.

> Кровь моя холодна.
> Холод ее лютей

> реки, промерзшей до дна.
> Я не люблю людей. (К: 109)

> (My blood's cold.
> Its coldness is sharper
> than a river, frozen solid.
> I don't love people.)

In the first three lines of this stanza, there are resonances of the poem that Mandelstam wrote in 1916 (in which Petersburg's early springtime is commensurate with the January of Brodsky's poem) where he first acknowledged Persephone as a controlling presence:

> Мне холодно. Прозрачная весна
> В зеленый пух Петрополь одевает,
> Но, как медуза, невская волна
> Мне отвращенье легкое внушает.[20]

> (I am cold. Transparent spring
> Dresses Petropolis in green down
> But, like a medusa, the Neva wave
> Fills me with slight revulsion.)

The cold-bloodedness and 'slight revulsion', the river, the conjunction of 'tenderness and heaviness'[21] in a dying city are all elements that contribute to the making of 'Natiurmort'. The essential difference – the antithesis and completion in Brodsky's *tessera* – is that the presiding force of darkness in 'Natiurmort' lacks the teleological support of a mythological figure which is present *throughout*, as in Mandelstam's Petropolis poem. When the supernatural does emerge in the *final* section of 'Natiurmort', the effect is disjunctive, for it announces poetic closure.

The fourth section of 'Natiurmort' commences explicitly and firmly: 'Veshchi priiatnei'. Things are preferred to people, and darkness is preferred to light,[22] for light only illuminates the dust

> Пыль. И включенный свет
> только пыль озарит. (К: 110)

> (Dust. And a light switched on
> only illuminates dust.)

The Complicity of the Real

The motivating idea of this poem depends upon a form of 'reversed commonplace':[23] in the first instance man's activity may serve to disturb the dust, but ultimately it is the dust that disturbs man. It disturbs, because, according to section five, it is the 'flesh of time; flesh and blood':[24]

> Ибо пыль — это плоть
> времени; плоть и кровь. (K: 110)

It is through time that man is tested, for 'time is created by death' ('Vremia sozdano smert'iu' [K 59]), and in 'Natiurmort' it is his death, which, in a macabre parody of Renaissance mimesis, holds a mirror up to nature – to the poet's mouth – to see how he 'endures non-being':[25]

> как я переношу
> небытие на свету. (K: 110)

Man is mortal. The directness of Mandelstam's simple sentence 'A man dies'[26] and Brodsky's 'They [people] will die./All. I also shall die'.[27] – both attest to the starkness of the fact. But a thing takes up space rather than time, for (whatever non-Euclidean physics may say) in the sensuous universe of poetry space is solid:

> Вещь есть пространство, вне
> коего вещи нет. (K: 111)
>
> (A thing is space, outside
> of which there is no thing.)

As an instance of the spatial property of things, Brodsky takes an object central to the poetic world of Mandelstam, (the) stone:

> Он неподвижен.
>
> (It is immobile.)

The stone in Brodsky, as in Mandelstam, is not only the antithesis of all that man is, but, in its mineral quality, it also stands in inorganic (unchanging) opposition to the vegetable world of (organic) growth. 'Living nature' is represented in the triad of nouns that introduce the eighth section:

Дерево. Тень. Земля ... [28] (K: 111)

(Tree. Shade. Earth . . .)

Tree and *earth* menace man in the same way as the 'black horse' does in Brodsky's earlier poem. The insubstantial shadow between tree and earth reminds us, on the one hand, that both 'tree' and 'earth' are associated with transformation.[29] On the other hand, their duality is still part of 'living nature', since this is the kind of shade that cannot exist without a sun:

Тень. Человек в тени,
словно рыба в сети. [30] (K: 111)

(Shade. Man in shade,
Is like a fish in a net.)

In section nine, immobile things – things without roots – represent *nature morte*, which appears in a 'metaphysical' triad in contrast to the 'natural' triad of life: 'skull, skeleton, scythe' ('cherep, skelet, kosa') The tenth, and final, section represents an unexpected shift of register from the metaphysical to the religious (which, as an established, referential framework, is equivalent to the mythic in *Tristia*). Mary asks Christ:

ты мой сын или Бог?
То есть, мертв или жив? — (K: 112)

(Are you my son or God?
That is, dead or living?)

To which Christ replies with a baffling remark that there is no difference, living or dead, son or God, he is hers: 'Ia tvoi'.

If, as has often been asserted, post-tsarist literature in Russia is marked by the advent of Blok's *The Twelve*, then one may safely say that enigmatic religious conclusions that open up new horizons are as old as Soviet poetry itself. The offering of Self may be construed as the offering of the poem.[31] In any case, it is a Modernist technique[32] that in this instance allows Brodsky to deny an absolute distinction between the living and the dead, a denial already implicit in the oxymoron of *nature morte* (and its English equivalent, still life).

WORD AND CULTURE

In his celebrated essay of 1921, 'The Word and Culture' ('Slovo i kul'tura'), Mandelstam wrote:

> Poetry is the plough that turns up time in such a way that the abyssal strata of time, its black earth, appear on the surface. There are epochs, however, when mankind, not satisfied with the present, yearning like the ploughman for the abyssal strata of time, thirsts for the virgin soil of time . . . I want Ovid, Pushkin, and Catullus to live once more, and I am not satisfied with the historical Ovid, Pushkin, and Catullus.[33]

The 'fish in a net' simile from 'Natiurmort', quoted above, contains an allusion to a Pushkinian subtext:[34]

> Не разумел он ничего,
> И слаб и робок был, как дети;
> Чужие люди за него
> Зверей и рыб ловили в сети...
>
> (He understood nothing
> And was weak and timid, as children are,
> Strange people for him
> Caught wild animals and fish in nets . . .)

What is significant in view of the commentary that follows on 'Babochka' is not merely that these lines from Pushkin's 'Gipsies' are also quoted by Mandelstam in 'Slovo i kul'tura',[35] but that the 'root' of this branching subtext, the unnamed 'he' of the first line in the quotation above, refers to the exiled Ovid – the author of 'Metamorphoses' and 'Tristia'.

In his poem, 'Babochka', Brodsky demonstrates that the 'thirst for the virgin soil of time' exists for him as well. He takes up an image venerable enough to be classed as an archetype, and attempts to revitalise it. To mention only the most obvious of 'references, allusions, linguistic and figurative parallels' from antiquity, the *butterfly* evokes ideas of 'soul' (the Greek *psyche*),[36] of 'transformation' (Chuang Chou's dream),[37] and of 'death' (Ovid's 'funereal butterfly'),[38] all of which converge (at the apex) at the point of *non-being*.

Although Mandelstam does not use the 'butterfly' as a major

symbol in his poetry, there is a clear 'recognition' of the 'soul/butterfly' identification in 'Slovo i kul'tura'. The 'bee', which functions similarly in the poetry of Mandelstam, is preferred for its association with Persephone.[39]

'BABOCHKA' (AND TIME)

'Babochka' is a fourteen-stanza poem in which each stanza has the appearance on the page of a butterfly's outline. This circumstance, immediately obvious to the reader, is an appropriate graphic device to support the poem's insistence that the silent butterfly *shows* rather than tells. The poem takes the form of an apostrophe to the ephemera of its title. The *topos* of life's brevity competes with the *topos* of the protean quality of existence for thematic dominance in a prolonged, lyric meditation that focuses (from the rhetorical question in the first line of the poem to the answer arrived at in the concluding stanza) on the fragile insect hovering on the brink of non-being. The device at its core involves another 'reversed commonplace': it is not so much 'a day in the life of . . .', as 'a life in the day of . . .', the poet-observer.

'Babochka', in exploring the interface of life and death as a means of articulating the metaphysical perplexity of the lyrical persona, commences where 'Natiurmort' leaves off. There are several details that reinforce the thematic inter-connection between the two poems, among which the reference to 'natiurmort' (in stanza 4), the image of caught fish (also in stanza 4), and the night/light opposition (particularly in stanzas 5 and 12) clearly belong. The difference in titles is indicative, however, of a contrast in the treatment of the theme, for whereas 'Natiurmort' takes its terms of reference from an art-form that is regarded as primarily spatial, 'Babochka' draws upon an archetypal emblem of the last stage in a life-cycle that is, by definition, primarily temporal.[40] As in 'Byl chernyi nebosvod . . .' ('The black night sky . . .'), the intensity of focus is dependent essentially upon the fusion of a dominant physical image and a dominant abstract condition. The difference here is that what identifies it as 'metaphysical' is the 'oversaturation' of time and not, as in the earlier poem, of space

The juxtaposition of the notions of ephemeral life ('No ty zhila lish' sutki') ('But you lived only a single day')) and tombstone death – which is reckoned by the subtraction of the lesser from the greater number on the slab to determine the duration of life in years – is a device that links Brodsky with the conceits of the English Metaphysicals, but in choosing the image of the butterfly, he grafts the 'metaphysical' branch on to the stem of the Ovidian 'metamorphic' view, an outlook on existence encapsulated in the Latin poet's often-quoted aphorism: *Tempus edax rerum*.

The 'idea that lies behind the thing'[41] manifests its influence in the opening stanza at the level of sound-orchestration of which the fulcrum is the *grusti/gorsti* (sorrow/hollow (of the hand)) pairing. Although such an acoustic device is a stock-in-trade of the post-symbolist craftsman, one recognises in Brodsky's use of sound-texture the specific presence of Mandelstam inasmuch as other subtextual appeals are made, in the same stanza, to a poem from the *Tristia* volume: 'Voz'mi na radost'. . .' ('Take for joy . . .'). When it is recalled that *radost'* and *ladoni* ('joy' and 'palms (of the hand)') are the starting-points for this lyric poem by Mandelstam on the transformational potency of the dead bee,[42] then a whole network of subtextual allusions begins to insinuate itself. The striking simile for grasping the meaning of existence that introduces *Less than One* has already been quoted, but what is no less remarkable is the fact of its resemblance to the opening statement of Mandelstam's essay 'Batum': 'Batum in its entirety resembles an object easily fitting into the palm of your hand'.[43] Handling tests 'veshchnost'' (but not 'vechnost'' ('eternity')), 'konkretnost'', 'material'nost'', as Mandelstam's example of the 'blind man's joy' demonstrates.[44] On the basis of these and other passages, it is reasonable to conclude that an extensive parallel exists between Madelstam and Brodsky in their deployment of *tactile imagery for emotive effect*.

To return to the opening exhortation of 'Voz'mi na radost' . . .' ('Take for joy . . .'), it may be noticed that it contains an echo of the closing lines of an earlier poem, one that Mandelstam wrote in 1916 (and which was addressed to Tsvetaeva, a poet much admired by Brodsky): 'Primi zh' ladoniami moimi/ Peresypaemyi pesok.' ('Take, then, from my palms/The sand poured out'.) Mandelstam's *sand* in *Tristia* is commensurate with Brodsky's *dust* – the dust of things that have crumbled in the seepage of time. More pertinently, the root of the epithet that Mandelstam adopts in the image of 'pere*sy*paemyi pesok' is cocooned within the 'ras*sy*palas'') of the ninth line of 'Babochka.'[45] The Russian verb 'rassypat'', which in its reflexive form may be used to describe both the disintegration of things into dust and the 'crumbling' of bread, is applied in the 'metaphysical' image that concludes 'Slovo i kul'tura': 'Wheat must be scattered through the ether.'[46]

Metaphorically, the whole of 'Slovo i kul'tura' is contained within an ascending parabola that moves from the sprouting grass mentioned in the opening sentence of the essay[47] to the scattered wheat of the last sentence[48]. As such Mandelstam's vision is towards future life and regeneration as opposed to the 'drift towards death' of the 'dust' imagery of 'Babochka'. It is only when it becomes possible to identify Brodsky's 'dust of things' as *pollen* (that is, as the Russian 'pyl'tsa'), that an affirmative edge to his metaphysics is offered:

> Так делает перо,
> . . .
> не пыль с цветка снимая,
>   но тяжесть с плеч. (С: 37)

> (So moves the pen,
> . . .
> not taking dust from the flower,
> but heaviness from the shoulders.)

Taking away, subtracting, reducing (to 'less than one') are actions that have the force of ontological negatives, outweighing the positive act of lyrical enlargement ('vziavshi lupu' ('having taken up the magnifying glass;) in this poem, and they establish the butterfly's proximity to *nebytie*.

The butterfly is 'more fleshless than time,/ more soundless':

> Бесплотнее, чем время,
>   беззвучней ты. (С: 36)

If *time*, as I have argued, occupies an intermediate level in Brodsky's poetic universe, then it follows that the *butterfly* of this poem, in being deprived of both sound and flesh (like the 'soul' although Brodsky does not take up the metonymic reference in this poem), functions as a mediating agent between 'being' and 'non being'. Non-being denies the presence of time and words. It denies, it does not transcend. (Brodsky refuses the velleities of the Hegelian *Aufhebung*.)[49] There is none of the teleological warmth of

Mandelstam's mythocentric system[50] in the flat assertion of finality in 'Babochka':

> мир создан был без цели,
>   а если с ней,
>   то цель — не мы. (C: 37)
>
> (the world was created without an end,
>   and if with one,
>   that end is not us.)

In stanza six of 'Babochka', Brodsky refers to the world where the butterfly is 'like a thought about a thing' ('kak mysl' o veshchi'), the world where 'we are the thing itself' ('my – veshch' sama'). The analogy of the word, which 'wanders freely around the thing, like the soul [as Psyche] around an abandoned, but not forgotten body' is Mandelstam's equivalent.[51] It is not so much invoked here, as revoked, for an 'antithetical meaning' is given to the 'primal words': *veshch'* ('thing') and, indirectly, *dusha* ('soul').

It is appropriate, then, that 'Babochka' terminates with a lyrical meditation on 'Nothingness', *Nichto*. Likened to a 'frail barrier' ('kak legkaia pregrada'), between void and self, the butterfly represents the 'antithetical completion' of Mandelstam's poetic image of the soul, Psyche-life.[52] Brodsky revisionary task is done. The image emerges as imago.[53]

Notes

1. K. Taranovsky's essay 'Concert at the Railroad Station: The Problem of Context and Subtext' (in his *Essays on Mandel'štam*, Cambridge, Mass., 1976 pp. 1–20) has done much to establish *subtext* in the current critical lexicon as meaning 'poetic reminiscences' and 'other voices'. Compare the entry under *subtext* in V. Terras (ed.), *Handbook of Russian Literature* (New Haven, 1985), pp. 452–3.
2. Mandelstam has written 'Tsitata ne est' vypiska. Tsitata est' tsikada' and '. . . otnyne utoliaiut ne tol'ko fizicheskii, no i dukhovnyi golod'. See O. Mandelstam *Slovo i kul'tura: Stat'i* (Moscow, 1987) (hereinafter referred to in the notes as SK) pp. 113, 40. An English translation is to be found in *Mandelstam: The Complete Critical Prose and Letters* J.G. Harris (ed.) (Ann Arbor, 1979) (hereinafter referred to in the notes as CCPL) pp. 401, 113.
3. Brodsky's essay on Mandel'štam's poetry. In a shorter version, the

essay was originally published as an introduction to *Osip Mandelstam: 50 Poems*; translated by Bernard Meares (New York, 1977). The meaning of Mandelstam for Brodsky is communicated eloquently by this essay, and clearly needs no gloss. The importance of Petersburg, and its 'metaphysical' appeal as an 'abstract' city, is also obvious from many of the essays collected in *Less than One*. For Brodsky's evaluation of Dostoevsky's place in Russian literature, see the essays 'The Power of the Elements' and 'Catastrophes in the Air' in *Less than One*.

4. Crucial to Bloom's notion of 'antithetical criticism' is the assertion that 'the meaning of a poem can only be a poem, but *another poem – a poem not itself*. And not a poem chosen with total arbitrariness, but any central poem by an indubitable precursor, even if the ephebe *never read* that poem. Source study is wholly irrelevant here; we are dealing with primal words, but antithetical meanings, and an ephebe's best misinterpretations may well be of poems he has never read'. *The Anxiety of Influence: A Theory of Poetry* (New York, 1973) p. 70.
5. *The Anxiety of Influence*, p. 70.
6. *The Anxiety of Influence*, pp. 66, 71. It is clear from Bloom's remarks that the *tessera* is not the same as the *subtext* (which is always known to the later poet). It is certainly not the case that the erudite Brodsky 'has never read' all the poems of Mandelstam to which I refer in this essay. Indeed, he has explicitly asserted the centrality of reading in his claim that 'man is what he reads' (L: 365). Nevertheless, two salient factors remain valid: each poem by Mandelstam that I discuss is a 'central poem by an indubitable precursor' and we are 'dealing with primal words, but antithetical meanings'. *Clinamen* – Bloom's first revisionary category (or 'ratio'), by which a 'poet swerves away from his precursor' (*The Anxiety of Influence* p. 14) – is also a prominent feature in Mandelstam (for example, in the poem 'Silentium', where issue is taken with Tiutchev) and in Brodsky (an obvious instance occurring in the sixth sonnet of the Mary Stuart sequence: 'Ia vas liubil . . .'). Brodsky has written that the 'most awful thing about service to the Muses is precisely that it does not tolerate repetition – either of metaphor, subject, or device' (L: 187).
7. See SK: 170 (CCPL: 63)
8. CCPL: 69, 71 (SK: 50, 52)
9. 'Whatever a work of art consists of, it runs to the finale which makes for its form and denies resurrection. After the last line of a poem nothing follows except literary criticism' (L: 123). For an account of Mandelstam's belief, see his essay 'On the Nature of the Word' (CCPL: 117–32) (SK: 55–67) and the essay-fragment 'Pushkin and Scriabin' (CCPL: 90–95) (not included in SK). I have discussed the motif of resurrection in the poet's 'Leteiskie stikhi' (Berlin, 1923) in L. Burnett, 'The Survival of Myth: Mandel'shtam's "Word" and Translation', in T. Hermans (ed.) *The Manipulation of Literature: Studies in Literary Translation* (London, 1985) pp. 181–4. See also Ronen *An Approach to Mandel'štam* (Jerusalem, 1983) p. 257.
10. Gumilev (in *Apollon* No. 1, 1916) was the first to comment on an abrupt change in Mandelstam's style in 1912, which he described as a

movement away from Symbolism to Acmeism. Of Mandelstam's first phase, Gumilev wrote: 'The poet strives towards the periphery of consciousness, to prehistoric chaos, into the kingdom of metaphor, yet he does not harmonize it according to his own will as do those who believe in all the doctrines; rather he is only frightened by the incompatibility between it and himself'. (Translation quoted from *Nikolai Gumilev on Russian Poetry*, David Lapeza (ed.), Ann Arbor, 1977 p. 163.) For an amplification of Gumilev's remarks, see C. Brown *Mandelstam* (Cambridge, 1973) pp. 178–81. Mandelstam's post-Symbolist shift of 1912 is covered well in the discussion of *Stone* in a recent study by C. Isenberg, *Substantial Proofs of Being: Osip Mandelstam's Literary Prose* (Columbus, Ohio, 1987) pp. 17–23.

11. There is a good translation and discussion of this poem in Peter France, *Poets of Modern Russia* (Cambridge, 1982) pp. 198–202.
12. 'It was the sense of an oversaturated existence that the young Mandelstam was trying to convey in his first two collections, and he chose the portrayal of overloaded time as his medium' (L: 125).
13. Unless otherwise indicated all translations from the Russian are my own. For the original, see SK: 170–2.
14. *Comparative Criticism*, 7, p. 211. The Russian text has 'Delo vsegda v printsipe. V idee, a ne veshchi kak takovoi . . .' (*Mramor*, Ann Arbor, 1984 p. 19).
15. Persephone is to be understood (as Kerényi has argued) as constituting the *uniqueness* of the individual and the *enthralment to not-being*. (See Burnett, 'The Survival of Myth', in T. Hermans (ed.) *The Manipulation of Literature* London, 1985, pp. 187–8). Brodsky employs the Persephone mythologem in the long poem, 'Pamiati T.B.' ('To the Memory of T.B.') (K 19–28), but not as a constructional factor, as it is used in Mandelstam.
16. Compare Isenberg's discriminating analysis of Mandelstam's poetic development from *Kamen'* to *Tristia* in *Substantial Proofs of Being: Osip Mandelstam's Literary Prose*: pp. 25–28 (note 10). As Brodsky crudely, but correctly, said of Mandelstam in 'The Child of Civilization': 'When space ended, he hit time'(L: 139).
17. See, particularly, E. Etkind, *Materiia stikha* (Paris, 1978) pp. 114–117 and L. Loseff, 'Iosif Brodskii's Poetics of Faith', *Aspects of Modern Russian and Czech Literature* A.B. McMillin (ed.) (Columbus, Ohio, forthcoming) for 'Natiurmort'; M. Kreps, *O Poezii Iosifa Brodskogo* (Ann Arbor, 1984) pp. 31–50 for 'Babochka'; and V. Polukhina, *Joseph Brodsky: A Poet for Our Time* (Cambridge, 1989) pp. 152–6, 182–94 for both poems.
18. The neologism 'supersist' is offered in response to Brodsky's coining of 'supertext' (L: 182).
19. Compare Mandelstam's line (from 'Grifel'naia oda' ('The Slate Ode'): 'Ia nochi drug, ia dnia zastrel'shchik' ('I am night's friend, day's skirmisher'). For a commentary on this line and its relation to other references to *night* in Mandelstam's poetry, see Ronen, *An Approach to Mandel'štam* pp. 198–200.
20. Mandelstam's 1912 poem 'Ia vzdragivaiu ot kholoda . . .' ['I'm shiv-

ering from cold'] – from his Symbolist phase, anticipates the metaphysical climate of 'Mne kholodno' and belongs, as does the later poem, to the tradition of Petersburg as an 'abstract' city.
21. See Mandelstam's poem 'Sestry – tiazhest' i nezhnost', odinakovy vashi primety . . .' ['Sisters – heaviness and tenderness, your signs are the same . . .'] (1920). Here the 'tenderness' and the 'heaviness' are represented by the green world of 'transparent spring' and, in the last line of the poem, 'emerald' water.
22. The 'black' or 'night' sun image of *Tristia* has been discussed by several critics. See, particularly, Taranovsky *Essays on Mandel'štam*, pp. 54–5; 150–2.
23. The phrase 'reversed commonplace' ('protivopolozhnoe obshchee mesto') is borrowed from Bazarov in Turgenev's *Fathers and Children*. (For the Russian text see *Polnoe Sobranie Sochinenii i Pisem* VIII (Moscow, 1964) p. 324.) Semantic and lexical reversals are among Brodsky's favourite rhetorical devices. Two examples of lexical reversal are sufficient to demonstrate the general principle: (1) the fourteenth sonnet in the Mary Stuart sequence begins: 'Liubov' sil'nei razluki, no razluka/dlinnei liubvi'. ('Love is stronger than parting, but partings/ are longer than love'.) and (2) the third section of 'Kolybel'naia treskovogo mysa' ('Cape Cod Lullaby') begins: 'Odinochestvo uchit suti veshchei, ibo sut' ikh to zhe/odinochestvo'. ('Solitude teaches the essence of things, for their essence is that self-same/solitude'.) It is to be noticed that, in each of these illustrative examples, violation of line-boundary (*enjambement*) contributes to the total effect of 're-verse' or 'echo'. As for semantic reversal, the very title of 'Natiurmort' depends upon a 'reversed commonplace', namely a denial of the lyrical truism of 'living nature'.
24. For Brodsky, it is 'death' that is voracious, for Mandelstam 'time'. In 'Slovo i kul'tura', Mandelstam states: 'Slovo – plot' i khleb. Ono razdeliaet uchast' khleba i ploti: stradanie. Liudi golodny. Eshche golodnee gosudarstvo. No est' nechto bolee golodnoe: vremia.' 'The Word is flesh and bread. It shares the fate of bread and flesh: suffering. People are hungry. Still hungrier is the state. But there is something even hungrier: time'.) In their respective uses of *plot'* and *vremia* (*flesh* and *time*), Mandelstam and Brodsky provide a clear example of the adoption of 'primal words, but antithetical meanings'.
25. Mandelstam's 'mirror' of non-being in 'Kogda Psikheia-zhizn' spuskaetsia k teniam' ('When Psyche-life descends to the shades') (1920) – 'Dusha ne uznaet prozrachnye dubravy,/Dokhnet na zerkalo i medlit peredat'/Lepeshku mednuiu s tumannoi perepravy'. 'The soul will not recognise the transparent thickets,/She will breathe on the mirror and delay giving up/The copper disc from the misty crossing') – is derived from a mythological subtext, dependent ultimately upon the controlling presence of Persephone.
26. Line 3 of 'Sestry – tiazhest' i nezhnost', odinakovy vashi primety . . .' ('Sisters – heaviness and tenderness, your signs are the same . . .') reads: 'Chelovek umiraet. Pesok ostyvaet sogretyi'. ('Man dies. Warmed sand cools'.) Line 12 of 'Venitseiskoi zhizni mrachnoi i

besplodnoi . . .' 'Of gloomy and barren Venetian life . . .') (1920) reads: 'Umiraet chelovek'. ('A man dies'.).
27. 'Oni [liudi] umrut./Vse. Ia tozhe umru'. 'Natiurmort', Section 2.
28. Here 'Derevo' ('Tree') stands, as it were, at the top of the organic line, whereas 'Zemlia' ('Earth') (which holds the roots of the tree) reaches down into the next line of the stanza.
29. In the essay 'Slovo i kul'tura' ('The Word and Culture'), for example, a tree is associated with a dryad (SK: 39 (CCPL: 112)), and earth with time (SK: 40 (CCPL: 113)).
30. Compare Mandelstam's netted swallows in 'Sumerki svobody' ('The Twilight of Freedom') (1918): 'Skvoz' seti – sumerki gustye –/Ne vidno solntsa i zemlia plyvet'. ('Through the nets – thick twilight – /The sun is not visible and the earth is afloat'.)
31. Mallarmé's 'Don du Poëme' and Mandelstam's 'Voz'mi na radost'' ('Take for joy') are but two well-known variations on this theme.
32. The last line of 'Natiurmort' ('Syn ili Bog, ia tvoi' ('Son or God, I am yours')) is an example of what Barbara Smith classifies as a Thematic Device of Unqualified Assertion. Her description of closure that involves 'monosyllabic diction' and an 'oracular assertion of an utter and ultimate verity' is applicable here. See *Poetic Closure: A Study of How Poems End* (Chicago, 1968) pp. 182–6, 195.
33. CCPL: 113. For the Russian text, see SK: 40–41. I have discussed the significance of this 'earth' metaphor in the general context of Mandelstam's poetics in the early 1920s in Burnett, 'The Survival of Myth', in T. Hermans (ed.), *The Manipulation of Literature*, (London, 1985) 171–73.
34. Although Turgenev may seem an unlikely 'precursor' for Brodsky, the appropriateness of the metaphor near the end of *On the Eve* should not be overlooked. Turgenev wrote: 'Death is like a fisherman, who has caught a fish in his net and leaves it for a time in the water: the fish still swims, but the net is around it, and the fisherman will pull it out – when he wishes.' ('Smert', kak rybak, kotoryi poimal rybu v svoiu set' i ostavliaet ee na nei, i rybak vykhvatit ee – kogda zakhochet' (*Polnoe Sobranie Sochinenii i pisem* VIII: 166)).
35. SK: 39 (CCPL: 112). Mandelstam has misquoted slightly, without altering the sense.
36. '*Anima*, the Latin word for soul . . . originally designated the breath of life known in Greek as *Psyche*. Of the four elements *air* was most closely linked with the soul on the basis of both its inherent constituent and the medium through which it travels. Like air, the soul is intangible and invisible, penetrates and cannot be delimited'. Quoted from S. Nalbantian, *The Symbol of the Soul from Hölderlin to Yeats: A Study in Metonymy* (London, 1977) p. 1. The equation of 'butterfly' and 'soul' resurfaces in each literary era. In nineteenth-century Russian literature, Zhukovsky's long poem 'Motylek i tsvety' ('The Butterfly and the Flowers') constitutes a sustained neo-Platonic allegory that employs the equation.
37. 'Last night Chuang Chou dreamed he was a butterfly . . . He does not know whether he is Chou who dreams he is a butterfly or a butterfly

who dreams he is Chou. Between Chou and the butterfly there was necessarily a dividing; just this is what is meant by the transformation of things'. Quoted from A.C. Graham, *Chuang-Tzu: The Inner Chapters*, (London, 1986) p. 61.
38. The original text, from *Metamorphosis* XV, is:

> Quaeque solent canis frondes intexere filis,
> Agrestes tineae, res observata colonis,
> Ferali mutant cum papilione figuram.

Horace Gregory (in Mentor Classics, New York, 1958 p. 425) translates: 'And over here the white-spun caterpillar/Cradles himself within a living leaf/(And this familiar to all country people)/ To change into a tombstone butterfly'.
39. Poe's 'Ulalume – A Ballad', which served Mandelstam as subtext (see Burnett, 'The Survival of Myth', in T. Hermans (ed.), *The Manipulation of Literature* (London, 1985) pp. 177–8), employs the analogy of 'soul/butterfly'. Pushkin links *motylek* and *pchely* in *Eugene Onegin* 2: 21. See Taranovsky, 'Bees and Wasps', in *Essays on Mandel'štam*, pp. 83–114 and L. Burnett, 'Heirs of Eternity: An Essay on the Poetry of Keats and Mandelstam, *Modern Language Review*, LXXVI (1981), pp. 396–419 for detailed discussions of the 'bee' analogy in Mandelstam.
40. Since Brodsky has written that 'the past, whether personal or historical, has been taken care of by the words' own etymology' (L: 125), it is not beside the point to note that *babochka* and *babushka* ('grandmother') have been linked etymologically, on the basis of the idea that 'the soul of one who dies continues life in the form of a butterfly'. See M. Vasmer, *Etimologicheskii slovar' russkogo iazyka*, I (A–D) (Moscow, 1964), p. 100.
41. See note 14 *supra*.
42. The 'dead bee' image was the nexus of an ideological-poetic debate of the period c.1910–1922. See N.A. Nilsson, 'The Dead Bees: Notes on a Poem by Nikolaj Gumilev', *Orbis Scriptus: Festschrift für Dimitrij Tschizevskij zum 70. Geburtstag* (Munich, 1966) pp. 573–580.
43. CCPL: 229.
44. In 'Slovo i kul'tura', Mandelstam wrote: 'Ne trebuite ot poezii suguboi veshchnosti, konkretnosti, material'nosti. Eto tot zhe revoliutsionnyi golod' (SK: 42) ('Do not ask of poetry any particular substantiality, concreteness, materiality. It is the self-same revolutionary hunger'.) This injunction was directed at the 'doubting Thomas', who *looks for* the consolations of proof and causality. The true laying-on of hands is reserved for the *blind* man: 'Slepoi uznaet miloe litso, edva prikosnuvshis' k nemu zriachimi perstami, i slezy radosti, nastoiashchei radosti uznavaniia, bryznut iz glaz ego posle dolgoi razluki' (SK: 42) ('A blind man recognises a beloved face by barely touching it with seeing fingers, and tears of joy, the true joy of recognition, will fall from his eyes after a long separation' (CCPL: 116). This passage from 'Slovo i kul'tura' serves as a gloss on the reference to 'zriachikh pal'tsev styd'

('the shame of the seeing fingers') in the poem, 'Ia slovo pozabyl . . .' ('I have forgotten the word . . .') (1920).
45. It is worthy of note that Brodsky makes a reference to 'word-root dialectics' in his essay on Tsvetaeva, 'A Poet and Prose' (L: 186).
46. 'Nuzhno rassypat' pshenitsu po efiru' (SK: 43). Taranovsky has referred to a suggestion by Omry Ronen that the subtext for this image is to be found in the 'mystical philosophy' of G.I. Gurdjieff (see *Essays on Mandel'štam*: pp. 5–6), but this is an unlikely source for the Acmeist poet. A more credible subtext for the image of *resurrected* wheat in Mandelstam occurs in 1 Corinthians, XV, 36–45.
47. 'Trava na peterburgskikh ulitsakh – pervye pobegi devstvennogo lesa, kotoryi pokroet mesto sovremennykh gorodov' (SK: 39). ('Grass on the streets of Petersburg – the first sprouts of a virgin forest that will cover the site of modern cities' (CCPL: 112)).
48. This is the last sentence in Mandelstam's 1928 collection of essays, *O Poezii* [*On Poetry*], which the new Soviet edition prints. In the earlier versions (of 1921 and 1922), there is one more sentence that reflected the spirit of the earlier time: 'Classical poetry is the poetry of revolution'(CCPL: 116).
49. Das *Aufheben* stellt seine wahrhafte gedoppelte Bedeutung dar . . . es ist ein *Negiren* und ein *Aufbewahren* zugleich . . .', Hegel, *Phänomenologie des Geistes*, A, ii: 'Die Wahrnehmung'.
50. 'Hellenism is . . . the transformation of impersonal objects into domestic utensils, and the humanizing and warming of the surrounding world with the most delicate teleological warmth' (CCPL: 127–8). Mandelstam precedes this statement with another quotation taken from the 'Ovid section' of Pushkin's *Gipsies*. For the Russian text, see SK: 64.
51. For the Russian text, see SK: 42.
52. For Psyche-Life to cross the ontological threshold, she (or the poet) is ultimately involved in *recognition* and *return*, as the twin-poem to 'Kogda Psikheia-zhizn' . . .' (When Psyche-Life . . .'), namely 'Ia slovo pozabyl . . .' ('I have forgotten the word . . .'), makes clear. The 'frail barrier' between void and self in Mandelstam's poetic cosmos depends upon the assumption of non-being as an *a priori* condition. The same metaphysic pertains in *Kamen'* when the poet (in 'Silentium') enjoins Aphrodite to *remain* as foam (i.e. unformed), so that the word may *return* into music (and the primordial unity consonant with non-being).
53. The SOED defines Imago as 'The final and perfect stage or form of an insect after its metamorphoses; the "perfect insect"'.

3
Politics/Poetics
Lev Loseff

Brodsky once happened to say: 'Politics and poetry do have something in common – the letter *p* and the letter *o*'. A literalist might point out other common letters as well, and also that poetry in general, and Brodsky's poetry in particular, always has political motifs – whether hidden or exposed – and that any text influences its reader's political conduct in some measure. Brodsky is merely reminding us here of poetry's autonomy and priority as a type of ideological activity.[1] This is particularly important for him as a Russian poet, inasmuch as the tradition of dealing with literature in political terms has been unusually long-lived on Russian soil.

It would appear that the political part of Brodsky's credo was formulated later than his aesthetic, existential-philosophic, and religious views. The formulation took place in the process of writing poetry and gradually consolidated itself into a series of invariant motifs and stable verbal imagery. This unique poetico-political philosophy took shape, basically, in the five years between 1965 and 1970. It was reflected, first of all, in such poems as 'Letter in a Bottle' (1965), 'A Stop in the Desert' (1966), 'A Speech on Spilt Milk' (1967), 'A Letter to General Z' (1968) and 'The End of the Belle Epoque' (1969).[2] The following are some observations on the emergence of political imagery in these texts.

THE PARADOX OF APOLITICALNESS

'My existence is paradoxical . . .' says Brodsky on the threshold of the New Year, 1967.[3] In the poet's life, this was a moment for summing up both his youth and his poetic apprenticeship. The three preceding years had been ones of severe trial. Government persecution, to which Brodsky had been subjected even earlier, had intensified in the second half of 1963; he was forced to flee from city to city, hiding from the police. Then followed arrest, prison, weeks spent in a mental hospital for psychiatric tests, the travesty of a trial, transit by rail in a prison car, a year and a half of exile in a remote northern village. Many Russian poets both before and after Brodsky have travelled that same road of suffering. The paradox one could see in Brodsky's case was that before his arrest Brodsky had written hardly anything 'criminal', practically nothing of the sort that other poets had been arrested and jailed for. Political, and even historical, motifs are very rare in Brodsky's early work.

This author can recall how his boss at that time – the late V.V. Toropygin, a writer absolutely loyal to the Soviet regime and the member of the nomenklatura – spoke with sincere surprise about the Brodsky poems he had read: 'It turns out that not only are they not anti-Soviet, they're not even avant-garde; they're straight out of the classics'! However the other side of Brodsky's paradox was that the polity sensed something subversive in the very linguistic matter of his verse even before he introduced any political themes. Much later Brodsky will say that a writer 'exposes the dead-end philosophy' of the given utopia by writing 'in the language of the given utopia'.[4] Just what was so antithetical to the Soviet utopia of the 1960s kind in the poetic idiom of the young Brodsky?

Basically this idiom was nothing other than a successful attempt at transplanting English (more broadly – Western-European) 'metaphysical' poetics to Russian soil. Russian poetry (in the modern sense, i.e. from Trediakovsky and Lomonosov on) made its appearance and entered into a dialogue with Western poetry a century after the decline of baroque. The reanimation of baroque poetics and transplant performed by Brodsky did not degenerate into mere pastiche because the poetic practice of Russian modernism in the generation preceding Brodsky had in many ways already begun to approximate the baroque, or 'metaphysical', poetics at work three centuries earlier. If the English modernists – T.S. Eliot, first of all – consciously returned to their roots, then in the Russian modernists – in Mayakovsky, Tsvetaeva, Pasternak – one can observe isomorphic poetic phenomena despite the absence of any national roots of that sort. Brodsky superbly grasped the connection between twentieth-century modernism and seventeenth-century metaphysical verse, and paid tribute to his English teachers with two commemorative pieces: 'Great Elegy for John Donne' (1963) and 'On the Death of T.S. Eliot' (1965).

Tendency toward dialectics expressed in complex developing metaphors is what characterises baroque poetics first of all. Or as Tsvetaeva, Brodsky's immediate predecessor in Russian poetry, put it: 'A poet begins his speech from afar, and the speech takes him too far'.[5] This is exactly what happens to Brodsky in all the pieces we are going to discuss: he begins with some casual or playfully imagined situation and ends with an accumulation of striking images depicting the historical dead-end in which his country finds itself.

'LETTER IN A BOTTLE' (1965)

This long poem dates back to the period when Brodsky was avidly enjoying unfolding the possibilities of a newly acquired style.

The obvious genre models for 'Letter in a Bottle' are Rimbaud's 'Le bateau ivre', known to Brodsky in Benedict Livshitz's excellent translation, and Gumilyov's 'The Lost Streetcar' – especially the latter. 'Letter in a Bottle' shares a general design with Gumilyov's 1921 poem: a quest for understanding one's own stance represented by the extended metaphor of a surrealistic journey through a terrifying historical reality. As in 'The Lost Streetcar', Brodsky's description of the journey is interrupted by a lyrical digression in the form of direct address to the beloved.[6]

The element of play stands out in this poem with an ever greater fragmentation of passages toward the end, separated by the unrhymed and a-rhythmical comment размыто (washed out). The playful atmosphere though is set in the very beginning, when the author introduces a sort of verbal equivalent of an antique map cartouche into his seascape: Leviathans, Sirens and Two-Faced Janus. In these emblems, in combination with such turn-of-the-century technological achievements as the Smith & Wesson handgun, Marconi's radio, or Zeiss binoculars, the 1960s reader immediately sensed a frolicksome stylisation of the *belle epoque* – a taste developed by the illustrators working for the Polish magazine *Przekroj*, then popular with the young Russian intelligentsia, by the films of Czech animator Karel Zeman, and later by the Beatles. However, unlike stylisers, Brodsky preserves the emblematic value of his mythological figures: his Janus is still the deity of the dead of winter (January) who 'faces death with one face and life with the other', and his Leviathans certainly nudge the reader towards Hobbes.[7]

The backbone of the poem consists of a complex metaphor extending over 279 lines: the Country appears in the guise of a ship and the Author in the guise of a Passenger.

> ⁵ Но так как нос корабля на Норд,
> а взор пассажир устремил на Вест
> (иными словами, глядит за борт),
> сложность растет с переменой мест.
> И так как часто плывут корабли,
> ¹⁰ на всех парусах по волнам спеша,
> физики «вектор» изобрели.
> Нечто бесплотное, как душа.
>
> ⁴⁵ Прошу лишь учесть, что хоть рвется дух
> вверх, паруса не заменят крыл [...] (O: 148–9)

(But since the ship's bow points North,/while the passenger's gaze points West/[in other words, he looks overboard],/the complexity grows with the change of places./And since the ships often run/over waves in full sail,/the physicists invented 'vector',/something incorporeal, like soul./ . . . Please take into consideration that, although the spirit strives to go/up, sails cannot replace wings.)

This extended metaphor (conceit) continues over the course of the entire poem and provides for plot development: the ship is ice-bound, the passenger freezes, drowns. But this plot is merely a frame around principal content – a farewell to the world, which cannot come to help:

> ⁷⁷ На азбуке Морзе своих зубов
> я к вам взываю, профессор Попов,
> и к вам, господин Маркони ... (O: 150)

> (In the Morse code of my teeth/I appeal to you, Professor Popov,/and to you, Mr. Marconi . . .)

The inventors of modern means of communication are followed by the Pilot-Saviour Lindbergh, and gradually the list of farewells grows to include ironic mention of those who either come to mind accidentally, or else are remembered from schoolbooks, or else are inventors, scientists, philosophers, and writers genuinely dear to the author. Besides those mentioned above, the following make their appearance in 'Letter in a Bottle': Newton, Shakespeare, Edison, Faraday, Archimedes, Freud, Marx, Lev Tolstoy, Einstein, Boyle and Mariotte, Kepler, Mendel, Darwin, Kant, Feuerbach, Rabelais, St Francis, and Erroll Flynn. This list of accidental celebrities outlines, albeit in a facetious manner, the contours of a great Western civilisation towards which the passenger directs his gaze.

(The intruder in this highbrow company, Erroll Flynn of the pirate movies, performs a function here that is not merely comic. He also embodies biographical reality – out from the behind of the carnival mask of the Passenger peeks the live, vulnerable author, in whom the impressions of a young and tender age live on.)[8]

'Farewell to the West' takes up lines 77 through 140 and 197 through 214, after which comes the finale, the farewell to the beloved (215–79). The grand 'Farewell to the West' is interrupted (lines 141–96) by a passage in a different key – not ironic but purely lyrical – which might be called 'The Dream':

> [141] Снился мне холод и снился жар,
> снился квадрат мне и снился шар,
> щебет синицы и шелест трав. (О: 152)

(I had a dream about the cold and about the heat,/I had a dream about a square and about a sphere./[About] a tomtit chirping and grass rustling.)

We should note (this will serve again later on) that the images of warmth and summer, as well as the motif of hope, appear in the dream. In the metaphorical 'reality' of the poem it is cold that conquers: the ship is lost, the letter unfinished, its writer perishes.

Since water is Brodsky's constant metaphor for freedom, the internal scheme on which 'Letter in a Bottle' is based can be presented as *the water turns to ice – movement is arrested.*[9]

'A STOP IN THE DESERT' (1966)

This title – another formula of arrested movement (a paraphrase of the title common in painting: 'Rest on the Flight into Egypt') –

Brodsky eventually gave to the entire collection summing up his early work (the book came out in 1970).

'A Stop in the Desert' stands stylistically apart from the rest of the poems examined here: with the exception of the title, there is hardly a trope to be found in it. On the contrary, there is a noticeable tendency to de-metaphorise such stereotypical metaphors of common speech as 'inanimate object', 'doglike loyalty', or 'to bear a cross'. This is characteristic of Brodsky: as a rule, the poetics of his religious verse lacks the striking rhetorical constructions so typical of the most of his other verse (cf. 'Nunc Dimittis' or the 'Christmas' poems of various years).

'A Stop in the Desert' takes the form of a straightforward description and emotionally restrained meditation on certain aspects of Russian history. The description was certainly perceived as realistic by the author's contemporaries and countrymen. Leningraders remember the demolition of the Greek church in 1966 and the construction, in its place, of a large concert hall in the spirit of timidly modernistic post-Stalin architecture. Strolling the city in search of unusual architectural perspectives ('and at some late hour I sat/on the ruins of an apse') was quite common among young intellectuals, many of whom could even give the name and address of 'a certain Tatar family'. One of the daughters in the family was an exceptional beauty.

However, the unadorned and seemingly photographic style of 'A Stop in the Desert' is in essence no less conventional and even less theatricalised than the surrealistic style of 'Letter in a Bottle'. The difference lies in that here the theatricalness, the convention and the symbolism of detail are hidden, and are suggested to the reader casually.

> [1] Теперь так мало греков в Ленинграде,
> что мы сломали греческую церковь,
> дабы воздвигнуть на свободном месте
> концертный зал. (O: 166)

(There are so few Greeks now in Leningrad,/that we tore down the Greek Church,/to build in the empty space/a concert hall.)

The author is indicated by the first person pronoun, and of course a significant part of the poem is made up of unconstrained personal reminiscences, but although 'I' and its corresponding verbal forms are used, the poem begins, none the less, with 'we'. That is, the 'I' of the poem is immediately offered as part of the 'we' and the author takes care that the subject of his historical discourse be perceived not as an individual but as a nation:

> [40] Когда-нибудь, когда не станет *нас*,
> точнее — после *нас*, на *нашем* месте
> возникнет тоже что-нибудь такое,
> чему любой, кто знал *нас* ужаснется.
> Но знавших *нас* не будет слишком много. (O: 167)

(Some day, when we will be no more,/more precisely – after *us*, in *our* place/also will emerge something/that will terrify anyone who used to know *us*./But there will be not too many of those who used to know *us*. [*Italics added*.])

The 'I' of the poem turns out to be distinct from the autobiographical 'I'. The real Joseph Brodsky certainly does not identify himself with those who were destroying the city's architectural monuments and could in no way have said: 'We tore down the Greek church'. The poem's 'I' is dual: the author sometimes appears as an individual in opposition to the faceless majority and sometimes as the rhetorical personification of this very majority.

Neither is the poem's logic quite so simple and logical as it seems at first glance. The conventional narrator declares in a convincing tone that the Greek Church was torn down because there was no need for it: a lack of parishioners. The real author knows all too well that this church, located, incidentally, not too far from his own home, has not been active for years. And not because there were not enough Greeks in Leningrad but because there could not have been any at all, inasmuch as since the Second World War they had belonged to the 'punished peoples' category. Behind the neighbours of Greek extraction who quietly disappeared from the neighbourhood loom the ancient Greeks, the bearers of Hellenistic heritage and of Christianity.

Brodsky's ostensibly straightforward, colloquially intoned narrative conceals a number of inobtrusive but clever poetic devices aimed at making details ambiguous and thus enriching a reader's perception with historico-philosophical associations. Or else Brodsky coaches his reader in seeing everyday experience on a grand scale. Take the following example:

¹⁷ Все началось с татарских разговоров;
а после в разговор вмешались звуки,
сливавшиеся с речью поначалу,
но вскоре — заглушившие ее.
В церковный садик въехал экскаватор
с подвешенной к стреле чугунной гирей. (О: 166)

(It all started with some Tatar conversations;/and then some sounds intruded into conversation,/first they merged with the speech,/but soon – they drowned it./An excavator rolled into the church garden,/with an iron wrecking ball hanging from its bow.)

Within the blank verse a kind of anagrammatic 'rhyme' can be heard: *TATARSKikh RAzgOVOROV-eKSKAVATOR*.[10] This 'rhyme' is certainly a loaded one: everyday conversations among the author's Tatar friends, Tatar speech, 'rhyme' with the sound of destruction, the wrecking ball striking the walls of the Greek Church. An otherwise inadmissibly ridiculous pun, *gírey-Giréy*, the latter being the name of the Crimean khan dynasty frequently mentioned in Russian literature, flickers by in this context.

In 'A Stop in the Desert' Brodsky's historical vision acquires a particularly Solovyovian tinge: *tatarshchina* (Tatar-stuff), 'Asia', is turning Hellenistic-Christian civilisation into ruins. In a way the same vision of the Apocalypse according to Vladimir Solovyov, i.e. in the form of invasion out of Asia, delineates all the poems discussed here.[11] It remains only to emphasise that in Brodsky's work 'Asia' and all its synonyms stand for collectivism, that the invasion occurs not only in the outer world but in the inner one, turning a personality into a mote of dust, replacing 'I' with 'we'.[12]

'A SPEECH ON SPILT MILK' (1967)

The title of this poem, albeit understandable, sounds a bit strange in Russian, which has no direct equivalent of the English proverb 'No use crying over spilt milk'. Perhaps in choosing the calque instead of some similar Russian saying, Brodsky paid an oblique tribute to the source of the genre he adopted here: such publicistic poetic monologues as W.H. Auden's 'Song for the New Year' or 'A Communist to Others'.

The bulk of this long (40 eight-line stanzas) poem consists of a Karamazovian monologue, a sarcastic flood of simile, metaphor and hyperbole aimed at exposing ideas of managing history and organising general happiness as anti-human. Developing his own philosophical anthropology, the poet puts an equal sign between all those teachings which, from his point of view, give preference to the collective over the individual and which are attractive because they are founded on the promise of salvation from suffering, on the promise of bliss, euphoria.

This motif steals into the colloquial, accidentally rhymed lines of the very first stanza as an odd metaphor:

> [1] Я пришел к Рождеству с пустым карманом.
> Издатель тянет с моим романом.
> *Календарь Москвы заражен Кораном.* (К: 6)

(I arrived at Christmas with empty pockets./My publisher's dragging his feet with my novel./*The Moscow calendar is contaminated with the Koran* [italics added.])

The mention of a calendar in a Christmas poem is natural, but it takes some effort for the reader to look at the phases of the moon shown on an ordinary Soviet calendar and see, as the poet does, the symbol of Islam. The Muscovite blend of the Christian and the Asian is not an unknown motif in Russian poetry (cf. Esenin's famous nostalgic lines: 'I love this city of elms,/Albeit aged and grown flabby:/Golden dreamy Asia/Has rested on its domes'.[13]). But Brodsky's Moscow is obviously a metonymical one, it stands for a certain type of social order and the political philosophy behind it. No wonder that we encounter the next mention of Islam in 'A Speech on Spilt Milk' in the context of a virulently satirical attack on Marxist political economy:

> [117] Тьфу-тьфу, мы выросли не в Исламе,
> хватит трепаться о пополаме. (К: 10)

(God forbid! we've not been raised in Islam;/enough of that 'half-and-half' talk.)

In his criticism of Marxist political economy, Brodsky is undoubtedly following such renegade critics of Marxism as Sergey Bulgakov and Berdyaev. It is their ideas that he quotes so concisely: 'Labour is not a market commodity,/to say so is to offend the workers' and 'Labour is the goal and the form of being'.[14]

Although Brodsky's wrathful invectives against Marxist market theory, Eastern religions, and drug addiction may give an impression of random potshots, of near-incoherence, what he is saying is not alogical but is in fact the idea of labour-as-commodity taken to its logical end: if labour is not man's lifelong destiny but only something to be sold in exchange for idleness and pleasure then the ideal humanity strives for is to do no work at all, and experience uninterrupted pleasure. So Buddhist Nirvana, drug highs, and the bliss promised to the inhabitants of Muhammad's paradise are all placed on the same footing. (Of course, both Buddhism and Islam are taken here in their 1960s pop-culture versions.)[15]

The poem is not confined to apocalyptic prophecy, a vision of approaching entropy. Its internal drama is based on the conflict between action and inaction. Not only active evil is repulsive but non-resistance to evil as well: 'Gentlemen, could you at least smash a couple of windows'! There is a parallel to this in the external plot itself: the author 'sits on a chair', too lazy to take even uncomplicated everyday steps in order to have a better time on New Year's Eve, but he does overcome his own idleness by an activity on a higher plane – poetic meditation.

As always with Brodsky, the poem's composition is one of the most important elements of content. One ought to pay particular attention to the division of 'A Speech on Spilt Milk' into three parts and to the interconnection of motifs encountered in the concluding stanzas of each part (stanzas 9, 31, and 40).

The first and the second part of the poem end with a wintry night-time cityscape outside the author's window:

> [9] Ночь. Шуршание снегопада.
> Мостовую тихо скребет лопата.
> В окне напротив горит лампада.
> Я торчу на стальной пружине.
> Вижу только лампаду. Зато икону
> я не вижу. Я подхожу к балкону.
> Снег на крыши кладет попону.
> И дома стоят, как чужие. (К: 8)

(Night. Rustling of snowfall./Shovel quietly scratching pavement./An icon-lamp lit in the window across the street./I'm stuck on the steel spring./I can see only the lamp. But the icon/I cannot see. I'm coming to the balcony./Snow covers roofs with its blanket./And the houses stand, estranged. [. . .]

> [31] Ночь. Переулок. Мороз блокады.
> Вдоль тротуаров лежат карпаты.
> Планеты раскачиваются, как лампады,
> которые Бог возжег в небосводе
> в благоговеньи Своем великом
> перед непознанным нами ликом
> (поэзия делает смотр уликам),
> как в огромном кивоте. (K: 14)

(Night. Alley. [Leningrad] Siege frost./The Carpathians along the sidewalks./Planets swaying like icon-lamps/which God has lit in the firmament/in His great piety/before the image not apprehended by us/(Poetry reviews the evidence),/like in a giant icon-case.)

While these vignettes parallel each other as pictures of cold micro- and macrocosms, the stanza that concludes the third part of 'A Speech on Spilt Milk' and the whole poem sharply contrasts them. In fact, there is no obvious logical connection between it and the text that immediately precedes it. (Brodsky has more than once used striking non-sequiturs as conclusions; see e.g. the closing of 'Nature Morte'.) Moreover this stanza is framed by quotation marks, which makes its status in the poem even more special:

> [40] "Зелень лета, эх, зелень лета!
> Что мне шепчет куст бересклета?
> Хорошо пройтись без жилета!
> Зелень лета вернется.
> Ходит девочка, эх, в платочке.
> Ходит по полю, рвет цветочки.
> Взять бы в дочки, эх, взять бы в дочки.
> В небе ласточка вьется". (K: 16–17)

('The green of summer, oh, the green of summer!/What does the burning bush whisper to me?/It would be nice to stroll without a vest!/The green of summer will return./A little girl walks, oh, in a scarf./She walks around the field picking little flowers./ If only I could adopt her as my daughter, oh, as my daughter./A swallow hovers in the sky'.)

This stanza is marked not only by the disappearance of anger, irony, and resignation but also by such features as emotive interjections, exclamation marks and endearing diminutive suffixes – all highly unusual in Brodsky's poetry.

It is possible that quotation marks are introduced here because Brodsky indeed 'quotes' something, namely an approximation of a sentimental folk song (hence the repetitions and 'oh' interjections). There is also here a semi-quotation from one of Mandelstam's tenderest poems, 'What grasshopper-watch sings . . .', where lines 8 and 9 read: 'It is [my] daughter-swallow/who unbent my canoe'. But above all, the non-sequiturs, stylistic contrast and quotation marks all serve to remove the concluding stanza from the rest of the poem, and to place it in another reality: this is a dream of warmth in the midst of frozen waking.

Brodsky's lyrical meditation on Russian history, based primarily on oppositions of *reality/dream, cold/warmth, Asia/Russia,* and *rest/ movement,* has a precedent in modern Russian poetry. One would inevitably recall Blok's widely anthologised *The river spreads out. It flows sadly and lazily* . . . – the first part of the triptych, *On Kulikovo Field*. The reality of Blok's poem is 'permanent battle' and, first and foremost, rapid movement. In the perspective of this movement Blok sees warmth overcoming night's coldness: 'We'll light up the distant steppe with fires . . .' and the victory of Russia's 'holy banner' over the 'steel of khan's sabre'. But most importantly, the movement, the impetuous galloping of Russia, will never end. In one of the most quoted lines of Russian poetry Blok resolutely resolves the *movement/rest* opposition in favor of the former: 'And the permanent battle! Rest exists only in our dreams.' As we have seen, both Blok and Brodsky derive their historical vision from Vladimir Solovyov and exploit basically the same imagery – but to opposite ends. What is 'reality' for Blok is 'dream' for Brodsky and vice versa. In Brodsky, the victory of 'Islam', cold and immobility is not the result of the poet's personal pessimism

'LETTER TO GENERAL Z.' (1968)

On the eve of his forced exile, in June of 1972, when Brodsky wrote in his letter to Brezhnev: 'There will be neither me who is writing this letter nor you who is reading it [. . .]'[17] he was in a way quoting himself. 'General! Unfortunately there is only one life' – this is from 'Letter to General Z.', written about three years earlier. Out of all the pieces under consideration here, 'Letter to General Z.' is closest to political allegory, a response to the occupation of Czechoslovakia. Brezhnevism's political rhetoric ('The USSR has extended a fraternal helping hand to the people of Czechoslovakia') is directly parodied here:

> [45] [...] сюда нас, думаю, завела
> не стратегия даже, но жажда братства;
> лучше в чужие встревать дела,
> коли в своих нам не разобраться. (K: 31)

([. . .] what has brought us here, I believe, is/not even strategy but striving for brotherhood;/it is better to meddle in the affairs of others/when we cannot manage our own.)

Predictably, Brezhnev's aggressive ventures are depicted in images of dead ends, of getting stuck in the mud, of the utter impossibility of further movement: 'We've been sitting in the mud for so long . . .', 'our cannons, with their barrels buried in the ground . . .', 'we've walked ourselves into a blind alley'. Pictures of bad roads, or no roads, of inactivity, aimlessness abound in the poem. They are so graphic that the text at times resembles a film script:

> [19] Наши пушки уткнулись стволами вниз ...

> [25] Офицеры бродят, презрев устав,
> в галифе и кителях разной масти. (K: 30–1)

Politics/Poetics

> [86] Снайпер, томясь от духовной жажды,
> то ли приказ, то ль письмо жены,
> сидя на ветке, читает дважды (К: 32)

(Our cannons, with their barrels buried in the ground . . .; officers are wandering about/in unmatched tunics and breeches despite the regulations [. . .]; The marksman, athirst in spirit,[18]/ reads something a second time:/either an order or a letter from his wife)

Brodsky himself links this finely detailed style to the period's *Zeitgeist*. 'To be sharp-sighted in this epoch means to see dead-end things sharply,' – he would write somewhat later ('The End of the Belle Epoque', December 1969).

What we do not find among the expected images here are images of cold and freezing. The Arctic ocean is replaced by some equatorial swamp. The author himself points out this substitution in the poem's first stanza:

> [1] Генерал! Наши карты — дерьмо. Я пас.
> Север вовсе не здесь, но в Полярном Круге.
> И Экватор шире, чем ваш лампас.
> Потому что фронт, генерал, на Юге. (К: 30)

(General! Our maps[19] are shit. I pass./The North isn't here at all but within the Polar Circle./And the Equator is wider than the stripe on your uniform breeches./Because the front, General, is in the South.)

It might seem that the choice of the backdrop is linked to Antoine de Saint-Exupéry's famous 'Letter to General Z' written in war-time Africa. That is partly true, but the overall plot design of 'Letter to General Z.' is nothing other than a wide-ranging extension of the generally accepted metaphor, 'the law of the jungle'. The following passage from a poem written at roughly the same time, 'Adieu, Mademoiselle Veronique', can serve as commentary:

> [58] прими же сегодня как мой постскриптум
> к теории Дарвина, столь пожухлой,
> эту новую правду джунглей. (О: 171)

(Take it today as my postscriptum/to Darwin's so very withered theory,/this new truth of the jungle.)[20]

Inasmuch as Brodsky has chosen to write the poem as an epistle, the representation of both the writer and his addressee in 'Letter to General Z.' merits special attention.

The pronoun defining the author is, in the direct sense of the word, ambivalent: as in 'A Stop in the Desert', it is sometimes 'I', sometimes 'we'. Depicting the historical dead end toward which his homeland is headed, Brodsky makes himself a character in his own allegory. In this connection we can once again turn to 'Adieu, Mademoiselle Veronique' where we find this self-commentary:

> [51] Ты, несомненно, простишь мне этот гаерский тон. Это — лучший метод сильные чувства спасти от массы слабых. *Греческий принцип маски снова в ходу.* [21] (О: 171)

(You will, undoubtedly, forgive me this/jestful tone. This is the best method/for rescuing strong feelings from the mass/of weak ones. *The Greek principle of the mask/is again in vogue.* [Italics added.])

Even more curious is Brodsky's treatment of the addressee. Although, unlike most of Brodsky's poems, this allegory has an addressee who can be unequivocally deciphered – L.I. Brezhnev – one of the fundamental and explicit motifs of the poem is the illusory nature of that very addressee.

> [97] Генерал! я вам должен сказать, что вы вроде крылатого льва при входе в некий подъезд. Ибо вас, увы, не существует вообще а природе. Нет, не то чтобы вы мертвы или же биты – вас нет в колоде. (К: 33)

¹⁰⁹ Генерал, я скажу вам еще одно :
Генерал! Я взял вас для рифмы к слову
"умирал"[...] (K: 33)

¹²⁷ Генерал! Вас нету, и речь моя
обращена, как обычно, ныне
в ту пустоту, чьи края – края
некой обширной глухой пустыни,
коей на картах, что вы и я
видеть могли, даже нет в помине. (K: 34)

(General! I must tell you, that you are/something like a winged lion at the entrance/to some doorway. Because you, alas,/do not exist in nature at all./No, it is not that you are dead/or covered – you are just not in the deck. . . . General, I'll tell you something else: General! I took you because you rhyme with the word/*umiral* [was dying] . . . General! You don't exist, and my speech/now as usual is addressed/to the void whose edges are the edges/of a vast wild desert,/of which there is nary a mention/on maps that you or I could see.)

The recurring motif of a card game serves the same purpose as these direct assertions of the addressee's non-existence. Brodsky consistently resorts to puns on gambling terms, thus managing to create the dizzying effect of a dislocated, 'unreal' reality.

Russian *karty* means both 'maps' and 'cards'. 'In the very first line of the poem *karty* can be read both as playing cards and maps: 'General! Your *karty* are shit. I pass' (are they playing cards?). But in the second line: 'The North isn't here at all but within the Polar Circle' (are they maps?).

Chervi means 'hearts' as a card term and 'worms' otherwise. The third stanza begins with 'We've been sitting in the mud for so long/that the king of *chervi* is already rejoicing [. . .]'

The 'Ace of diamonds' used to be a patch on convicts' garb. In stanza 11: 'Let them attach an ace of diamonds/between my shoulder blades'.

In the 12th stanza: 'I don't want to die for/two or three *kings* whom/I've never ever seen [. . .]'

In the 13th stanza: 'I'm/bored with the *krestovy pokhod*'. *Krestovy pokhod* means 'crusade' and *krestovy* as a card term means 'clubs'.

Card terminology is used unambiguously in the 17th stanza:

'[You're not] beaten, you're just not in the deck' and in the last one: 'General! Even a house of cards is a pigsty'.

The epigraph[22] says: 'Your Excellency, war is an empty game./ Good luck today, a hole[23] [in the skull] tomorrow'. As we have seen, Brodsky's mostly ambiguous metaphorical system treats this game as a double game. The deck is marked: the king with his little red heart is not a symbol of love or marriage but of death and decay; the ace of diamonds turns into a convicts' brand, etc. Thus in this poem the traditional mythical connection between the card play and the forces of evil is actualised.

In the epigraph the game is defined as *empty*. The General, i.e. the addressee, is also eventually defined as a zero, a unit of emptiness. Once again in Brodsky's work we are dealing with the widespread Christian – especially Eastern Orthodox Christian – concept of evil (devil) as the absence of good.[24] The very initial Z. designating the poem's addressee is apparently not just the mathematical symbol for the unknown (why not X?) but also the initial for *zero*. A final possibility should not be excluded – that the very name 'General Z.' is compounded from the characters' names in Vladimir Solovyov's *Three Conversations*, where one of them is called 'General' and another 'Mr Z.' In that case we are dealing with a reference to Solovyov's last prophecy: the coming of the Antichrist.[25]

CONCLUSION

The discourse with which Brodsky was addressing political issues in the 1960s was engendered by Vladimir Solovyov (and to a lesser degree by other turn-of-the-century Russian philosophers) and was thus akin to the poetic discourse of the Silver Age. It is no wonder that some survivors of that period welcomed Brodsky as a poet reaching back to 1921 and starting from where Blok and Gumilyov left off.[26] We shall not discuss here the affinity of Brodsky's poetico-political philosophy with that of Akhmatova – it seems to be self-evident. But even when Brodsky defies Blok on a historical issue, they still share the same vision and rhetoric. Like Silver Age poetry, Brodsky's poetry in the 1960s is decidedly chiliastic. He believes that he is witnessing what Blok and others had a foreboding of (hence his paradoxically formulated idea of *post aetatem nostram*[27]). This sets Brodsky apart from his poet contemporaries. Famous bards of the 1960s – Akhmadulina, Evtushenko, Okudzhava, Voznesensky *et al.* – who sometimes attacked the Soviet regime in a more direct way than Brodsky ever did, but their rhetoric never dared to violate the lines drawn at the 20th Party Congress (de-Stalinisation, 'return to the Leninist norm', etc.).

It would be naive to credit Brodsky with 'inventing' the rhetoric of anti-*zastoi* (stagnation) which gained currency in Soviet society some twenty years later, but we have seen that this was exactly what Brodsky came up with at the very beginning of the Brezhnev's era when he was trying to pinpoint the essence of a new *Zeitgeist*.

In the following years Brodsky seldom chose purely political topics. However, the air of political, or rather historical, reality is always present in his work, including even utterly lyrical pieces. A reader familiar with Brodsky's *oeuvre* cannot help discerning these overtones whenever images of cold, arrested movement, Asia or illusion appear in a Brodsky poem.

'The End of the Belle Epoque' (1969) serves as a good illustration to our topic – the formation of a thematic figurative lexicon – primarily because here the *zastoi* motifs come thick and fast.

This elegy is one of the gloomiest and simultaneously most lyrical of Brodsky pre-emigration poems. Theatrical devices, masks are hardly used here. 'I, one of the deaf, balding, moody envoys/of a second-rate nation [. . .]] says the author at the beginning – but here the masquerade ends, and is followed by a lyric monologue. If we tried to synopsise the poem stanza by stanza, we would see the 'historico-political' imagery being organically integrated into it.

Stanza 1. The author goes downstairs to get a paper.

Stanza 2. Cityscape in the evening. Everything seems illusory ('victory of mirrors').

Stanza 3. The mental expansion of the cityscape. Enumeration of attributes of Russian life begins with the generalisation: 'Everything [here] is meant for winter'.

Stanza 4. Enumeration of 'things Russian' continued with emphasis on their weightiness: 'Even wicker chairs are fastened here/with bolts and nuts'.

Stanza 5. Meditation on man's ontological unfreedom.

Stanza 6. The crude thought that love is no way out of the existential cul-de-sac: what lies between a beautiful woman's legs is the 'end of perspective'.

Stanza 7. Meditation on being locked into the country; the author returns to his apartment.
Stanza 8. Meditation on suicide and inevitable failure of escape attempt because the escapee is 'crazy from frost'.
Stanza 9. The author reads his paper; meditation on the death penalty: 'a man lying face down by the brick wall'.
Stanza 10. Meditation on history. The origin of the current situation back in the days when the nation was formed, when not distinguishing between a man and an object ('[they did not distinguish between] those who fell out of cradles and the pipes falling [from their mouths]'[28]) was commonplace. In Brodsky's world this lack of concern for the individual is, as we know, characteristic of 'Asia', here dubbed 'white-eyed Chud'.[29]
Stanza 11. Coda. A crude antithesis to one of Brodsky's favorite metaphors from *The Lay of the Igor Campaign*: '[one ought to] ooze like a gob on a wall'.[30] A dinosaur is introduced, an image from a monstrous, pre-human life (similar metaphors lie concealed at the beginning of Solzhenitsyn's *Gulag Archipelago* and in Shalamov's story 'Lend Lease'). The last three lines, with their mention of the green, the bird and with the songlike interjection 'oh', echo the ending of 'A Speech on Spilt Milk'.

The word 'wall' (in Russian *stena*, which is not just semantically but also phonetically and, perhaps, etymologically close to *ostanovka*, 'stop') occurs three times in the poem: 'prison walls [meant for winter]' in the third stanza, the man lying 'face down by the brick wall' in the ninth and 'a gob on a wall' in the eleventh.

The poems which have been discussed here do not make a cycle in the traditional poetic sense of the term. I put them together because, in my view, they show how Brodsky's ideas about history and society have been formed and shaped into a limited set of invariable motifs and verbal images.

Among the motifs the generic one is undoubtedly oppostion: *movement/immobility*. Other essential motifs connected with it paradigmatically are the oppositions: *warmth/cold, life/death, water/ dryness, man/thing, reality/illusion*. The latter gives the otherwise elementary paradigm a typically Brodskian twist: the material world of things is dead and illusory. This idealistic revelation first came to Brodsky even before the period described here. In his rather confused, youthful long poem 'Procession' (1962) there is one remarkable passage, the dialogue between Chestnyaga (A Square Fellow) and the Chorus. Chestnyaga proclaims the principles of

Faith, Love, Good Labour and Lofty Aspirations to which the Chorus responds with gutter language. The Chorus's response is emphatically 'realistic'; it depicts *real* life where people cut each other's throats in their daily struggle. 'This is what life is like', concludes the Chorus. 'But it is more like death', Chestnyaga answers.[31]

The above mentioned paradigm is, by itself, elementary. The richness of the verbal imagery in which it is manifested is what strikes a reader of Brodsky. The poet's inexhaustible and extremely disciplined fantasy never fails to create new images of individual people and things, open sea and cluttered apartments, sunlit courtyards and wintry landscapes, etc., etc.

In each of the poems we have discussed there are other important motifs and images not mentioned in this specialized commentary. For example, the erotic is almost always interwined with the political in these poems. But it has not been this author's task to draft a mental map of Brodsky's creative mind. That is impossible and unnecessary. This article was meant to show how a poet gives expression to his people's vague budding political feelings.

Notes

1. Most recently in his Nobel speech (1987).
2. In this article the poems 'Letter in a Bottle' and 'A Stop in a Desert' are quoted from Iosif Brodsky, *Ostanovka v pustyne*, New York: Izdatel'-stvo imeni Chekhova, 1970; 'A Speech on Spilt Milk', 'A Letter to General Z'. and 'The End of the Belle Epoque' from Iosif Brodsky, *Konets prekrasnoy epokhi*, Ann Arbor: Ardis, 1977. The quotations are followed by our interlinear translation and the first line of each quotation is numbered to indicate its place within the poem.
3. 'A Speech on Spilt Milk'.
4. In Andrey Platonov, *The Foundation Pit* (Ann Arbor: Ardis, 1973), p. x.
5. '*Poetry*' (1923); Marina Tsvetaeva, *Stikhotvoreniya i poemy v pyati tomakh*, t.3 (New York: Russica, 1983), p. 67.
6. In 'Post aetatem nostram' (1970) there is a simile borrowed from Gumilyov's 'The Lost Streetcar'. Gumilyov writes about the executioner with 'udderlike face', Brodsky about the Vicegerent 'whose face resembles a purulent udder' (*Konets prekrasnoy epokhi*, p. 91).
7. Cf. in 'A Speech on Spilt Milk': [164]'(one can find it in Hobbes)'.
8. Cf. Sonnet 2 in 'Twenty Sonnets for Mary Stuart' (Iosif Brodsky, *Chast' rechi* (Ann Arbor: Ardis, 1976), p. 51).
9. On Brodsky's constant metaphors see Valentina Polukhina, *Joseph Brodsky: A Poet for Our Time* (Cambridge, 1989).

10. Phonetically this anagram is even fuller: ZG (raZGovorov) is a voiced equivalent of voiceless SK (tatarSKikh).
11. See 'Tri razgovora' in Vladimir Solovyov, *Sobranie sochineniy*, Petersburg: 'Prosveshchenie' (n/d) t.10, pp. 81–221. Brodsky had the YMCA-Press reprint of Solovyov's collected works in his library.
12. Cf. 'Flight from Bysantium' in Joseph Brodsky, *Less Than One*, New York: Farrar, Straus, Giroux [1986], pp. 396–446. See also Thomas Venclova's article in this collection.
13. 'Da! Teper' resheno. Bez vozvrata . . .' (1922–23); Sergey Esenin, *Sobranie sochineniy v 5 tomakh*, t.2, Moscow: 'Khudozhestvennaya literatura', 1966, p. 119.
14. See e.g. Sergey Bulgakov, *Filosofiya khozyaystva*, Moscow: Put', 1912 (reprint: New York: Chalidze Publications, 1982), pp. 242–43 and 307–21.
15. One can find more reverential treatment of Islam by Brodsky in his 'Pamyati T.B.' (*Konets prekrasnoy epokhi*, pp. 19–28). Incidentally, Brodsky says that his first meaningful encounter with poetry was reading, following his mother's advice, *Gulistan* (*The Garden of Roses*) by Saadi in Russian translation (*Less Than One*, p. 488).
16. It should be noted that in Blok we have not only the opposition 'Russians vs Tatars' but also the expression of Russian 'Tatarism' in the spirit of the then budding Eurasian movement.
17. Quoted by Ia. Gerchin in *Neva* no. 2, 1989, p. 166.
18. 'Athirst in spirit . . .' – Brodsky ironically quotes the first line of Pushkin's 'The Prophet' (1826).
19. A pun. See discussion of this punning image below.
20. 'Proshchayte, madmuazel' Veronika', *Ostanovka v pustyne*, p. 171. That Brodsky kept an eye on the main geopolitical shift of the century, replacement of the East-West conflict with the North–South one, is also evident in 'A Speech on Spilt Milk' (lines 148–52) and in 'Adieu, Mademoiselle Veronique' where lines 2–5: 'meatgrinders/are becoming a luxury item available to small nations–/after great many combinations/Mars is moving closer to palms' (*Ostanovka v pustyne*, p. 169).
21. *Ostanovka v pustyne*, p. 171.
22. To the question 'Where did this epigraph come from?' Brodsky said that he does not remember, 'from one novel or another'.
23. *Dyra* (a hole) in Brodsky's poetic idiolect is more than once used in the meaning of a mortal wound.
24. Perhaps the most influential text in which this concept of evil was explained for Brodsky's generation was Pavel Florensky's 'Iconostasis', which circulated in samizdat.
25. Solovyov, *op. cit*.
26. This idea is emphatically expressed at the end of Victor Veidle's article 'Peterburgskaya poetika' in N. Gumilyov, *Sobranie sochineniy*, t.4, Washington: Izdatelstvo knizhnogo magazina Victor Kamkin Inc., 1964, pp. xxxv–xxxvi.
27. For literary parallels of this motif one should look not at the famous conclusion of Eliot's 'The Hollow Men' but rather at Czeslaw Milosz's poem 'Piosenka o koncu swiata' (Czeslaw Milosz, *Poezje*, Warszawa:

Czytelnik, 1981, p. 88) with its emphasis on the ordinariness of post-Apocalyptic world.
28. This opposition might sound strange in English but in Russian it is reinforced by a pun: *lyul'ka* (cradle) and *lyul'ka* (Cossack smoking pipe).
29. *Chud'* with its constant epithet in Russian folklore *beloglazaya* (white-eyed) was a Finnish tribe which had come from Asia and made one of the ethnic components of the future Russian nation. Note another connection with Blok: in Blok's *Rus' moya, zhizn' moya, vmeste l' nam mayat'sya?'* (1910) *Chud'* is also mentioned as an ancestor of Russians (this is not particularly common) (Aleksandr Blok, *Sobranie sochineniy v 8 tomakh*, t.3, Moscow-Leningrad: GIKhL, 1960, p. 259).
30. Brodsky's crude parody of the proverbial 'To run/to flow like a thought/ a squirrel around the tree'; this squirrel/thought (mysl') makes many appearances in Brodsky's poetry.
31. Iosif Brodsky, *Stikhotvoreniya i poemy*, New York: Inter-Language Literary Associates, 1965, pp. 189–92.

Translated by Jane Miller

4
Variations on the Theme of Exile
George L. Kline

I

Joseph Brodsky has said: 'Perhaps exile is the poet's natural condition . . . . I felt a certain privilege in the coincidence of my existential condition with my profession'.[1] Growing up in Leningrad, that most deliberately willed and un-Russian of cities, was a rehearsal for the condition of exile: 'If it's true that every writer has to estrange himself from his experience to be able to comment upon it then the city [St Petersburg/Leningrad], by rendering this alienating service, saved them a trip'.[2]

Jane Knox, who has known the poet for more than twenty years, has noted that 'Brodsky's critics and those who were just acquainted with him have always been struck by the fact that a "condition of banishment" was a constant trait of his spiritual-cultural make-up', adding that, long before Brodsky left Russia, his reaction, as a poet, to the world around him was one of alienation.[3]

In exile a poet is 'alone with his language':

> For one in our profession [Brodsky declares], the condition we call exile is, first of all, a linguistic event: an exiled writer is thrust, or retreats, into his mother tongue. From being his, so to speak, sword, it turns into his shield, into his capsule [presumably in the sense of a space-capsule or time-capsule]. What started as a private, intimate affair with the language, in exile becomes fate – even before it becomes an obsession.[4]

I shall distinguish in Brodsky's work three different groups of 'poems of exile':

1. Those poems written during his 18-month internal exile, in

the tiny village of Norinskaia[5] in the Archangel Region of Northern Russia (March 1964 to November 1965). The dates of the poems in this group range from late March 1964 to October 1965.
2. Those poems, including several major ones, written in February and March 1972, in anticipation of the permanent foreign exile which in fact began for Brodsky in June of that year.
3. Those poems written during his permanent exile, mostly in the United States, but including several written in England and Italy, beginning in November of 1972 and continuing with special emphasis on the periods of 1974–77 and 1980.

For convenience I shall refer to these three groups of poems of exile simply as the 'first group', the 'second group', and the 'third group'.

All three groups of poems exhibit certain general themes: loss, pain, shock; the experience of separation, and of solitude. Certain more specific themes characterise the different groups.

In the first group there is the sense of 'being overboard', of finding oneself in 'no-man's land', of going deaf and going blind. Significantly, there is no mention of the poet's being or becoming 'mute'; that is a theme reserved for the early poems (1972–73) of the third group, in particular the powerful '1972'. Added to this is the threat of madness and loss of memory, or at least of specific memories. In one important poem of this group there is the experience of shipwreck, of going down for the last time, of facing imminent destruction and death.

In the second group there is a poignant anticipation of profound personal loss – loss of the woman the poet loves, who is the mother of his young son, and of that son – where the loss of memory becomes an inability to discriminate within the flow of time. Its most painful expression is the inability of the father to recall the age of his distant son whom he has not seen for many years. Other poems in this group raise the question of the hugeness, impersonality, and amorality of the 'Empire' in opposition to the free, or freedom-seeking, individual, especially the individual artist or poet.

The third group exhibits the hitherto unexpressed themes of growing old, growing decrepit, dying, lapsing into silence (in the sense of *molchanie* or 'non-speaking'), of losing the absolute control of one's native language which is essential to the profession of the poet.

The focus in the poems of the third group on the themes of aging, losing one's hair and teeth, growing deaf, lapsing into *molchanie*, cannot, I think, be explained solely in terms of the difference in Brodsky's age in the two cases. At the beginning of the first group he was twenty-four; at the beginning of the third group he was thirty-two, a difference of only eight years. Although he had indeed experienced serious health problems both in Leningrad and Ann Arbor the difference lies in large part in the finality and irreversibility of his banishment from his country, his culture, and, in a sense, his language.

There was, of course, much more severe trauma in the case of the permanent exile abroad, expressed in part by the fact that the 'dry' period, the period during which Brodsky was unable to write, was four times as long in the case of the third group of poems of exile as in the case of the first – eight months as compared to two.

He had written a poem ('Squeezing the Ration of Banishment') in the Archangel transfer prison on 25 March 1964. Two months later, in Norinskaia, he wrote several of the poems of the first group, two of which are dated, respectively, 17 May and 24 May, the latter being Brodsky's twenty-fourth birthday.

In contrast, the last poems written before his permanent exile abroad date from February and March of 1972 – and they include such major works as 'The Funeral of Bobo', 'Letters to a Roman Friend', 'Song of Innocence and Experience', *'Nunc Dimittis'*, and 'Odysseus to Telemachus' – and were followed by severe culture shock and a full eight months during which Brodsky was unable to write a single poem. He spent a week with me at my summer cottage in the Berkshires in July and several days with me at Bryn Mawr and in New York in October; we also spoke quite frequently by telephone during this period (he was in Ann Arbor). My clear and painful impression was of a poet who feared that he might *never* write again. In the event, his concern proved groundless: in mid-November he composed 'In the Lake District' and in December the long and powerful poem '1972'. Since that time, of course, his poetic output has been both steady and strong.

Certain poems of the third group exhibit a set of related themes of being a 'complete nobody', of taking (being forced to take?) 'memory-deadening' pills, of having lost not only memory (as in the first group), or one's only son (anticipated in the second), but also one's homeland.

Variations on the Theme of Exile

Certain later poems of the third group, dating from 1974–76, exhibit an identification, or close association, of the poet with three major historical figures, who have in common the fact that they were mistreated – disgraced, exiled, or executed – by the country or city which they loved and served with devotion and effectiveness. The three are Dante, Mary Queen of Scots, and the Soviet Second World War hero Marshal Georgi Zhukov.

II

In sections II, III, and IV, I shall, in turn, discuss and quote from the principal poems of the three groups.

'New Stanzas to Augusta' (1964)[6] finds the poet fearing the loss of his five senses, and even the loss of his mind. He is *zakhoronennyi zhiv'em* ('buried alive'), *bez pamiati, s odnim kakim-to zvukom* ('without memory, with only a certain [inner] sound') (O: 156). Brodsky exclaims:

Что ж, пусть легла бессмысленности тень
в моих глазах,... (О: 157)

(What does it matter that a shadow of mindlessness has crossed my eyes . . .?) (SP: 58)[7]

Лишь сердце вдруг забьётся, отыскав,
что где-то я пропорот. ... (О: 157)

(But my heart pounds suddenly when I discover that somewhere I am torn.) (SP: 58)

И вот бреду я по ничьей земле
и у Небытия прошу аренду. (О: 158)

Here I wander in a non-man's land
and take a lease on non-existence.) (SP: 59)

Вот я стою в распахнутом пальто
и мир течёт в глаза сквозь решето,
сквозь решето непониманья.
Я глуховат. Я, Боже, слеповат. (О: 159)

(Here I stand, my coat thrown open,
letting the world flow into my eyes
through a sieve of incomprehension.
I'm going deaf. O God, I'm going blind.) (SP 60, revised)

'A Letter in a Bottle' (1965), also written in Norinskaia, exhibits the linked themes of shipwreck, running aground, sinking to the bottom, and the utter isolation from which one can attempt to escape only by sending such a futile 'letter' – here pictured as being 'received' with many of its key lines 'washed out' by sea-water.

Я честно плыл, но попался риф,
и он насквозь пропорол мне бок.
Я пальцы смочил, но Финский залив
вдруг оказался весьма глубок. (O: 149)

(I sailed with honor, but my frail craft
wounded its side on a jagged reef.
I wet my fingers; the Finnish Gulf
suddenly proved to be very deep.) (SP: 107)

Снег повалил тут, и я застрял,
задрав к небосводу свой левый борт,
как некогда сам 'Генерал-Адмирал
Апраскин'. Но чем-то иным затёрт. (O: 149)

(Snow was now falling; I'd run aground
on the dark reef, my port side was high –
like the *Admiral Apraskin*[8] of naval renown –
though not by what she was stranded by.) (SP: 107)

Вода, как я вижу, уже по грудь,
и я отплываю в последний путь.
И, так как не станет никто провожать,
хотелось бы несколько рук пожать.   (0:151)

(I see that the water is now chest-deep.
And I must bed down for my final sleep.
Since no one is coming to say good-bye,
I'll shake several hands now, definitively.) (SP: 109)

Variations on the Theme of Exile

Снилось мне также, что лошадь ржёт.
Но смерть — это зеркало, что не лжёт. (O: 152)

(I dreamed I was hearing a horse's neigh.
But death is a mirror that does not lie.) (SP: 110)

я вижу, собственно, только нос
и снег, что ундине уста занёс
и нежный бюст превратил в сугроб.
Сейчас мы исчезнем, пловучий гроб[7] (O: 152)

(All that I see now is my ship's bow.
The figurehead's mouth is concealed by snow.
Her delicate breast is a white snowbank.
This frail floating coffin will soon be sunk.) (SP: 111)

когда на скромном своём корабле
я, как сказал перед смертью Рабле,
отправляюсь в "Великое Может Быть"...
(размыто) (O: 153)

(while I in my modest and halting way
set sail, in the words of old Rabelais,
for the shadowy shore of the 'Great Maybe'.[9]
(washed out) (SP: 112)

Я слух и желудок не смог сберечь:
я нахлебался и речью полн...
(размыто)

Меня вспоминайте при виде волн!
(размыто)

Что парная рифма нам даст, то ей
мы возвращаем под видом дней.
Как, скажем, данные дни в снегу...
Лишь смерть оставляет, мадам, в долгу.
(размыто)

Что говорит с печалью в лице
кошке, усевшейся на крыльце,

снегирь, не спуская с последней глаз?
"Я думал, ты не придёшь. *Alas!*" (O: 155)

(I couldn't protect my stomach or ears.
I've now drunk my fill and I'm choked with speech.
                                        (washed out)
Remember me, madam, whenever the sea . . .
                                        (washed out)
What couplets may bring me I must pay back
in days or in hours on my lonely track –
for instance, these days in the snowy waste.
It's death alone, madam, that can't be repaid.
                                        (washed out)

What did the sorrowful bullfinch chirp
to the cat that had climbed to the poor bird's perch?
He said, without shifting his eyes from his foe's,
'I thought you weren't coming. You're here. Alas!')
                                    (SP: 114, revised)

III

Certain poems of the second group introduce a historical, mythological, and political dimension to Brodsky's reflections on the fate of the exiled poet. In the words of a recent critic: as a result of Brodsky's 'poetic reinterpretation there is a 'making contemporary' of myth, its appropriation by modern culture; the reader, through the myth, hears the poet's narrative about time and about himself'.[10]

The category of 'Empire', introduced in '*Post aetatem nostram*' (1970), is here expanded. (There will be a further expansion in certain poems of the third group. See section IV below.) 'Empire', as Lev Loseff has recently noted, is for Brodsky a universal realm with no distinct geographical or historical boundaries; it is impersonal, alienating, godless[11] – in opposition to the free, or freedom-seeking individual. Such an individual, however, – called simply 'the Greek' in '*Post aetatem nostram*, – is not yet explicitly identified as a poet.

That identification, and the contrast between the turbulent capital – center of power and intrigue – and the relatively safe and tranquil provinces, is drawn in 'Letters to a Roman Friend' (March 1972). This poem is neither an imitation of nor an adaptation from Martial.[12] There are some borrowed elements: the Roman friend's name, Postumus, is one used by Martial. But the principal similarity is one of condition: the poet in exile. Martial (ca. 40 – ca. 104), who was born in Spain, had a brilliant literary career in Rome, but then, disillusioned and embittered, returned to the provincial obscurity of Spain to spend the last half-dozen years of his life (from 98 AD).

Brodsky's poem makes it clear that it is safer – if one is fated (as both Martial and Brodsky were) to live one's life in a great Empire – to live quietly, even obscurely, as remote as possible from the centres of power, violence, and intrigue.

> Если выпало в Империи родиться,
>   лучше жить в глухой провинции у моря.
>
> И от Цезаря далёко, и от вьюги.
>   Лебезить не нужно, трусить, торопиться. (С: 12)

(If one's fated to be born in Caesar's Empire
let him live aloof, provincial, by the seashore.
One who lives remote from snowstorms and from Caesar
has no need to hurry, flatter, play the coward.)
                                            (PS: 53)[13]

The 'storms', of course, are political and cultural rather than natural or cosmic.

That the author of the 'Letters' is a poet, or at least a writer, is suggested in two rather subtle ways. He says that he is sending *books* – perhaps his own, although that is not explicitly stated – to his friend in Rome. And at the end there is a mention of the 'zelen' lavra' ('green of the *laurel* tree') in connection with discussion of the author's (poet's) imminent death:

> Скоро, Постум, друг твой, любящий сложенье,
>   долг свой давний вычитанию заплатит.
> Забери из-под подушки сбереженья,
>   там немного, но на похороны хватит. (С: 13)

> (Soon, dear Postumus, your friend who loves addition
> will pay off his debt, his old debt, to subtraction.
> Take my savings, then, from underneath my pillow –
> though not much, they'll pay the cost of my interment.)
> (PS: 54)

The mention of a volume – presumably the *Historia Naturalis* – by Pliny the Elder in the final stanza of the poem is puzzling, despite the fact that Pliny the Younger, nephew and literary executor of Pliny the Elder, had written a moving account of Martial's death, until one realises that Martial had described the waste slopes of the recently active Mt Vesuvius and, in particular, that Pliny the Elder (23–79) had been killed in that volcanic eruption, the famous explosion that buried Pompeii and Herculaneum. Brodsky had spoken more than once of volcanos in general and Vesuvius in particular as destructive forces which threaten both persons and cultures. For example, there is this early (1962) unrhymed sonnet:

> Мы снова проживаем у залива,
> и проплывают облака над нами,
> и современный тарахтит Везувий,
> и оседает пыль по переулкам,
> и стёкла переулков дребезжат.
> Когда-нибудь и нас засыпет пепел.
> Так я хотел бы в этот бедный час
> приехать на окраину в трамвае,
> войти в твой дом,
> и если через сотни лет
> придёт отряд раскапывать наш город,
> то я хотел бы, чтоб меня нашли
> оставшимся навек в твоих объятьях,
> засыпанного новою золой. (O: 45)

> (Once more we're living on the Gulf [of Finland];[14]
> and clouds of black smoke drift, daily, above us.
> Our own Vesuvius has cleared its throat;
> volcanic ash is settling in the side-streets.
> Our windowpanes have rattled to its roaring.
> Some day we too will be shrouded with ashes.
> And when that happens, at that awful moment,
> I'd like to take a streetcar to the outskirts

of town and find your house;
and if, after a thousand years,
a swarm of scientists should come here
to dig our city out, I hope they'll find me,
cloaked with the ashes of our modern epoch,
and everlastingly within your arms.) (SP: 46, revised)

In 'December in Florence' – Brodsky's 'Dante' poem (to be discussed in Section IV below) – we find this claim:

...вблизи вулкана
невозможно жить, не показывая кулака; ... (C: 111)

(. . . near a volcano
one cannot live without shaking a fist at it, . . .)
(trans. Maurice English and George L. Kline, *Shearsman*, 1982, p. 19)

The second theme adumbrated – through myth – in the second group of poems of exile is an even more personal and poignant one, although it is presented with no trace of self-pity. This is Brodsky's permanent separation from his son. In the poem 'Odysseus to Telemachus' (February–March 1972)[15] we listen as Odysseus, somewhere on the long journey home from Troy, addresses his son:

Не помню я, чем кончилась война,
и сколько лет тебе сейчас, не помню.

Расти большой, мой Телемак, расти.
Лишь боги знают, свидимся ли снова.
Ты и сейчас уже не тот младенец,
перед которым я сдержал быков.
Когда б не Паламед, мы жили вместе.
Но может быть и прав он: без меня
ты от страстей Эдиповых избавлен,
и сны твои, мой Телемак, безгрешны. (C: 23)

(I can't remember how the war came out;
even how old you are – I can't remember.

Grow up, then, Telemachus, grow strong.
Only the gods know if we'll see each other
again. You've long since ceased to be that babe

before whom I reined in the pawing bullocks.
Had it not been for Palamedes' trick
we two would still be living in one household.
But maybe he was right; away from me
you are quite safe from all Oedipal passions,
and your dreams, my Telemachus, are blameless.) (SP: 168)

IV

The first poem of the third group, which dates from November 1972, bears the title 'In the Lake District'. It expresses both the frustration of being unable to finish a poem and a poignant sense of increasing decrepitude and a final sadness. Here are a few excerpts:

> ... я, прячущий во рту
> развалины почище Парфенона, ...

> ... — я жил
> в колледже возле Главного из Пресных
> озёр, ...

> Всё то, что я писал в те времена,
> сводилось неизбежно к многоточью.
> Я падал, не расстёгиваясь, на
> постель свою. И ежели я ночью
> отыскивал звезду на потолке,
> она, согласно правилам сгоранья,
> сбегала на подушку по щеке
> быстрей, чем я загадывал желанье. (С: 28)

(... there I, whose mouth held ruins more abject than any Parthenon ...

... was living at a college near the most renowned of the fresh-water lakes; ...

Whatever I then wrote was incomplete:
my lines expired in strings of dots. Collapsing,
I dropped, still fully dressed, upon my bed.

> At night I stared up at the darkened ceiling
> until I saw a shooting star, which then,
> conforming to the laws of self-combustion,
> would flash – before I'd even made a wish –
> across my cheek and down onto my pillow.)
> (PS: 67, revised)

The sense of isolation and of an impending solitary and unmarked death is powerfully expressed in an untitled poem of the same period, which ends:

> Здесь снится вам не женщина в трико,
> а собственный ваш адрес на конверте.
> Здесь утром, видя скисшим молоко,
> молочник узнаёт о вашей смерти.
> Здесь можно жить, забыв про календарь,
> глотать свой бром, не выходить наружу
> и в зеркало глядеться, как фонарь
> глядится в высыхающую лужу. (C: 30)

> (The dreams you dream are not of girls half-nude
> but of your name on an arriving letter.
> A morning milkman, seeing milk that's soured,
> will be the first to guess that you have died here.
> Here you can live, ignoring calendars,
> gulp Bromo, never leave the house; just settle
> and stare at your reflection in the glass,
> as streetlamps stare at theirs in shrinking puddles.)
> (PS: 61–2)

Brodsky's first major poem of the third group, called simply '1972' (completed in December of that year), is notable, on the one hand, for its formal inventiveness,[16] and, on the other, for its saturation with allusions to Russian history and culture. It expresses an almost overwhelming sense of irrecoverable loss, of the impending end, of growing old and lapsing into silence. It echoes the equation of speech and life, and of silence and non-speaking (molchanie), put forward in the long and complex poem 'Gorbunov and Gorchakov' (1965–1968), which falls between the first and second groups of poems of exile.[17] That earlier poem includes these remarkable lines:

> Молчанье — это будущее дней,
> катящихся навстречу нашей речи, . . .
> с присутствием прощания при встрече.
> Молчанье — это будущее слов, ... (О: 206)

(And silence is the future of all days
that roll toward speech; yes, silence is the presence
of farewells in our greetings as we touch.
Indeed, the future of our words is silence . . .) (SP: 147)

> Молчанье есть грядущее любви; (О: 206)

(Silence: the future fate of all our loving . . .) (SP: 147)

> Молчанье — настоящее для тех,
> кто жил до нас. ... (О: 206)

(And silence is the present fate of those who
have lived before us. . . .) (SP: 147)

> Жизнь — только разговор перед лицом
> молчанья". ... (О: 206)

(Life is but talk hurled in the face of silence.) (SP: 147)

The association of life and speech, and death and silence, also appears in a major poem of the second group, *Nunc Dimittis* (February 1972). The dying of St Simeon is evoked with great sensitivity:[18]

> ... Одежд и чела
> уж ветер коснулся, и в уши упрямо
> врывался шум жизни за стенами храма.
>
> Он шёл умирать. И не в уличный гул
> он, дверь отворивши руками, шагнул,
> но в глухонемые владения смерти.
> Он шёл по пространству, лишённому тверди,
>
> он слышал, что время утратило звук. (С: 22)

> (... The wind stirred his robe
> and fanned at his forehead; the roar of the street,
> exploding in life by the door of the temple,
> beat stubbornly into old Simeon's hearing.
>
> He went forth to die. It was not the loud din
> of streets that he faced when he flung the door wide,
> but rather the deaf-and-dumb fields of death's kingdom.
> He strode through a space that was no longer solid.
>
> The rustle of time ebbed away in his ears.) (PS: 56–7)

In '1972' these associations and oppositions become both less metaphorical and more painfully personal. Brodsky declares:

> старенье есть отрастанье органа
> слуха, рассчитанного на молчанье.
>
> Старенье! В теле всё больше смертного.
> То есть, ненужного жизни. ... (С: 25)

(to grow old is to lose the use of the organ/of hearing, an organ directed toward silence. Growing old! In the body there is more/and more of what is mortal. I.e., what is of no use to life. ... .)

In plain language: the increasing deafness of the old is a rehearsal for the non-speaking which is death, the silence which is eternity.[19]

Brodsky goes on to present a stark catalogue of what he is losing; the losses are both physical or psychological and cultural or spiritual:

> ... Можно сказать уверенно:
> здесь и скончаю я дни, теряя
> волосы, зубы, глаголы, суффиксы, ... (С: 26)

(... One can say with certainty: I shall end my days here, losing my hair and teeth, my verbs and endings.)

Moreover, the poet is 'chashi lishivshis' v piru Otechestva' ('deprived of [my] chalice at the feast of [my] Fatherland').

Despite the searing sense of loss, I find no self-pity in this poem. It is not, Brodsky says explicitly, a *vopl' otchaian'ia* ('howl of despair') but rather *pervyi krik molchaniia* ('the first shriek of [my] non-speaking'). The central, and most dreaded loss, is cultural and literary, symbolised by the loss of '[my] verbs and endings', i.e., that total control and command of his native tongue which is essential to any poet. A closely related point is stated in the first line of '1972'. 'Ptitsa uzhe ne vletaet v fortochku' ('The bird no longer flies in through the ventilation pane' [in a typical northern Russian storm window]), in other words, the muse is no longer entering the poet's study, inspiring his poetic creativity.

Loseff has put forward the intriguing hermeneutical hypothesis that in such works as '1972' there are 'two Brodskys', (1) the Brodsky who vividly describes, and laments, the thinning of his hair, the loss of his teeth, etc., and (2) the Brodsky who – representing the role and calling of the poet – passes judgement on the first Brodsky.[20]

The pervasive sense of traumatic loss is movingly expressed in 'Lagoon' (early 1973), Brodsky's first 'Christmas' poem of the third group, set in Venice.

> И восходит в свой номер на борт по трапу
> постоялец, несущий в кармане граппу,
>   совершенный никто, человек в плаще,
> потерявший память, отчизну, сына; ... (С: 40)

> (And a nameless lodger, a nobody, boards the boat,
> a bottle of grappa concealed in his raincoat
>   as he gains his shadowy room, bereaved
> of memory, homeland, son. . . .)
> (PS: 74; trans. by Anthony Hecht)

Brodsky had, of course, visited Venice – and in good season Rome, Florence, Ravenna, Paris, London, Mexico City, etc. The local color of all these places – with special stress of their architecture – appears in one or another of his poems. But, as Loseff has noted, the role and status of a traveller or tourist is quite different from that of an exile, even though both are 'away from home'. The traveller looks around him with greedy eyes; the exile looks rather within himself at the receding image of his homeland'. The traveller sees many countries; the exile sees only one: *'non-homeland'*. Despite Brodsky's planetary displacements since June 1972 – Loseff concludes – he has not *travelled* but has simply *lived in exile*.[21]

Three major poems of the third group introduce a new theme: Brodsky's identification with certain major historical figures, in particular: Dante, Mary Queen of Scots, and Marshal Georgi Zhukov. What these three have in common, despite their obvious differences of country, language, career, social role, and sex, is *mistreatment* – disgrace, exile, imprisonment, execution – by the city or country which they had served and which eventually 'rehabilitated' them, restoring their honour and reputation. Such 'rehabilitation' is clearest and most complete in the case of Dante, least clear and complete in the case of Zhukov. Mary Stuart presents the further complication that it was Elizabeth of England rather than a Scottish sovereign who had her executed. So if one considers England and Scotland to be separate powers, her fate was rather different from the fates of Dante and Zhukov. But if England and Scotland are considered to be two realms within a single (United) Kingdom, then her fate closely parallels theirs.

Brodsky's identification with such historical figures is, not surprisingly, most complete in the case of Dante and had been prefigured in an important poem of the second group. 'The Funeral of Bobo' (February–March 1972). That poem ended with these lines:

> И новый Дант склоняется к листу
> и на пустое место ставит слово. (С: 9)

> (And a new Dante leans over a sheet of paper,
> placing a word in a previously empty place.)

'On the Death of Zhukov' (1974) mentions Zhukov by name; Mary Stuart is mentioned several time (by first name only, to be sure) in the text of the 'Twenty Sonnets to Mary Queen of Scots' (1974); but Dante is not mentioned even once in 'December in Florence' (1976). Loseff suggests that this may be a device for intensifying the identification of the two poets.[22] Whether or not that is the case, many details clearly mark this as Brodsky's 'Dante' poem. I quote a few brief excerpts:

> Человек превращается в шорох пера по бумаге, в кольца,
> петли, клинышки букв и, потому что скользко,
> в запятые и точки. ... (C: 112)

(People turn into scratches of pen on paper, into the
stitching of letters,
their tiny wedges and hooks; and – since it is
slippery work – into commas and periods. . . .)
(trans. Maurice English and George L. Kline, *Shearsman*,
1982, p. 20)

> ощущая нехватку в терцинах, в клетке
> дряхлый щегол выводит свои коленца. (C: 112)

(A goldfinch, out of the tremble of wires he's caged in
feebly runs through the terzinas of his tune.)
(trans. English and Kline, p. 20)

> и щегол разливается в центре проволочной Равенны. (C: 112)

(A goldfinch's voice flows out from its cage in Ravenna.)
(trans. English and Kline, p. 20)

The first passage sounds a familiar – and, in a sense, traditional – Brodskyan theme: that through his poetry the poet can overcome the destructive power of time and death. What the poet leaves behind is his 'chast' rechi', his 'part of speech' or 'language part'.[23] The second passage refers specifically to Dante (without, of course, mentioning him by name). The monument to Dante in Ravenna, the city in which he lived in exile from his native Florence, is enclosed in a cage-like cast-i-ron grillwork.

The parallels between the lives, careers, and fates of the two exiled poets are catalogued in the final stanza:

> Есть города, в которые нет возврата.
> Солнце бьётся в их окна, как в гладкие зеркала. То
> есть, в них не проникнешь ни за какое злато.
> Там всегда протекает река под шестью мостами.
> Там есть места, где припадал устами
> тоже к устам и пером к листам. И

там рябит от аркад, колоннад, от чугунных пугал;
там толпа говорит, осаждая трамвайный угол,
на языке человека, который убыл. (С: 113)

(There are cities in this world to which one can't return.
The sun beats on their windows as though on polished
                                              mirrors.
And no amount of gold will make their hinged gates turn.
Rivers in those cities always flow beneath six bridges.
There are places in those cities where lips first pressed
                                              on lips
and pen on paper. In those cities there's a richness
of colonnades, arcades, and scarecrows cast in iron.
There are crowds besieging trolley stops are speaking
in the language of a poet who has been long gone.
       (trans. English and Kline, p. 21, revised)

Both Florence and St Petersburg/Leningrad are characterised by an abundance of arcades, colonnades, and statues ('scarecrows cast in iron'). In Dante's time there were six bridges in Florence (one has been added since), the exact number of bridges in Brodsky's native city.[24] The last two lines assert a bold – perhaps overstated – parallel between the way Dante shaped the Italian literary language, now spoken by ordinary Florentines as they board their streetcars, and the way Brodsky has shaped the contemporary Russian literary language. The fundamental point, however, is that each poet – though abused and exiled – has made a permanent contribution to the language, literature, and culture of the homeland that has mistreated him.

The 'Twenty Sonnets . . .' (1974) are too complicated and various for detailed discussion here.[25] But the shared fate of Queen and poet is clearly delineated. Brodsky, or his poetic persona, imagines that he and Mary Stuart became lovers, that he took her back to Russia at a time when trade was being initiated between Scotland and Russia. The point is perhaps clearest in Sonnet 8:

        На склоне лет, в стране за океаном
        (открытой, как я думаю, при Вас),
        деля помятый свой иконостас
        меж печкой и продавленным диваном,
        я думаю, сведи удача нас,
        понадобились вряд ли бы слова нам:

> ты просто бы звала меня Иваном
> и я бы отвечал тебе 'Alas!
>
> Шотландия нам стала бы матрас.
> Я б гордым показал тебя славянам.
> В порт Глазго, караван за караваном,
> пошли бы лапти, пряники, атлас.
> Мы встретили бы вместе смертный час.
> Топор бы оказался деревянным. (С: 54) [26]

(I'd spend my last years in my distant homeland/ (opened to commerce in your reign, I'd guess),/ dividing an unkempt iconostas/ between my Russian stove and battered divan;/ there you and I would find our happiness./ We'd need no universe of words to live in:/ you'd call me simply 'Ivan'/ and I would plainly answer you 'Alas'.// Your Scottish shires would serve as lovers' beds./ I'd introduce you, Mary, to proud Slavs – and their ships would crowd the port of Glasgow, laden with bast-shoes, satins, honeyed gingerbreads./ We'd face our death together; and the heads-/ man's blade would turn out to be wholly wooden.)

The *prima facie* puzzling final lines should, I think, be interpreted not in the sense that the axe turned out to be 'harmless' or 'make-believe' but in the rather different sense that the fate of the poet and of Mary Stuart has been set in a Russian mode, assimilated to what was often referred to as 'dereviannaia Rus'' ('old wooden Russia').

Brodsky's imagining of Mary Stuart as his beloved seems to me to symbolise the unity of their fates. And in suggesting that she would call him simply 'Ivan' – the commonest of Russian names – while he would reply simply 'alas', Brodsky is saying that the doomed lovers would not need a common language. These two elemental words would suffice. On the other hand, a secondary allusion may be – as Loseff has suggested[27] – to Ivan IV ('The Terrible') (1530–84), contemporary on the throne of Mary Queen of Scots (1542–87). A relevant historical fact is that it was Ivan IV who established the first commercial as well as diplomatic ties between Russia and England, going so far as to propose marriage to Queen Elizabeth I.

The opening stanza of 'On the Death of Zhukov' (1974) depicts a funeral with full military honours:

Вижу колонны замерших внуков,
гроб на лафете, лошади круп.
Ветер сюда не доносит мне звуков
русских военных плачущих труб.
Вижу в регалии убранный труп:
в смерть уезжает пламенный Жуков. (C: 44)

(Columns of grandsons, stiff at attention;
gun carriage, coffin, riderless horse.
Wind brings no sound of their glorious Russian
trumpets, their weeping trumpets of war.
Splendid regalia deck out the corpse:
thundering Zhukov rolls toward death's mansion.)[28]

There follows an account of Zhukov's glorious victories in the Second World War (which the Russians call the 'Great Fatherland War'), and then of his disgrace and neglect by an ungrateful country.

Кончивший дни свои глухо, в опале,
как Велизарий или Помпей. (C: 44)

(. . . And his last days
found him, like Pompey, fallen and humbled –
like Belisarius banned and disgraced.) (PS: 78)

In the same passage (stanza 2) the name of Hannibal is also mentioned – like Belisarius and Pompey, a general who had brilliantly served his country but then suffered disgrace and exile.

Kalomirov takes Brodsky to be evoking and celebrating military commanders as such, and asks why Napoleon is not included in his catalogue.[29] The answer seems to me to be twofold. On the one hand, the commanders mentioned by Brodsky – and in particular Zhukov – fought wars of defence. On the other hand, they were treated ungratefully by their own countries, disgraced or exiled by their own governments. Napoleon fits neither of these criteria: his wars were aggressive; and his exile was brought about not by France, but by France's enemies, who had defeated Napoleon at Waterloo.

At the end of Brodsky's poem the parallel between soldier and poet is made explicit. The military leader brings his people a 'gift' of victory, of freedom; the poet brings a 'gift' of poetry, of words. The two contributions are treated with equal ingratitude.

> ... У истории русской страницы
> хватит для тех, кто в пехотном строю
> смело входили в чужие столицы,
> но возвращались в страхе в свою.
>
> Маршал! поглотит алчная Лета
> эти слова и твои прахоря.
> Всё же, прими их – жалкая лепта ... (С: 44–5)

(. . . Russian history holds, as is fitting,
space for the exploits of those who, though bold,
marching triumphant through foreign cities,
trembled in terror when they came home.

Marshal! These words will be swallowed by Lethe,
utterly lost, like your rough soldier's boots.
Still take this tribute, though it is little, . . .) (PS: 79)

Derzhavin, the eighteenth-century poet Brodsky most admires, wrote a celebrated poem on the death of Marshal Suvorov (May 1800). Its title is 'Snegir' ('The Bullfinch'). The bullfinch's song is said to resemble the sound of a military fife.[30] The meter of Brodsky's poem, with a caesura in each line, echoes Derzhavin's meter in suggesting the slow interrupted beat of a military funeral march. Characteristically, Brodsky does not name Derzhavin in this poem, but he ends the poem with the word, 'snegir', clue enough for any cultivated Russian reader.

'Plato Elaborated' was written in February 1977, thirteen years to the month from the beginning of Brodsky's Leningrad trial for 'social parasitism'. The title, directly borrowed from Richard Wilbur's 'Lamarck Elaborated', refers to the Platonic proposal that poets – at least those not subject to the discipline of the political authorities – be banished from the ideal city-state. Plato's views are 'elaborated' or 'further developed' (the Russian title is 'Razvivaia Platona') in the sense that an 'ideal' city is depicted – with gentle irony and occasional biting wit – from which in the end, poets are violently eliminated. Presumably Brodsky has in mind such passages as these from Plato's *Republic*:

'we can admit no poetry into our city save only hymns to the gods and the praises of good men' (607^a). . . . we should be justified in not admitting [the poet] into a well-ordered state, because he stimulates and fosters this [irrational] element in the soul, and by strengthening it tends to destroy the rational part . . . (605^b). We should send [the poet] away to another city, after pouring myrrh down over his head and crowning him with fillets of wool (398^{a-b}) (trans. Paul Shorey).

Brodsky is imagining, in a personal, almost confessional way, what would have happened to him if he had remained in the Soviet Union, or perhaps what would have happened to him if he had returned there from his foreign exile.[31]

Here is the end of the poem:

И когда бы меня схватили в итоге за шпионаж,
подрывную активность, бродяжничество, менаж-
а-труа, и толпа бы, беснуясь вокруг, кричала,
тыча в меня натруженными указательными: "Не наш!"

я бы втайне был счастлив, шепча про себя: "Смотри,
это твой шанс узнать, как выглядит изнутри
то, на что ты так долго глядел снаружи;
Запоминай же подробности, восклицая "Vive la Patrie!" (U: 10)

> (And when they would finally arrest me for espionage,
> for subversive activity, vagrancy, for *ménage
> à trois*, and the crowd, boiling around me, would bellow,
> poking me with their work-roughened forefingers,
> 'Outsider, we'll settle your hash!' –
>
> then I would secretly smile, and say to myself, 'See,
> this is your chance to find out, in Act Three,
> how it looks from the inside – you've stared long
> enough at the outside –
> so take note of every detail as you shout, '*Vive la patrie!*)
> (PS: 131)

Brodsky reduces the charges to absurdity by placing the obviously trumped-up charge of capital crimes (espionage, subversion) in the same list with the true but trivial charge of unconventional sexual behaviour (*ménage à trois*) and the tendentious and irrelevant charge of social parasitism (vagrancy).

The penultimate stanza contains a unique reference to the hostile reaction of the crowds outside the Leningrad courthouse where Brodsky was being tried during February and March of 1964.[32] As he was being brought into the courthouse for each day's proceedings, and taken away at the end of the day, people pointed at him and shouted – among other unpleasant things – '*ne nash*' (lit. '[you're] not [one of] ours'), in other words, 'you're an outsider, an alien element [chuzhdy element]' – to use the sinister Stalinist expression.

V

Few poets have expressed the sense of loss, separation, and estrangement more powerfully than Brodsky. Yet there is in his poetry a courageous acceptance of the pain and absurdity of human existence, and a kind of 'being-at-home' in 'not-being-at-home' in the world. This results in both a special serenity and a deep sense of gratitude in much of his poetry. The question may be raised: gratitude for what? For the gift of life? Or for the gift of poetic talent? Kreps thinks that, at least in 'Conversation with an Angel' (1970), it is 'gratitude to Heaven for his talent'.[33] The general object of the poet's gratitude, I suspect, is closer to what Loseff identifies in another connection, namely, 'creativity, or even more broadly – the life of the artist as a creative act'.[34] Perhaps more broadly still, it is the unity of life and poetry – to use a formula put forward by Zhukovsky and made central by Pasternak in *Dr Zhivago*.

In what follows I offer five examples from poems ranging in date from 1965 to 1982.

The first 'Christmas poem' of the first group – '1 January 1965' – opens with a sense of bitter loss and isolation, symbolised by the Christmas tree and empty stockings:

> Волхвы забудут адрес твой.
> Не будет звёзд над головой. (O: 115)

> (The Wise Men will unlearn your name.
> Above your head no star will flame.) (SP: 86)

> И молча глядя в потолок,
> поскольку явно пуст чулок, ... (O: 115)

> (You glare in silence at the wall.
> Your stocking gapes. No gifts at all.) (SP: 86)

But the poem continues:

> Пусть он звучит и в смертный час,
> как благодарность уст и глаз
> тому, что заставляет нас
> порою вдаль смотреть. (O: 115)

> (Let it sound in my hour of death –
> as gratefulness of eyes and lips
> for that which sometimes makes us lift
> our gaze to the far sky.) (SP: 86)

And it ends with these words:

> И, взгляд подняв свой к небесам,
> ты вдруг почувствуешь, что сам –
> чистосердечный дар. (O: 115)

> (– But suddenly, lifting your eyes
> to heaven's light, you realise:
> your *life* is a sheer gift.)[35] (SP: 86)

Five years later, in 'Conversation with an Angel' (1970) Brodsky declares:

> Благодарю...
> Верней ума последняя крупица
> благодарит, ... (K: 65)

(I give thanks . . . Or rather, the last atom of my mind gives thanks . . .)

The last of the 'Twenty Sonnets' concludes with these lines:

> Ведя ту жизнь, которую веду,
> я благодарен бывшим белоснежным
> листам бумаги, свёрнутым в дуду. (С: 60)

(Leading the kind of life I lead,/I'm grateful now to what were once/blank sheets of paper, rolled into a flute.)

The 'flute' or '[shepherd's] pipe' (duda, dudka, or dudochka) symbolises poetic creativity, as in Akhmatova's poem 'The Muse' (1924), in Brodsky's '1972' (C: 26; PS: 65), and his 'Lullaby of Cape Cod' (C: 100; PS: 108).

In a powerful poem written on his fortieth birthday ('24 May 1980'), Brodsky catalogued the adventures, losses, and disasters that have filled his life:

> Бросил страну, что меня вскормила.
> Из забывших меня можно составить город. (U: 177)

(I've abandoned the country that nourished me./One could create a city from people who have forgotten me.)[36]

> жрал хлеб изгнанья, не оставляя корок. (U: 177)

(I've wolfed down the bread of banishment, not even leaving a crust.)

But, in the closing lines, Brodsky goes on to declare:

> Но пока мне рот не забили глиной,
> из него раздаваться будет лишь благодарность. (U: 177)

(Until my mouth is wholly stopped up with clay,/nothing but gratitude will issue from it.)

The twelfth in Brodsky's group of 'Roman Elegies' with these lines:

> Наклонись, я шепну Тебе на ухо что-то: я
> благодарен за всё; ... (U: 116)

(Bend down, and I'll whisper something in your ear: I/am grateful for everything . . .)

Variations on the Theme of Exile   81

The stress on gratitude for the gift of existence and the gift of poetic genius brings Brodsky close to Pasternak with his 'astonishment at the miracle of existence', in the words of Andrei Siniavsky.

VI

A striking formal feature of several of Brodsky's most important poems of exile, especially of those of the first and third groups, is their use of triple rhymes, a clear echo of Dante's 'terza rima'. The rhyme scheme of the *Divine Comedy* is ABABCBCDC ... (all rhymes being feminine), which is highly appropriate for his long cantos, averaging between 130 and 150 lines, and not divided into stanzas. Brodsky's stanzas which contain triple rhymes range in length from six to nine lines. He plays many changes on triplicity, none of them identical with 'terza rima', but all of them reminiscent of it. I shall briefly identify the rhyme schemes of five of the poems discussed in this paper.

1. '1 January 1965' has eight-line stanzas and the the rhyme scheme *aaacbbbc*, (all rhymes being masculine), where the same *c* recurs in the first and third stanzas.
2. '1972' has eight-line stanzas and the rhyme scheme *AAACBBBC*, where the rymes are all dactylic rather than feminine (in one or two cases the C is feminine, but there are no masculine rhymes). This is a somewhat 'tighter' rhyme scheme than 'terza rima', any given eight-line section of which – contains two *As*, three *Bs*, two *Cs*, and one *D*.
3. 'On the Death of Zhukov' has six-line stanzas. In the first stanza the rhyme scheme is *AbAbbA*; in stanzas 2–5 the rhyme scheme is *AbAbAb*.
4. 'December in Florence' – perhaps the most 'Dantesque' of Brodsky's poems – has nine-line stanzas and the rhyme scheme *AAABBBCCC* (entirely feminine rhymes).
5. 'Plato Elaborated' has four-line stanzas grouped into sets of four, which constitute a numbered part or section of the poem. The rhyme scheme is *aaXa, bbXb*, etc., where 'X' indicates an unrhymed feminine ending.

The triple dactylic rhymes of '1972' are what Brodsky calls 'destructive' (razrushitel'nye). They involve a 'destructive' semantic movement – a 'slide' or 'fall' – from the first rhyme position to the second, and from the second to the third. Each rhyme position has a rigidly associated semantic or symbolic level: the first level is spiritual/moral; the second is psychological/emotional; the third physical/biological. Admittedly, this striking device works more clearly and effectively in some cases than in others. In the appendix on p. 87 I have listed five stanzas (out of a total of sixteen) where the destructive rhymes work particularly well. I shall discuss only three of these five examples in any detail.

The first triple rhyme in the stanza is 'fortochku/koftochku/kostochku'. The 'fortochka' is the ventilation pane in a storm window through which the bird (i.e. muse) no longer enters the poet's study. In other words, his poetic creativity has dried up. The 'koftochka' is the blouse which a young woman to whom he wishes to make love refuses to take off. In other words, his sexual attractiveness has also faded. The 'kostochka' is a cherry-pit on which he will slip, but not fall, since he is now moving too slowly. In other words, his biological/physical energy has been drained.

The first triple rhyme in the third stanza is 'raskaialos'/skalilos'/karies', two verbs and a noun. 'Raskaialos''' ('repented') operates at the spiritual/moral level. The statement about the body's having repented of its passions may be ironic, but that does not change the level at which this process operates, namely, repentance in the face of approaching death. 'Skalilos''' ('bared its teeth', i.e., 'laughed') operates at the psychological/emotional level. The poet's emotional responses – laughing, crying – were in vain. 'Karies' ('caries', i.e., 'tooth decay') obviously operates at the physical/biological level, symbolising the disintegration of advancing age.

The first triple rhyme in the eighth stanza is 'trusosti/trudnosti/trupnosti'. Here the possibility of suicide is broached. 'Trusost''' is the cowardice or moral weakness which keeps one from taking one's own life. In second position, the 'trudnost''' ('difficulty') is the psychological difficulty of self-destruction, of overcoming the powerful instinct of self-preservation. (Brodsky refers to the crossbeam – *perekladina* – from which he is *not* going to hang himself and describes the train wheels clattering fast, in a clear allusion to Anna Karenina's suicide.) In the third position is the unusual term 'trupnost''', literally 'corpseness' or 'corpselike condition', i.e. the future biological deadness which is reflected in the present moral weakness and psychological inertia.

There is nothing quite like Brodsky's 'destructive' rhymes in

Russian poetry. Quite understandably, the poet was eager to present this work to an English audience. But those who had translated his other poems, including myself, regarded this one – despite its originality and power – as untranslatable, since not just the rhymes (triple, dactylic) but their three-part semantic slide or fall is an essential and unrenderable aspect of the poem.

Brodsky's own version, done with Alan Myers, does retain the dactylic rhymes and approximate rhymes, including compound slant rhymes. But dactylic rhymes are not at home in serious English poetry as they are in Russian. What is more regrettable, the 'destructive' aspect of the triple rhymes is generally lost in the Brodsky-Myers version. 'Fortochku/koftochku/kostochku' is rendered as 'nowadays/noble place/nobody's'; 'starenie/struenie/stroenie' as 'senility/chilly tea/vicinity'; 'trusosti/trudnosti/trupnosti' as 'cowardice/enterprise/old device'; and 'otchaian'ia/odichaniia/molchaniia' as 'deep distress/wilderness/speechlessness'. This last is somewhat less objectionable than the others. In my judgement, the most nearly successful rendering is that of 'raskaialos'/skalilos'/karies' as 'proclivities/activities/cavities'. 'Cavities' is fine; unfortunately, both 'proclivities' and 'activities' are much too general, too unspecific, to be effective.[37]

VII

The distinguished Czech novelist in exile, Josef Skvorecky, has made a helpful distinction between two contrasting modes of being a writer in exile, that of Ovid and that of Conrad. He recommends that, rather than wasting oneself in nostalgia for one's unrecoverable homeland – like Ovid in Scythia yearning for Rome – one should throw oneself into the language, literature, and culture of one's adopted country – like the Polish-born Joseph Conrad, living in England and writing in English.

It is clear that Joseph Brodsky has done precisely that, throwing himself with notable energy and imagination into the literature and culture not just of America and England but of the West more generally. Not all important Russian writers in exile have taken this course; Siniavsky and Solzhenitsyn are prominent counter-examples. But, unlike them, Brodsky has always been, and remains today – like Goethe – in every respect a 'good European'.

Notes

1. From an interview conducted by Giovanni Buttafava, *L'Espresso*, 6 December 1987, p. 156. Although the interview was conducted by transatlantic telephone, in Russian, it has been published only in Italian. The Italian text of the quoted passage reads: 'L'esilio, forse, è la condizione naturale del poeta. . . . Sentivo una sorta di grande privilegio in questa coincidenza fra la mia condizione esistenziale e la mia occupazione.'
2. 'A Guide to a Renamed City' in *Less Than One: Selected Essays* (New York: Farrar, Straus, Giroux, 1986), p. 79.
3. 'Ierarkhiia *drugikh* v poezii Brodskogo' in L.V. Loseff, ed., *Poetika Brodskogo* (Tenafly, NJ: Hermitage, 1986), p. 160.
4. 'The Condition we Call Exile', *New York Review of Books*, 21 January 1988, p. 18.
5. Although Brodsky himself spells the name of his exile village 'Norenskaya' (see *A Part of Speech*, New York: Farrar, Straus, Giroux, 1980, p. 8), the *Espresso* interview mentioned in Note 1 contains a photograph of Brodsky and Anatoly Naiman standing beside the sign identifying that town, where the spelling is clearly 'Norinskaia' (see p. 156). As Brodsky has pointed out, the pronunciation is about the same for both spellings.
6. The title refers to Byron's 'Stanzas to Augusta' (which Pasternak had translated into Russian): in both cases an exiled poet addresses a loved woman who remains behind – in Byron's case, his sister; in Brodsky's, the 'M.B.' to whom this poem is dedicated.
7. Here, and in all subsequent quotations, the translations of Brodsky's poetry, unless otherwise identified, are my own. In the case of published translations the source is given by use of a siglum; in the case of a very few unpublished verse translations, diagonals are used to mark line divisions; in other cases 'plain prose versions' are given, without such diagonals.
8. The Russian cruiser *Admiral Apraksin* – named for Count F.M. Apraksin (1661–1728), chief of the Admiralty under Peter the Great – ran aground in the Gulf of Finland in 1900.
9. In response to Cardinal Châtillon's inquiry about his health, the dying Rabelais wrote: '*je vais quérir un grand peut-être*'.
10. Michael B. Kreps, *O poezii Iosifa Brodskogo* (Ann Arbor, Mich.: Ardis, 1984), pp. 147–8.
11. 'Niotkuda s liubov'iu . . .: Zametki o stikhakh Iosifa Brodskogo', *Kontinent*, No. 14 (1977), p. 325.
12. Loseff's claim that this poem consists of 'imitations of, and free translations' from Martial strikes me as overstated (cf. 'Niotkuda s liubov'iu', p. 325). The subtitle given to this poem – 'Iz Martsiala' ('From Martial') – in *Chast' rechi*, a volume co-edited by Loseff, is misleading, although Brodsky's and Loseff's aim in using it was to suggest that various themes and images had been borrowed from classical Latin poets – Ovid and Horace as well as Martial. The subtitle is omitted, with Brodsky's full approval, in *A Part of Speech*, p. 52.

13. For a discussion of this, and related passages, focused on the notion of *zrelishche* ('spectacle'), in comparison with *'Post aetatem nostram'*, see Kreps, *O poezii Iosifa Brodskogo*, p. 243.
14. The Russian *zaliv* ('bay' or 'gulf') could refer to the Gulf of Finland, on which Leningrad is located. But the reference to Vesuvius makes it clear that the Bay of Naples is also intended. There is a fairly transparent reference, expressed by the words *sovremennyi . . . Vezuvii* (lit. 'a [or 'the'] contemporary Vesuvius'), to air-polluting industry.
15. For a close and sensitive reading of this important poem, see Kreps, *O poezii Iosifa Brodskogo*, pp. 153–7.
16. For a discussion of the strikingly original triple 'destructive' rhymes of this remarkable poem, see Section VI below.
17. Concerning 'Gorbunov and Gorchakov' see my introduction to *Joseph Brodsky: Selected Poems* (1973), pp. 20–22; Carl R. Proffer, 'A Stop in the Madhouse: Brodsky's 'Gorbunov and Gorchakov', *Russian Literature TriQuarterly*, 1 (1971), pp. 342–51.
18. Brodsky has said of St. Simeon: 'He is tired of living. Having to live so long – until the birth of the Christ Child – has been a kind of punishment for him'. When I mentioned that the line 'The roaring of time ebbed away in his ears' anticipated the passage in '1972' about 'growing old' as involving a dulling of the 'organ of hearing' which prepares it for silence, he replied: 'Yes, but also in the sense that as the body grows older it fills up with silence – with organs and functions that are no longer relevant to its life'. When I noted the continuity of this theme with that of 'Gorbunov and Gorchakov' – the association of life with speech and of death with silence – his answer was: 'I am very pleased, George, that you have noticed this connection, because it does indeed exist, and I consider it important' (see 'A Poet's Map of his Poem', Interview with Brodsky, *Vogue*, 162, 3 1973, p. 230).
19. As Kreps has noted, the 'fear of death' expressed in Brodsky's poems is 'posthumous': 'it is not death itself, i.e., the experience of dying, as a physiological act [or phenomenological experience] that frightens him, but the thought, while one lives, of one's posthumous non-being, nothingness' (*O poezii Iosifa Brodskogo*, p. 91).
20. 'Niotkuda s liubov'iu', p. 309.
21. *Ibid.*, p. 320. For a somewhat different view of the Brodsky poems set in Venice, Florence, Mexico City, etc. – a view which, in a certain sense, stresses their 'touristic' dimension – see Kreps, *O poezii Iosifa Brodskogo*, pp. 178–93.
22. 'Niotkuda s liubov'iu', p. 320. For helpful discussions of these three poems see the following:
    'December in Florence': Kreps, *O poezii Iosifa Brodskogo*, pp. 180–90; 'Twenty Sonnets to Mary Queen of Scots': anonymous Soviet author (now revealed to be Giorgi Vasiutochkin of Leningrad) in *Poetika Brodskogo*, pp. 16–37; A. Zholkovsky in *ibid.*, pp. 38–62; Loseff, 'Niotkuda s liubov'iu', pp. 325–6; 'On the Death of Zhukov': Kreps, *O poezii Iosifa Brodskogo*, pp. 130–3; A. Kalomirov, in *Poetika Brodskogo*, pp. 223–4.
23. Cf. Kreps, *O poezii Iosifa Brodskogo*, p. 254.

24. The six Leningrad bridges are listed by Loseff in 'Niotkuda s liubov'iu', p. 320.
25. They include an embedded quotation from Dante: *Zemnoi svoi put' proidia do serediny* (*Nel mezzo del cammin di nostra vita*) (the first line of Sonnet 3, echoing the first line of Canto I of the *Inferno*). Like Dante, who was thirty-five when he wrote that line, Brodsky was – after 24 May 1974 – in his thirty-fifth year, i.e., half way through a Biblical life-span of three score years and ten.
26. In form this is a 'Brodskyan sonnet', a *tour de force* with septuple rhymes: AbbA bAAb bAA bbA. Septuple rhymes may be viewed as including triple rhymes.
27. 'Niotkuda s liubov'iu', p. 308.
28. The word which I have translated as 'thundering' is *plamennyi*, lit. 'flamming', an echo of the word *pylaia* ('fiery', 'ardent') used by Derzhavin to describe Suvorov (see below and Kreps, *O poezii Iosifa Brodskogo*, p. 130). Derzhavin's description of the contrasted roles of Suvorov as *Skiptry davaia, zvat'sia rabom* ('bestowing scepters, [but] called a slave') is echoed in Brodsky's lines:

> смело входили в чужие столицы,
> но возвращались в страхе в свою. (С: 45)

> (. . . those who, though bold,
> marching triumphant through foreign cities,
> trembled in terror when they came home.) (PS: 78)

Suvorov, who in his final years commanded Russian and Austrian armies in campaigns against Napoleon, restored to their thrones monarchs whom Napoleon had deposed, but was himself in disfavour with his own monarch, Paul I. Similarly, Zhukov, as a bold conqueror marched at the head of his troops into enemy cities (lit. 'capitals', here primarily Berlin), but trembled in anticipation of mistreatment when he returned to Moscow, the capital of his own country.
29. A. Kalomirov, 'Iosif Brodskii (Mesto)' in *Poetika Brodskogo*, p. 224. Kalomirov assumes that Napoleon is 'too romantic and universal' for Brodsky's taste. He falls back on such vague and unsatisfactory criteria, presumably, because he has entirely failed to grasp Brodsky's reasons for including just those military leaders who *are* mentioned in this poem.
30. This is made explicit in the opening lines of Derzhavin's poem:

> Что ты заводишь песню военну
> Флейте подобно, милый снегирь?

> (Sweet bullfinch, why do you strike up a song of war, like that of the fife?)

31. At this time Brodsky told me of his nightmare about repeating the fate of Marina Tsvetaeva who, after more than fifteen years of exile in Prague and Paris, returned to the Soviet Union in 1939 and took her own life in 1941.
32. Allusions to the trial itself and to the trial judge Savel'eva may be found in certain poems of the first group.
33. *O poezii Iosifa Brodskogo*, p. 237.
34. 'Niotkuda s liubov'iu', p. 313.
35. A more literal translation, rendering *sam* as '[you] yourself' rather than 'life', would leave open the question of whether the poet's gratitude is for the gift of life or the gift of poetic talent.
36. Brodsky's expression *Brosil stranu* is a clear echo of Akhmatova's powerful poem of 1922, *Ne s temi ia, kto brosil zemliu* ('I'm not with those who have abandoned their land'). His reference to the *khleb izgnan'ia* ('bread of exile') echoes her line which, after mentioning the *izgnannik* ('exile'), declares: *polyn'iu pakhnet khleb chuzhoi* ('there's a smell of wormwood about alien bread').
37. See *A Part of Speech*, pp. 63–6.

APPENDIX: 'DESTRUCTIVE' TRIPLE DACTYLIC RHYMES IN BRODSKY'S '1972'

Rhyme position: →	First	Second	Third
Level: → Stanza	spiritual/moral	psychological/emotional	physical/emotional
1	(a) *fortochku* = 'ventilation pane in a storm window'	*koftochku* = 'blouse' [which a young woman refuses to remove]	*kostochku* = '[cherry] pit [on which I slip]'
	(b) that through which the bird (muse) no longer enters, i.e. failure of poetic creativity	loss of sexual attractiveness	exhaustion of physical and biological energy
2	(a) *starenie* = 'growing old'	*struenie* = [sluggish] flow [of the blood]	*stroenie* = 'shape': the [once handsome] shape [of (my) legs (now)] hurts my eyes]
	(b) moving toward silence and nothingness	cooling of the passions	physical ugliness that comes with age
3	(a) *raskaialos'* = [the body] 'has repented' (of its passions)	*skalilos'* = [the body] 'has bared its teeth', i.e. has laughed	*karies* = 'caries', 'tooth decay'

	(b) I have repented [as I face approaching death]	my emotional responses [laughing, crying] were in vain	disintegration of the body
8	(a) *trusosti* = 'timidity', 'cowardice'	*trudnosti* = 'difficulty' [of carrying out the act]	*trupnosti* = 'corpseness' 'corpselike condition'
	(b) moral weakness or inertia (which keeps one from commiting suicide)	psychological difficulty of self-destruction	[future] biological deadness, which is reflected in present moral weakness and psychological inertia
13	(a) *otchaian'ia* = 'despair'	*odichaniia* = 'going wild', 'going to seed'	*molchaniia* = 'silence'
	(b) this poem is not a howl of despair	... but the result of [my] going wild	... and the first shriek of [my] silence, i.e. the onset of my dying, lapsing into non-speaking

KEY
(a) transliterated Russian word and literal meaning;
(b) symbolic or metaphorical meaning in the given context

5
The Ironic Journey into Antiquity
Georges Nivat

The journey into 'antiquity' plays a cardinal role, not just in the poetics, but also in the imagination of Joseph Brodsky. The decapitated, antique statue with the sumptuous folds of its tunic or peplum which at one and the same time reveal and conceal the body, seems to me to be the fundamental image, that can, perhaps, provide the key to the 'Arts Poetica' of the poet of the 'Roman Elegies', of the 'Bust of Tiberius', or of the play 'Marble'. The marble toga is simultaneously life/folds, oblique unveiling of the body, modesty eternalised in stone – and total impersonalisation – solidification of life, a decapitated body which does not 'speak', save through the scarcely disclosed contours of its inner self . . . Brodsky's 'Ars Poetica' contains both of these elements: life seized in moments of eternity and the impersonality of the world, and of the man made solid, made into statue in this world.

The two prisoners in the play 'Marble' have the right to a certain number of busts of 'classics'. In their prison which is a 'lack of space' (nedostatok prostranstva) they have the right to these men of reknown frozen in marble. Publius declares that 'a text is a tattoo' (pis'mennost' i est' tatuirovka) but Art is, more usually, an imitating of the body, statuary, that is an ineffaceable movement of the body, frozen, 'made marble'. The Empire, declares Tullius, the more philosophical of the two prisoners, realises its significance by means of a 'desemanticisation of space' (obessmyslivanie prostranstva), that is to say the Empire unites the various, which is reduced to a common denominator, the common denominator of marble, statuary, the classical 'canon'. 'All the horror lies in the fact that people have more common than individual traits'.

The same character quotes, without giving his source, an epigram of Martial, which in Latin states: *Difficilis, facilis, incundus, acerbus es ideus Nec tecum possum vivere nec sinete*, which can be translated as: 'Crabbed but kind, pleasant and sour together, I can neither live with you, nor yet without you.' This epigram sums up the difficulty of living with the living, our nearest and yet our tormenter, and supplies the key to life's torments: *Nec tecum possum vivere nec sinete*.

Art, Statuary, Classicism are the only escape; marble renders cohabitation with the attractive/repulsive living finally 'livable'. Time himself is transformed into a grey statue and the poet Ovid into a poet of the 'grey', bleached vision, of statuary: he becomes O-vidii (the verb videt', to see, is heard) and his pleasant/irksome lament is 'marmarised' for eternity. This paradoxical seizing of Time and its contradictions is communicated, in antique statuary, through the robe's folds, the freedom of the dialectic of body and fabric, but frozen in marble slavery.

'What is the essence of the toga? Its folds. It is, so to say, a world unto itself. Which lives its own life. There is not the least relation with reality. Even with the toga's wearer. The toga is not made for the man, but the man for the toga'. This declaration of Tullius defines a man-toga, a man-classic, freed from his living model, who lives the life of the folds, of the rhythm of the envelope, of the art which envelopes the living.

In Brodsky's poetry too, we find the theme of the statue and of the toga's marble folds. First of all there are, of course, the poems which are directly linked with the play: 'The Bust of Tiberius', 'Post Aetatem Nostram'.

The proconsul's court is like a stage setting where statues have been placed

> The indifferent servants
> stared into the distance, like statues. (K: 88)

The poem 'Torso' affirms the superiority of the world-made-statue over the living world; when statuary dominates the living, 'you're in the Empire, friend' ('Ty v Imperii, drug') and Man is invited to step up into the empty niche and stand in for the statue, to lose his head, which '. . . from the shoulders/falls with the thud of boulders' (s plecha/skatitsia vniz, stucha.) and to become a classical torso, that exhibition of muscles, of folds, of impersonal power which is the Empire. The 'bust' is the 'symbol for the essential independence of brain/from body' (simvol nezavisimosti mozga/ot zhizni tela), the supremacy of effect over cause, the living, minus the individual psyche.

In his 'Roman Elegies' Goethe tries to make the stones speak:

> Saget, Steine, mir an, o sprecht, ihr hohen Paläste
> (Speak to me, stones, o say you lofty palaces.)

Brodsky's Roman Elegies are a succession of snapshots of the City in August. Hostage of stone, the City is petrified, and the apprentice poet he too, in that city, runs the risk of being turned to stone.

'The world is made of nakedness and foldings' (Mir sostoit iz nagoty i skladok). The folds are the dialectic of fullness and emptyness, of light and shadow, of absence and presence (that is of the paradoxical condition articulated by Martial, attraction/repulsion).

And at Rome, in the interplay of blinding sun and shadow-filled rooms, the poet feels himself becoming 'a relic', that is to say a bust, a torso, a living statue, deprived of head and hand.

> 'I was in Rome, I was flooded by light. The way
> a splinter can only dream about.[1]
> (Ya byl v Rime. Byl zalit svetom. Tak'
> kak tol'ko mozhet mechtat' oblomok!) (U: 116–17).

The poet is an intruder in Rome and is naked and vulnerable in his apartment, but he is going to be turned into a statue, 'as this city happily did in its childhood hour' and draped in a marble toga he too will become absence/presence, a fold of marble fabric;

> 'Still, the latter's richer with love than a face, that's certain'.[2]
> (V etikh posledhikh bol'she lyubvi, chem v litsakh.) (U: 111)

This solidification is conveyed to us through the use of surprising details: the figures on a dial criss-cross like the beams of an anti-aircraft battery; the drawing-rooms are covered in dust-sheets, a fly is a prisoner in a bottle, homeless statues contemplate the ruins. This world of marble relics finds a counterpart in the exiled Jewish poet, himself a relic, out of place no matter he finds himself, like the ulvular 'r' in the word 'Yevrei' (Jew).

August is the imperial month, it bears the name of Augustus; but here it becomes 'the month of drawn blinds' and of the 'sweating double in the mirror above the cupboard'. August is the month which blinds, (does he not have, facing him, the Colosseum with its hundred Argus-like eye-sockets) which blinds the statued Caesars and which blinds the poet, in short which is as depersonalising as antique statuary and classicism. It is the transformation into ruin, into relic or else into the yellowed snapshot (the 'Leica') that one will take with one into the hereafter, it is then the process of survival 'in the style of antiquity' which is at the centre of the Roman Elegies. The Seventh poem of the sequence tells us that Rome helps man to realise his finiteness; in Rome, city of Horace, one should 'calm down' (smirit'sia), one should think of oneself as a 'too cumbersome thought about oneself' and one should accept the idea of advancing towards a summing up of the whole, towards the semblance of achievement which is life, towards the statue, dismembered, but eternal.

All the themes of the Elegies are subordinated to that commanding image of the statue, dismembered and aggregate.

First, there is the theme of the Barbarian coming to Rome; the Russian-Jewish poet is a 'barbarian', a Scythian and, moreover, a Jewish Scythian. In 'Marble' the theme of distant Scythia and its poets is humorously introduced, a couplet of Anna Akhmatova's is quoted (without, of course, its source being indicated). In the Elegies there appears the theme of Tanais, the mythological name for the Don, the frontier river between Europe and Asia. The passage of the frontier, of the Roman *limes*, which maintained a harmonious order against barbarian diversity is a recurrent theme of Brodsky's (see the change of Empire in the 'Lullaby of Cape Cod'). The *limes*, the Tanais, here becomes ambivalent, firstly because the Scythian Barbarian comes from another empire which has succeeded Rome, from a third Rome, the Scythian empire, and then chiefly because this river is also identified with the Styx, it is the passage to the other world and into the future. The tenth elegy in that suite sums up all the themes of passage, passage from private life (shapeless, in threads, like the contours of Europe) to classicism, to the public and definitive statue of the self, and passage from the effect to the cause. That causal reversal is very typical of Brodsky's poetry, which forces us upwards, towards a prior passage, towards a 'hereinbefore', reversing the current of daily life, of its 'course' and of the course of Time and Causality. Thus one has to drink tea in order to open one's lips (and not the opposite) that is in order not to solidify, thus the blue jays fly off because of the glance at them from the window, etc . . . White paper, the throng of letters waiting to form themselves into words, and into a poem, that is yet another rite of passage, another *limes*.

> Rim, chelovek, bumaga; (U: 115)
> (Rome, a man, paper)

The passage can almost be invisible, just as Kazimir Malevich's square of white on white is quasi-invisible:

> Belyi na belom, kak mechta Kazimira,
> letnim vecherom ya, samyi smertnyi prokhozhii
> sredi razvalin, torchashchikh kak rebra mira, (U: 116)
> (White upon white, like the dream of Casimir,
> one summer's evening I, the most mortal of passers-by,
> amidst the ruins, which jut forth like the ribs of the world,)

This mortal who passes amidst the ruins, who is a poet, who is in love, is in a state of 'passage' towards the *limbo* of antiquity, a frozen, bleached immortality like that of the antique statue (white on white); his girlfriends are 'short-term goddesses', Lesbias and Cynthias, like the heroines of Catullus or Propertius, images of a life frozen for eternity, or rather 'fallen asleep' like the she-wolf nurse of Rome.

The final Elegy, also the most mysterious, accentuates the impression of death-passage. Death is already 'cutting the void for the poet', but the best proof of having existed is invisibility. Invisible like Malevich's white square, or like Christ during the three days between his death and his resurrection. Rome is also Christian Rome. The Crucified has superimposed himself in white upon Rome and casts a shadow on the relics of antiquity.

> Ty byl pervym's kem eto sluchilos', pravda? (U: 116)
> (You were the first to whom all this happened, were You?[3])

But what has happened? Well, the disappearance/reappearance, the most spectacular and most minuscule 'passage' in History.

> Chem nezrimei veshch, tem ono vernei,
> chto ona kogda-to sushchestvovala/na zemle, (U: 116)
> (The more invisible something is,
> the more certain it's been around,[4])

Is not this the central revelation of the Elegies? Their intersection with the laws of being and of Art? Invisible is the Resurrection, invisible is the immortality of the mortal. But the rite of 'passage' is omnipresent. The 'passage' is the small coin that one gives to Charon, it is the penny that one places upon the eye of a corpse, it is the white square that shows through the white of another square, it is the garland of elegies which crystalise in the chaos of things and words awaiting immortality, it is the sacred concealment of hidden forms: for example all those letters in words which are not pronounced, all those pitfalls in a language which reveal another language within.

> 'Kak ty zhil v eti gody?' – 'Kak bukva 'g' v 'ogo''. (C: 47)
> ('How did you live in those years?' 'Like the 'h' in 'oh-oh''.)
> (The Thames at Chelsea).

This is what is lacking, in the relic, in the debris, in the dismembered statue, which has been made eternal by its dismemberment. Brodsky's Rome is the centre of that Empire which has known how to make the debris eternal.

> Ya byl v Rime. Byl zalit svetom. Tak'
> kak tol'ko mozhet mechtat' oblomok!
> (I was at Rome. I was flooded by light.
> The way only a splinter can dream about.)

All revolves around this passage of debris into eternity away from the present (broken, sliced up, carried away by the wind which sweeps across the rubbish heaps) in to the future (in black and white, a strange 'negative', the statue dismembered but recombined).

The writing of poetry is the Poet's widow's mite, donated to Time. It is the coin that he gives to Charon. It is his payment to eternity, his Christ-like 'passion'. And Rome, to which he goes as a pilgrim in the steps of many predecessors, offers him the model of this 'passage' of the eternal passage of the fragment towards the whole: the statue dismembered but perfect, the marble toga, the relic, more living than life. With the statue the invisible counts as much as the visible; with the poem it counts even more.

Impersonality is deeply imprinted upon Brodsky's poetry. His friend Aleksandr Kushner, also takes the Roman statue as a guide to immortality, in 'The tie of things'.[5] 'What immortality, memory, success, power are, one could meditate upon in the company of a cracked bust', writes Kushner in a poem entitled 'In front of the statue' whose themes are astonishingly akin to those of Brodsky. But Kushner's poem, a meditation before the statue of the emperor Galba, who reigned for just one year, deals with the permanence of human nature. It includes another similarity with Brodsky's poetry: the enumeration of the emperors whose list 'lies down so spontaneously in the line of verse'. Enumeration is a fundamental component of Brodsky's poetry: the counting of the real, of history. The enumeration of the Greek Fleet in the Iliad and in Mandelstam's 'Bessonnitsa. Homer'. The long historical sequence means that there exists not just parallelism but complementarity: the long 'train' of things is made to enter the long 'train' of poetry. A list of things and of words amounts to the same thing in poetry. But Kushner debates the permanence of things. Brodsky, on the other hand, takes enumeration to the extreme, to the point of 'passage' towards another reality. His poetry of statement is also a poetry of ritual 'passage' towards impersonal immortality. The 'total' of the real (so many of Brodsky's poems beginning with his Great Elegy give us the impression that they are making a great summing up of the real) leads towards a backward glance which is forbidden to mortals as it was to Orpheus.

In an interview given to Annie Epelbouin[6] Brodsky defined the 'decentration' of his poetry. His love for the English poets from Donne to Elliot and Lowell, is a refusal of the egocentrism, of the sentimental anthropomorphism of European poetry (Romanticism, Germany, Russia). To cease to be the centre as victim or as actor – and to look at the world through an 'alien gaze'. In the end it is this 'alien gaze' that Brodsky's poetry is seeking for. His taste for ex-centricity (Chinese themes, Anglicised history, American mimesis, Antiquity), his love of towns of 'passage' (ports, great cities that have fallen on hard times) his predilection for windy or foggy spaces (the suburbs, the fog of San Pietro) are so many searches for the forbidden, Orphic, backward glance, the glance which ends in petrification, and which marks the 'passage'. Pasternak preached a vigilance of all the senses, he recommended to the poet not to sleep, to work, to struggle with sleep (see 'Night'). Brodsky is the complete denial of this religio-sentimental aesthetics. The Symbolist Poet in the mould of Pasternak is like an air-plane pilot, he climbs into the sky, he maintains a vigil while the world sleeps, he ascends towards the 'realiora', – superior reality. For Brodsky, certainly a son of Russian Symbolism, but a rebel son, who spurns prophecy, that imitation of Christ, of the Mage, of the pilot setting off into the hereafter, all is immanence, it is in the sluggishness of things that lies hidden the possible 'passage' to something else. In the 'Lullaby of Cape Cod' (a lullaby to induce sleep) dreams are just as much things as any other bit of reality, the undertow of the sea and the undertow of our dreams are the same (as in Mandelstam's 'Bessonnitsa. Homer'). It is not an event that one has to wait for, nor an epiphany, as has always been the case in Christian poetry, but a dismemberment which will project one into the eternal.

Brodsky's classicism objects to all mystical overcharging of the senses: on the contrary it admits loss, such as that admitted by the statue, and even implies dismemberment, just as the hereafter of the ancients implied a diminuation of being.

> What gets left of a man amounts
> to a part. To his spoken part. To a part of speech.[7]

Poetic discourse is like the statue; dismembered but forming an harmonious whole, composed of absence as much as of presence, of inattention as much as of concentration, of solitude as much as of space. In other words it lives because it is at the limits, because it constitutes a limit; a limitation and a limit. When in 'To Urania' the poet declares:

> Odinochestro est' chelovek v kvadrate. (U: 158)
> (Loneliness cubes a man at random)[8]

that solitary man becomes statue, enclosed in Malevich's square and raised by the power of two by that operation of 'deindividualisation' which is Brodskian solitude. The statue can be of frost, of cold. Winter and frost sung of by Brodsky becomes a classic sculpture in which 'time is the flesh of the silent cosmos' as his fourth Eclogue says. As for the prophecy of this Eclogue, as for the 'new order' which it is supposed to announce (as the fourth Eclogue of Virgil has been taken to announce the coming of Christ) it is neither the Kingdom to come nor the New Man, it is the black traces on the white snow, it is the millipede of the cyrillic alphabet on the white page, that is, the poem reduced to tracks in the snow, which remains black on the white ground 'as long as the whiteness lasts. And after'.

It is impossible to make a more succinct evocation of classical immortality: That 'And after' so prosaically incongruous, is the immortality of the relic, of the trace, of the solitude within being, it is Brodskian immortality . . . a torso draped in folds in the white block of time.

Notes

1. Translated by J. Brodsky, *To Urania: Selected Poems 1965–85*, Penguin; London, 1988), p. 69.
2. ibid., p. 64.
3. ibid., p. 69.
4. ibid., p. 69.
5. Predmetnaya sviaz', in A. Kushner, *Dnevnye sny*, (Leningrad, 1986), p. 55.
6. Extracts of that interview were published in *Le Monde*, 18 December 1987, p. 21.
7. Translated by J. Brodsky, *A Part of Speech*, OUP:, Oxford 1980, p. 105.
8. *To Urania*, p. 70.

Translated by Chris Jones

6

Notes on the Sonnets to Mary Queen of Scots
Peter France

I

Мари, шотландцы всё-таки скоты.
В каком колене клетчатого клана
предвиделось, что двинешься с экрана
и оживишь как статуя сады?
И Люксембургский, в частности? Сюды
забрёл я как-то после ресторана
взглянуть глазами старого барана
на новые ворота и в пруды.
Где встретил Вас. И в силу этой встречи,
и так как 'всё былое ожило
в отжившем сердце', в старое жерло
вложив заряд классической картечи,
я трачу что осталось русской речи
на Ваш анфас и матовые плечи. (С: 51)[1]

'Non angli, sed angeli', said a punning Pope centuries ago. Brodsky begins his sonnet sequence with an equally bad, but less complimentary pun: 'skoty'/Scots. The first line sets a tone – flippant, conversational, vulgar. As for the pun, the significant thing is surely the distance it establishes. The English language (Brodsky's adopted language) is heard with Russian ears, which detect new resonances in it, much as those often extraterritorial writers Beckett and Nabokov find a new strangeness in their imposed or self-imposed second languages. In this sequence, written in 1974 some two years after Brodsky left for America, a feeling of distance is always present, openly or covertly: distance between words and feelings, between past and present, between

Notes on the Sonnets to Mary Queen of Scots

individual and society, between the poet and his native land. The separation of exile is regularly likened to the execution of the queen.

So the sonnets, mingling Renaissance Scotland, modern Paris and post-war Russia, are full of non-Russian words that emphasise the separation of worlds. Sometimes they are left in their original form ('Alas' in Sonnet 8), more often adapted to Russian ('voploshchenie gudbaya' in Sonnet 14) or given a new Russian twist, as in 'ayne klayne nakht muzhik' (Sonnet 7), where the Russian peasant intrudes on the easy chic of Mozart. As for the 'little Hollywood-House castle' of Sonnet 9, I live only a mile from Holyrood House, but it takes a foreign ear to notice in the name overtones of Hollywood entirely appropriate to the glamorous legend processed by John Ford four years before the 1940 German film (*Das Herz der Königin*) which is one of the guiding threads in Brodsky's cycle.

One further example of the foreign word and its unexpected richness. In Sonnet 20, after a rational, discursive octet, comes the surprising single line:

> V Nepale est' stolitsa Katmandu.

Holyrood/Hollywood is fair enough, but why Katmandu of all places? It establishes the rhyme 'du' which is used four times in the final sestet to conclude the sequence resoundingly – and last of all repeated in the concise world 'dudu', the 'pipe' or flute of poetry. But beyond this, the word itself, as in a game of charades, falls apart and takes on new meaning. In English 'cat-man-do', but in Russian 'kat' (an old word for 'executioner') and 'manda' ('cunt').[2] So we are taken back to the murderous obscenities of Sonnet 13. Words – and especially proper names – are like accidental gifts, full of poetic possibility:

> Sluchaynoe, yavlyayas' neizbezhnym,
> prinosit pol'zy vsyakomu trudu.

The whole sequence arises out of a unforeseen meeting with a statue, and out of this chance happening the poet weaves a poem of destiny.

II

To return to the first sonnet. The second line sketches a falsely exotic tartan scene, mocking it with an extravagant clatter of k's. Scottish history and legend are seen throughout the sonnets in heightened colours which border on the absurd. There is clearly a gulf between the historical reality, whatever it was, and the lurid images we see in Sonnet 9 for instance. A gulf too between life as it is or was lived and the nobler productions of art. The French statue is particularly important here, offering a monumental, dead, yet powerfully affecting image of the executed queen. Life (or history) and art are situated on different planes.

This theme is pursued throughout the sequence, in Sonnet 12 for instance, but most strikingly in Sonnet 14, where the Indian God Siva, normally imagined by Western readers in the form of a dancing statue (frozen movement) is a six-armed force of passion – and passion, for all its power, is helpless in the face of time and unliving stone. The statue, a figure of absence and separation, outlasts the passion that lights up eyes and cheeks. And yet this stone 'idol' (Sonnet 18) is so powerful that it 'brings life' to the Paris gardens (Sonnet 1). Sonnet 3 in particular opposes everyday life and statuary, with the advantage going to the latter. The picture of the everyday world, comically represented by figures of ladies, gentlemen, policemen and bawling children, concludes in the exasperated obscenity of 'Idi na' – and then the tone changes. The emphatic 'I' which opens the sestet and the apostrophe to Mary – queen and statue – begin to lift the language to a more traditional level of nobility (already present in the Dantesque opening line, which was rapidly undercut by the bureaucratic language of line 2). 'Ne pokladaya ruk' is still fairly conversational and comes oddly after the verb *'stoyat"* (in place of the more normal 'rabotat"), but the following two lines, with their regular iambic rhythm, the beautiful metaphor of the garland of statues and the fairy tale language 'vo vremya ono' evoking long-dead queens, all this takes the reader briefly into the world of art – but then, typically, this in turn is mocked by the sparrow of the following line (and its unspoken droppings).

The last two lines of this sonnet are very interesting. They juxtapose two of the great art works of France. On the one hand the Pantheon, solemn place of memory, stone monument to the great, on the other Manet's *Déjeuner sur l'herbe*, the deliberately shocking picture where the naked woman is deprived of the timeless dignity of the nude by being set among clothed contemporaries in a local landscape. In a way Brodsky's disconcerting poems are to traditional poetry what Manet's picture was to classical painting. And of course it is now *Le Déjeuner sur l'herbe* that is 'famous'. Art at a second degree is made out of the deliberate juxtaposition of art and non-art. So it is with Brodsky's sonnet sequence, which achieves classic status while subverting classicism.

III

From the beginning the first sonnet, like most of those in the sequence, is clearly addressed to Mary (or rather the French Marie but not the German or Russian Maria). She is usually 'ty', but occasionally 'Vy' (implying a more formal and respectful stance); in Sonnet 6 the parody of Pushkin gives us 'vy' rather than 'Vy'. As for the 'I' of the poet, he makes his first open appearance in the second quatrain of Sonnet 1, although of course his presence is perceptible from the outset in the exclamation of line 1, the two rhetorical questions and the conversational syntax of line 5. As we see him first, he is an unpoetic poet, casually 'kak-to' strolling in Paris after a restaurant meal. The Paris restaurant will recur in Sonnet 7 as the object of a pathetic kind of ambition ('Paris by night'), and will be immediately devalued in depressing images of Soviet vulgarity. As for the poet's food, we may notice that Sonnet 2 refers literally to the food shortages of the post-war years, for which the womb-like pleasures of the cinema with its gorgeous images of love and death provided compensation. Sonnet 18 on the other hand, takes up the image metaphorically, the true food of the soul (love, beauty) being set against the insipidity of life.

Notice also that the poet of Sonnet 1 is compared to a ram – and indeed to the animal in the proverbial 'smotret' kak baran v novye vorota' (to gaze in stupid amazement). This is one of several thematic and metaphorical networks that bind the sonnets together. It is echoed in the verb 'razzhevyvat'' of Sonnet 18, the dull old ram chewing over tasteless fodder. But the ram may have other connotations. In Sonnet 13 he opens the poem vigorously in a picturesque Scottish world of barons and barren heaths (is there perhaps a play on the words 'baran' and 'baron' in Sonnet 5?). The ram's wool is suddenly, if ironically, invested with the mythological glamour of the Golden Fleece. The ram is powerful, sexually potent. But in Sonnet 11 we have read that Fate snatches the coat (literally the noble astrakhan) from the sheep and in Sonnet 19, with its disillusioned references to modern Scotland, the fleece has become the woollen goods of the craft shops. So the 'old ram' of Sonnet 1 is essentially a figure of decline and loss: he has said goodbye, he has lost his fleece. As Sonnet 3 says, he is like Dante, in the middle of life's way, lost. But he too meets his Beatrice in the shape of the statue. Hence the ennobling 'Vy' of line 9 and the possiblility of making poetry out of life's prose.

IV

The sestet of Sonnet 1 contrasts the old and the new, suggesting an elegiac stance that recurs intermittently throughout the sequence. The particular allusion is to Tyutchev, not just an allusion, but a quotation in inverted commas: 'Vse byloe ozhilo/ v otzhivshem serdtse'. This speaks of death and life, the new life (*vita nuova*) that a chance meeting can kindle in a clapped-out old ram. It is one of the time-honoured themes of poetry: love and beauty remembered, the imagined return of lost youth and the realisation that time cannot be reversed. The Tyutchev original, 'Ya vstretil vas, i vse byloe', addressed to Baroness Krudener, is with its companion piece, 'Ya pomnyu vremya zolotoe', a classic example of this elegant bitter-sweet poetry, and has achieved even wider currency by being set to music as a romance.

In quoting Tyutchev, Brodsky removes an inversion – the original reads 'v otzhivshem serdtse ozhilo', thus fitting it into his prosodic scheme, but also slightly lowering its dignity. This is only a very slight alteration, however, as compared to his wholesale deconstruction of Pushkin's 'Ya vas lyubil' in Sonnet 6. A. Zholkovsky has written in detail about this,[3] and there would be no point in repeating his analysis here (though I wonder if he is right to read the 'vy' of this sonnet simply as Mary, rather than an amalgam of Mary and the woman of Sonnet 4, who so resembled the dead queen?). Zholkovsky also points out in passing a number of other literary allusions in the sonnets, and it is certain that most of them are riddled with intertextual reminiscences. The most important thing is the sonnet form itself (see below), but in addition there are open or obvious references to Dante (Sonnet 3), Mozart (Sonnet 7), Schiller (Sonnet 12) and Pushkin's 'Osen'' (Sonnet 16). Somewhat less evident are allusions to Sappho (the raising of the roof in Sonnet 15), to Blok (the mackintosh of

Sonnet 4), to Akhmatova (the 'rubbish' of Sonnet 18) and to E.T.A. Hoffman (the 'khromoy bochar' of Sonnet 10). And beyond these there are endless echoes called up by forms, words and images. The actualisation of these will depend on every reader's experience – I personally cannot read the opening of Sonnet 7 without thinking of that great Baudelairean elegy, 'Le Cygne'.

So what are these quotations and allusions? Fragments shored against Brodsky's ruins? Certainly the effect is not unlike what we find in T.S. Eliot – and in many other modern poets. On the one hand there is a kind of derision (or self-derision) in the juxtaposing of the noble tradition and the depressing present.[4] The works of the classics are unavoidable for the educated modern reader, but they can no longer work as they once did. A barrier of destructive irony divides us from them. It is like the great curtain that separates the poet from the world of Racine in Mandelstam's 'Ya ne uvizhu znamenitoy 'Fedry''. The same poet's 'Grifel'naya Oda' is a poem made like an ode, refering to a famous (but unfinished and now obliterated) ode; it fails to be an ode, and in this failure lies its specific greatness. So Brodsky, before leaving Russia, wrote his beautiful 'Pochti Elegiya', a sort of wistful yet ironic homage to a collapsed tradition. He alludes to classics subversively, but at the same time, like Mandelstam, he stretches towards them. The juxtaposition does not just mean deflation; it lifts the present temporarily to a higher plane. As Brodsky says in his essay on Auden, the poet challenges time.[5] Sonnet 20 closes fittingly on the emblematic transformation of blank paper into flute.

V

Sonnet 1 ends with one of several remarkable metaphors in the sequence. The empty barrel of a gun (the poet's voice, throat) is stuffed with classical grapeshot (all the paraphernalia of traditional poetry, rhyme, meter, poetic diction, rhetorical figures). The gun, incidentally, will reappear as the potential implement of suicide in Sonnet 6, the modern replacement, together with censorship and exile, of the axe which is perhaps the dominant motif of the whole sequence. Here it is the poet who is doing the shooting – but at what? Celebrating the memory of the beautiful executed queen, he directs his fire against all the enemies of love and beauty, the Scottish barons, Elizabeth of England, the modern philistines, and most sinister of all the paralysed 'gensek' ('tvoy gensek', we note) of Sonnet 7 – General Secretary Stalin. And his ammunition? 'Chto ostalos' russkoy rechi'.

Language is arguably the central concern in all of Brodsky's poems. Just to stay within the Mary sequence, poem after poem shows the poet speaking, trying to speak, failing to speak. In Sonnet 4, for instance, the gullet stands for the poet's voice, stammering 'togo' his paradoxical thanks to a fate that destroys him. In a way the true hero of the sonnets is not Brodsky or Mary, but the Russian language itself.

Schematically, one could say that the sequence aims to fill the classical sonnet form (old bottles) with a new kind of language (new wine, or vinegar). Or rather the wine (the diction) is both old and new. It veers quickly and constantly from one end of the linguistic spectrum to the other. Archaic words, new words, cliches, poetic words, unprintable words, the language of romantic fiction, of Soviet bureaucracy, of the streets – they all jostle and compete. Zholkovsky has demonstrated in detail the process of linguistic 'snizhenie' in Sonnet 6, and one could show a similar process operating in almost any sonnet in the collection. The full richness is of course only perceptible to readers for whom Russian is a native language (and modern Soviet Russian at that). Foreigners are less well placed. For the translator in particular the problem is to know exactly how to place individual expressions – not to speak of the difficulty of finding English equivalents.

Take Sonnet 18 as an example of Brodsky's range:

> Для рта, проговорившего 'прощай'
> тебе, а не кому-нибудь, не всё ли
> одно, какое хлебово без соли
> разжёвывать впоследствии. Ты, чай,
> привычная к не-доремифасоли.
> А, если что не так – не осерчай:
> язык, что крыса, копошится в соре,
> выискивает что-то невзначай.
>
> Прости меня, прелестный истукан.
> Да, у разлуки всё-таки не дура
> губа (хоть часто кажется – дыра):
> меж нами – вечность, также – океан.
> Причём, буквально. Русская цензура.
> Могли бы обойтись без топора. (С: 59)

The poem starts with a distinctly poetic metonymy (mouth for person) – by no means a neutral figure of course, for the mouth is what we speak with, eat with, kiss with (this important image is picked up in the 'tongue' of line 7). This opening has something of the nobility of a classic maxim, but this is quickly undercut by the ordinariness of 'ne komu-nibud'' (there are many such flat expressions in the sonnets), by the popular and dismissive 'khlebovo' and by the rather trivial 'razzhevyvat''. The middle of the octet is conversational in a stylised way ('chay', 'oserchay'), though not entirely the language of everyday speech with the bizarre neologism 'ne-doremifasoli'. The last two lines, however, form a separate unit, not so much conversation as a vivid metaphorical statement about poetry, echoing Akhmatova's famous 'Kogda b vy znali, iz kakogo sora/Rastut stikhi'. The tone is not exactly elevated (notice again the deliberately vague 'chto-to', echoing 'kogda-nibud'' in line 2), but still perceptibly the language of poetry (with the archaic 'chto' introducing the comparison with a rat).

The sestet opens with a classic apostrophe (and the most traditional of poetic epithets, 'preslestnyy'). But in lines 10–11 – overriding the line ending – Brodsky brings in a popular quasi-proverbial expression, personifying 'razluka' (separation), but not in the exalted way we saw in Sonnet 14. The dismissive parenthesis of line 11, playing on the resemblance of 'dyra' and 'dura', only exacerbates this feeling of triviality (it is noticeable how often Brodsky uses parentheses for these vital off-hand personal remarks). Line 12 though, formed symmetrically, with the big words 'vechnost'' and 'okean' and the archaic 'mezh', comes across with the unironic strength of tragedy (I have tried to catch something of this in my translation by an echo of Marvell's 'To his Coy Mistress', and surely Marvell is a poet after Brodsky's own heart). And then, yet again, the casual prosaic voice breaks in 'prichem' and the timeless, placeless language of high poetry gives way to the grimly precise 'russkaya tsenzura'. The final line returns us once more to the axe of Mary's execution, but in a grim, almost humorous comparison of two fates which avoids all poetic grandiloquence.

Throughout this sonnet, and throughout the sequence, we are tossed between different styles or voices, voices associated with different times, places and speakers. It is like a manifestation in lyric poetry of the polyphony that Bakhtin attributed uniquely to the novel. As with the literary allusions discussed earlier, I do not think that the result is simply to deflate ancient tradition. Brodsky seems rather to propose a multiple perspective on a world which is endlessly various and contradictory. And in doing so he does not sabotage, but preserves and renews 'chto ostalos' russkoy rechi'.

VI

I have said nothing so far about the most striking formal feature of the work. This is that rare bird 'belaya vorona' in Russian poetry, the sonnet sequence. The form is no doubt partly inspired by the subject. The Renaissance was the time for such massive production of sonnets, and Mary Queen of Scots herself paid tribute to the genre.[6] But Brodsky, preoccupied as he is with the possibilities of complex and difficult prosodic forms, is clearly interested in the sonnet for its own sake as well. Before this work, he had written a number of so-called sonnets, i.e. poems in fourteen lines which bear that title. These generally flout most of the formal expectations provoked by the word. 'Velikiy Gektor', for instance, written in 1961, is an unrhymed poem in iambic pentameters with nothing like the traditional divisions of either the Shakespearean or the Petrarchan sonnet – and the same is true of the two other ostensible sonnets in *Ostanovka v pustyne*. In 1964–5, however, he wrote two regular sonnets 'Prislushivayas' k groznym golosam' and 'Ty, Muza, nedoverchiva k lyubvi'.[7] But the Mary Queens of Scots sequence represents a far more formidable undertaking, a series of twenty poems which outwardly at least conform to the stringent requirements of the classic form, and indeed exacerbate the difficulty.

The sonnet is not a favoured form in Russian poetry, though there have been exceptions in the twentieth century (Bal'mont, Vyacheslav Ivanov). Pushkin's 'Onegin stanza', with its regular rhyme scheme embracing fourteen tetrameters, comes somewhere close to it, and even though most of Brodsky's sonnets are in pentameters, one cannot help being reminded occasionally of 'Evgeny Onegin', especially in view of the shifting tone and multi-layered language I have noted. But basically I imagine Brodsky's main point of reference for the sonnet when he refers to 'classic grape-shot' must be the writers of France, Italy and England (with John Donne to the fore, no doubt).

What happens to the sonnet here is reminiscent of what one finds in some of Rimbaud's youthful sonnets (e.g. 'Ma Bohème'). Quite apart from the deliberate mingling and contrasting of stylistic levels, we find in Brodsky as in Rimbaud a combination of respect and subversion – though one suspects that in the case of the mature Brodsky the motivation is very different from that of the adolescent French poet. Apart from its length, the most obvious feature of the sonnet is its use of rhyme.[8] Whatever model one follows, the classic sonnet is tightly rhymed, the different sections being bound together by rhymes which are often used more than twice – four times in the Petrarchan octet. All of this is true of the Mary sonnets. None of them contains more than five rhymes for its fourteen lines and in three of them (Sonnets 8, 13 and 20) there are only two rhymes. In the strict classical manner, Brodsky makes things more difficult for himself by alternating masculine and feminine rhymes. What is more, he seems to go out of his way to ring the changes within this rigid form, for none of his sonnets exactly repeats the rhyme scheme of any other. Several of them (the first two for instance) are regular Petrarchan sonnets with an ABBAABBA pattern for the octet (but variants in the sestet), others invert this in various ways (Sonnets 11 and 14 begin ABBABAAB), and Sonnet 5 stands the form on its head with a quite original pattern (AABCBCBCBCBCCB). In addition to this, most of the rhymes are full ones, often drawing the reader's attention with ostentatious wit, for instance by rhyming a group of words with a single word 'ne drozh', no'/ 'beznadezhno' or by rhyming foreign words with Russian ones 'Place des Vosges'/ 'prigozh'. When in the last poem Brodsky notes his 'slabost' k okonchaniyam padezhnym', one is tempted to see the whole sequence in retrospect as an extraordinary display of verbal skill, the despair of any translator who should believe that all formal elements should be transferred from one language to another in poetic translation.

However it will clearly not do to write this off as sheer ostentation. The point is that in the classic sonnet the tight rhyme scheme generally echoes and reinforces a unified rhetorical structure, whereas Brodsky creates a striking tension between his prosodic exactness (which also includes, with only a few exceptions, a constant adherence to the iambic pentameter) and a syntactic and logical structure which is a far cry from that of the traditional sonnet (not to speak of the lexical subversiveness discussed above). Of course to talk of the 'traditional sonnet' is an absurd over-simplification: the fourteen-line form can be structured in many different ways from the accumulation and sudden reversal of 'The expense of spirit in a waste of shame' to the far more balanced antithesis of 'Shall I compare thee to a summer's day'. In general, though, the rhetorical features of enumeration, antithesis and repetition help the sonnet to unfold in a single dynamic movement, gathering momentum to the final denouement. In Brodsky's sonnets, by contrast, there are characteristically stops and starts, new departures, asides and conversational sentences which cross line barriers and disrupt the movement of the pentameters. If his style is generally characterised by the long and winding sentence, in Sonnet 9 he chops up the fourteen lines to create a mini-drama, with snatches of dialogue and changes of scene. Most of the sonnets have a certain thematic unity, it is true, yet one often has an impression of centrifugal chaos, most notably perhaps in Sonnet 11. And even when the poem moves purposefully towards an ending, as it does for instance in Sonnet 17 – consisting of a single sentence and written unusually in iambic tetrameters so as to increase the forward flow of words over line divisions – even here we see Brodsky break the eloquent build-up in full flight with the self-deprecating or mocking 'ne mogu tiradu/zakonchit' – v obshchem, tvoy parik'. The throw-away 'v obshchem' is echoed time and again in the use of stammering filler-words which put a brake on the poet's natural eloquence. And the same effect is created by the numerous colloquial expressions such as 'chay', 'mozhet', or 'skazhu tebe'.

And yet . . . In Sonnet 17, after the hiccup in the middle, the rhythm picks up again and the sentence is finished in fine style. Likewise in many of the sonnets the old patterns of enumeration, gradation, repetition and antithesis still work in spite of the many obstacles put in their way. Brodsky does not entirely deny himself (or us) the satisfactions of sonnet eloquence. He does not wring its neck, but keeps it alive, renewed by a chilling dash of realism or scepticism.

VII

The Mary sonnets are not just a collection of poems, they are a sonnet sequence (or cycle, to use the more normal Russian word). Readers of the sonnet sequences of Petrarch, Ronsard or the English sonneteers are often perplexed about the architecture of these works. Are they presented in a random order, or does the overall structure make up something like the plot of a play or novel? Brodsky has written many long poems, in which he has tackled the problem of giving shape to a mass of material without a narrative thread. In the case of the Sonnets I am not sure that I can see good reasons for the placing of each particular poem, but an overall movement can be traced, and as one reads and rereads one can see patterns forming which link all the sonnets in a complex web of associations, similarities and contrasts. Schematically it looks something like this:

1. Introduction. Paris scene; poet's meeting with the statue; the impulse for the sonnets.
2. Introduction. Retrospective; memory of seeing the film in Leningrad.
3. Paris scene filled out; statuary and everyday life.
4. Retrospective; the poet's former love; his fate compared to Mary's.
5. Mary's passions evoked against Scottish setting; no mention of the poet.
6. Pushkin parody, pursuing the theme of passion, but in relation to the poet.
7. Paris scene; global vision; Paris and Soviet man.
8. In America the poet imagines a meeting with Mary.
9. Dramatic vision of Mary's Scottish adventures; no mention of the poet.
10. Lyrical digression on time and death; no mention of Mary.
11. Chaotic vision of fate, as seen by Mary and the poet.
12. Reflexions on art and history via Schiller's *Maria Stuart*.
13. Scottish scene; Mary's execution and the cynical barons.
14. Reflexions on love, death and art.
15. Mary's execution and the reason for it – her beauty.
16. Lyrical digression; autumn, the melancholy of passing time; no mention of Mary or the poet.
17. Mary's execution; its impact on spectators and poet.
18. The poet and Mary; separation. Beginning of conclusion.
19. Modern Scotland and England compared to Mary's epoch.
20. Conclusion, addressed to reader; the film, statue and poetry.

It is easy to see how different threads are plaited together: the Paris scenes in Sonnets 1, 3, 7; personal memories in Sonnets 2, 4, 6; visions of Mary's Scottish adventures in Sonnets 5, 9, 11, 13, 15, 17, 19; imaginative lyrical and reflective digressions in Sonnets 8, 10, 12, 14, 16, 18 and the final sonnet. Paris serves as a starting point, but soon both Paris and the poet's memories give way to visions of Mary's fate, real and imaginary, and to an interwoven series of those reflexions on being and non-being, time and space, separation and love, which are so characteristic of their author.

VIII

But why Mary Queen of Scots? Why should the 'meeting' with the Paris statue, bringing back old memories of a German film, have given birth to this extraordinary sonnet sequence? These are questions for the author rather than the reader, no doubt, but we can at least reflect on what the choice may mean. It so happens, moreover, that this particular reader finds himself in Edinburgh as it celebrates the four hundredth anniversary of Mary's execution – and as luck would have it, these celebrations have included a screening of *Das Herz der Königin*, the 1940 film which Joseph Brodsky saw in Leningrad in 1948.

Mary is of course only one of Brodsky's rather numerous mythical or legendary heroes. He often writes of great figures – Isaac, Hector, Ulysses – about whom a halo of associations has formed. It is in part a way of writing about the self, of searching out grandiose parallels to one's modern experience. Such parallels inevitably work in different ways: they can enlarge and universalise the private predicament, giving it the glamour of antiquity, but conversely the juxtaposition may destroy the halo, or else mock the present by contrasting it with glorious images from the past. The twenty sonnets, incidentally, were later included by Brodsky in his 1983 volume, *Novye stansy k Avguste*, the collection of poems addressed between 1962 and 1982 to the woman who figures in many of his dedications as 'M.B.'; the figure of Mary, like those of Dido and Byron's Augusta, is thus in part at least a legendary transposition of a real contemporary. So much can in any case be guessed from Sonnets 4 and 6; a reading of the sonnets does not depend upon knowledge of the poet's private life.

Mary Queen of Scots (to use her local name rather than Brodsky's continental appelation) brings with her a wealth of images from history, literature, music and painting. She has attracted the most contradictory judgements, ranging from Froude's 'bad woman, disguised in the livery of a martyr', via Macdiarmid and Grassic Gibbon's 'well-intentioned but hysterical poodle' to Dr Johnson's 'such a Queen . . . as every man of gallantry of spirit would have sacrificed his life for'. For Scots she is an ambiguous folk-heroine, but her legend has spread far abroad to writers all over the world, among them Schiller, whose Romantic version of the story is derided in Sonnet 12, even while the poet is proclaiming the supremacy of Art over History.

Apart from Schiller's *Maria Stuart*, which does not seem particularly present in any of the sonnets except Sonnet 12, the two dominant images of the queen are the Paris statue and *Das Herz der Königin*. The statue shows the transformation of life into beautiful stone, the double-edged victory of art. With the film things are more complicated. Brodsky is writing about a childhood memory, presumably unrefreshed by subsequent exposure to this version of the story. It is an odd irony, adding a further twist to the whirlpool of cultures offered us, that this is an anti-English film made in Nazi Germany, with the Marlene Dietrich substitute Zarah Leander playing the queen, and for some reason (perhaps its anti-Englishness?) it was still being shown in the USSR three years after the defeat of Nazi Germany. The heavy and rather self-consciously beautiful film shows the crushing of a loving woman by the manipulations and prejudices of both the English and the Scots – here perhaps we can see the origins of the animus shown in the sonnets against the puritanical and brutal Scottish barons. It is a simplified romantic image, and was perhaps further simplified for Brodsky by the passage of time since 1948.

Zarah Leander may have taught the poet about 'tender feelings' (Sonnet 20), but tenderness does not have it its own way in the sonnets. Brodsky's Mary is not just the touchingly innocent Romantic victim of Carl Froelich's film or of nineteenth-century history paintings. His heroine is a sexy lady (see Sonnet 5) and from the point of view of the pig-headed Scots barons (since John Knox does not get a look in) a 'whore' or 'blyad' – a word which jars as much as it possibly could with the more romantic visions of the tragic queen. Not that Mary's sexuality is condemned; it is rather that the presentation of her has often a deliberately crude, cynical tone, pressing home on the reader the gap between lived reality and the purified image portrayed by statue and film. The statue of Sonnet 3 has a sparrow on its head, while the castle of Sonnet 9, set in a grim, sordid battlefield, is likened to a Hollywood set. Sonnet 17, after an eloquent build-up, culminates in a bathetic, yet moving allusion to Mary's fallen wig. Similarly Sonnet 19 ironically contrasts the tragedy of 1587 with the prosaic reality of

1974 (a Scotland of craft shops, tourist whisky and Loch Ness Monsters). Like the Renaissance sonnet form, the legend is subverted and dislocated – just as in the 1987 Edinburgh festival we had not only Schiller's *Maria Stuart*, but Liz Lochhead's less respectful *Mary Queen of Scots got her head cut off*.

But the romantic Mary is not eliminated altogether. It is the same as with the juxtaposition of different linguistic elements: modern irony does not rule out emotional involvement. For Mary is connected with art and with beauty; she is still the ideal, compared with which reality is insipid (Sonnet 18). The poet insists on her physical beauty, seeing in her the prefiguration of the woman he loved (Sonnet 4) and merging these two images together in his cynical yet passionate rewriting of Pushkin's 'Ya vas lyubil'. In Sonnet 8 he fantasises about an ideal meeting between queen and poet, a sort of ironical *Liebestod*. Brodsky and Mary might have met, for they are two of a kind.

Perhaps the main point is that made in the last three lines of Sonnet 15:

> Oni tebe zadelali svin'yu
> za to, chemu ne videli kontsa
> v te vremena: za krasotu litsa.

Mary's beauty, like Brodsky's poetry, falls victim to a brutal historical world, and it is through defeat, it seems, that the amorous queen reaches the heights of art:

> Chto delaet Istoriyu? – Tela.
> Iskusstvo? – Obezglavlennoe telo.

Brodsky never alludes openly to Mary's motto 'En ma fin est mon commencement' (which he may well have first met in its inverted form in Eliot's 'East Coker'), but one can easily imagine how it appealed to the poet who wrote in '1972 god':

> Tol'ko razmer poteri i
> delaet smertnogo ravnym Bogu.

In the end, then, for all the deliberate debunking of Romantic and poetic clichés associated with both Mary Queen of Scots and the classical sonnet, the 'Twenty Sonnets to Mary Queen of Scots' strike me as a perpetuation and renewal, rather than a refusal, of the old legend. Through their punning, dissonance, physicality and vulgarity, the commitment to love and beauty remains strong, as it was in Schiller or the Zarah Leander film. Brodsky is less the metaphysician here than in much of his work, more the poet of experience, memory and emotion. But above all, the master of language.

These have been a translator's notes. I have picked out aspects which seemed to me interesting without attempting to describe the whole of a very complex work, let alone to place it in relation to Brodsky's total poetic output. Translation is perhaps the only complete commentary. The translator, though limited by his or her own linguistic means, is obliged to make something of every single line. While I do not entirely share Brodsky's views on the translation of poetry,[9] I have rendered what I could of the shape and feel of the original – but faithfulness to the rhymes has defeated me. In any case, I am grateful to the author[10] and to Valentina Polukhina and Alan Myers for what they have done to make this translation less inadequate that it would otherwise have been.

Notes

1. Iosif Brodskiy, *Chast' rechi*, (Ann Arbor, Michigan: Ardis, 1977), p. 51. In this article I refer to the sonnets by number rather than giving page references.
2. L. Loseff, in a private communications, suggests that there is also here a punning reference to the Russian colloquial expression 'rezat' pravdu-matku' (to speak frankly).
3. See A. Zholkovskiy, '"Ya vas lyubil" Brodskogo: interteksty, invarianty, tematika i struktura', in *Poetika Brodskogo*, L.V. Losev (ed.) (Tenafly, New Jersey: Hermitage, 1986), pp. 38–62.
4. On this and many other aspects of the Mary sonnets see the rich anonymous article 'Pis'mo o russkoy poezii', in *Poetika Brodskogo*, pp. 16–37.
5. Joseph Brodsky, 'To Please a Shadow', in *Less than One* (Penguin, 1987), pp. 357–83 (p. 363).
6. There is some doubt about the authenticity of Mary's sonnets, particularly those addressed to Bothwell. In line 5 of Sonnet 2, Brodsky appears to be referring to Mary's own words when he writes 'kak ty by ne skazala', but I cannot trace the allusion – though one might see some connection here with Mary's famous motto 'En ma fin est mon commencement'.
7. These two sonnets were published in *Ekho*, No. 1, 1978.

8. For more details on the rhymes see the anonymous article referred to in note 3.
9. See Brodsky's article on the translation of poetry in the *New York Review of Books*, 7 February 1974. For a contrary view by an eminent French poet, see Yves Bonnefoy, 'On the Translation of Form in Poetry', *World Literature Today* (A Literary Quarterly of the University of Oklahoma), 1979, pp. 374–80.
10. See, however, Brodsky's *To Urania* (New York and London, 1988) for a revised translation of the sonnets by the poet and myself, in which he has managed to bring the English closer to the formal qualities of the original, and in particular the rhyme. I am most grateful to him for his permission to print my own version here as a part of my commentary on his writing.

APPENDIX: JOSEPH BRODSKY – TWENTY SONNETS TO MARY QUEEN OF SCOTS (1974)

1

Marie, I call them pigs, not Picts, those Scots.
What generation of what clan in tartan
could have foreseen you'd step down from the screen
a statue, and bring life to city gardens –
the Luxembourg to be precise? I came
here to digest a Paris lunch and stare
with the dull eyes of a decreipt ram
at the new gates and into ponds. And here
I met Your Highness. And to mark that meeting
and since 'all the dead past now lives anew
in my cold heart', by way of greeting
I'll stuff the old gun full of classic grape-
shot, squandering what remains of Russian speech
on your pale shoulders and your paler face.

2

The war to end no wars was over.
There was no fat to fry what food there was.
Marie, I was a boy then and saw Zarah
Leander go click-clacking to the block.
Whatever you may say, the axeman's blade
Makes molehills level with the lofty sky

Notes on the Sonnets to Mary Queen of Scots

A Joseph Brodsky manuscript page: Sonnet No. 14 from the cycle "Twenty Sonnets to Mary Queen of Scots" which was included in the Russian version of **A Part of Speech**.

The material appeared in Sven Birkert's interview with Brodsky entitled 'Art of Poetry: Joseph Brodsky', *Paris Review*, 24, Spring 1982, pp. 83–126. The manuscript page used was not numbered.

(cf. Apollo rising from the waves).
We came out from the pictures to the light,
But something called us at the hour of gloaming
Back to the 'Spartacus', whose plushy womb
is cosier than a European evening.
There the stars hang, the fairest a brunette,
two films are showing, with a queue for each.
And not a single seat.

3

I, who have travelled half my earthly road,
make my appearance in the Luxembourg
and contemplate the petrified grey locks
of thinkers and of scribblers; to and fro
they stroll, the ladies and the gents, a blue
mustachioed gendarme glistens in the green,
the fountain gurgles and the children bawl,
and who can I say 'fuck off' to? Not a soul.
And you, Marie, untiring, stand and stand
Among a wreath of stony lady friends,
the queens of France of once upon a time,
silently, with a sparrow in your hair.
You'd think the garden was a cross between
the Pantheon and the 'Déjeuner sur l'herbe'.

4

The beauty whom I later was to love
more tenderly than you loved Bothwell, shared
some features with you (automatically
I whisper 'Oh my God' as I recall
them) – only external features though – and we
like you did not make up a happy pair.
Wearing a mackintosh she went off somewhere.
To sidestep the straight line of destiny,

I cut across another line – whose edge
is sharper than a knife blade, the horizon,
Marie. With head held high above that thing,
not for the oxygen but the nitrogen

that seethes and bubbles in the swollen throat,
the larynx sort of offers thanks to fate.

5

Marie, the number of your lovers went
beyond the figure three, or four, or ten,
twenty, or twenty-five. For a crowned head
there's nothing that means more embarrassment
than hopping into bed with somebody.
(And that is why the monarchy is doomed,
while the republic stands against the flood,
a marble pillar of antiquity.)
And the Scots barons will never give an inch –
no joking about sex, their minds are shut.
It was beyond your Scottish lords to see
how throne and bed are different in law.
Oh rara avis of your century,
for your contemporaries you were a whore.

6

I loved you. And my love (or maybe
it's only pain) still stabs me through the brain.
The whole thing's shattered into smithereens.
I tried to shoot myself – using a gun
isn't so simple. And the temples: which one,
the right or left? Reflection, not the shakes,
kept me from acting. Jesus, what a mess!
I loved you with such strength, such hopelessness
may God send you in others – not a chance!
He may be capable of many things,
but – with Parmenides – won't reinspire
the fire in the blood, the bones' crunching collapse,
melting the lead in fillings with desire
to touch – 'your hips', I must delete – your lips.

7

Paris is still the same. The Place des Vosges
is still, as once it was (don't worry) square.

The Seine has not run backwards to its source.
The Boulevard Raspail is still as fair.
As for the new, there's music now for free,
a tower to make you feel you're just a fly,
no lack of people whom it's nice to meet,
but get your word in first, ask them 'how's life?'.

Paris by night, a restaurant . . . What chic
in words like those – a treat for vocal chords.
And in comes eine kleine nachtmuzhik,
an ugly cretin in a Russian shirt.
Cafe. Boulevard. The girl-friend in a swoon.
And General-Secretary-cripple-moon.

8

In my decline, in a land beyond the seas
(discovered in Your Highness' time, methinks),
splitting my old iconostas between
a stove and a divan with tired springs,
I muse how just a few words would have been
enough for us, if fate had crossed our paths:
you would have simply called me 'dear Ivan',
and I'd have answered with one word, 'Alas'.

Scotland would have become our mattress then.
I'd have displayed you to the haughty Slavs.
Port Glasgow would have seen a caravan
of satins, Russian cakes and shoes of bast
come sailing in. And we'd have met our fate
together. Cut short by a wooden axe.

9

A plain. Alarum. Enter two. The clash
of battle. 'Who are you?' 'And who are you?'
'Who am I?' 'Yes, you.' 'We are protestants.'
'And we are catholics.' 'So! Papists!' Crash!
And then the corpses lying all about,
the din of endless disputatious crows.
Then – winter, ornamented sleighs in snow,

a damask shawl: 'Damascus, where is that?'
'Where the peacock is fairer than his hen.'
'But even there he can't be made a queen.'
(A game of chess, an interlude in passion.)
Night in the little Hollywood-House castle.

A plain again. Time, midnight. Enter two.
And everything merges in their wolfish howl.

10

An autumn evening. With the Muse it seems.
Alas, not lifting her face toward the sky.
That's nothing new. On evenings such as these
everything cheers you, even the Red Star choir.
Today, as it changes into yesterday,
does not concern itself with the exchange
of writing paper, pen and dumpling broth,
or the lame Hamburg cooper's handiwork.
Time probably has no more confidence,
or hardly, in old, worn-out things that bear
the marks of stains and scratches than it has
in fresh-picked vegetables. Look how death
creaking the door will stand on the parquet
in a suburban coat moths have laid waste.

11

Clashing of shears, a chill runs through the veins.
Fate, coveting the fur coat on the sheep,
snatches our bridal crowns and royal crowns
alike. And specially takes off our heads.
Young men and their proud fathers, separations,
oaths of lifelong fidelity, farewell.
The brain feels like a skyscraper with tenants
who are so many strangers in their shell.
This is how twins go drinking in Siam,
one knocks it back, both go on the rampage.
There was no-one to cry to you 'Stand back!'
And you, 'I'm by myself and', Marie, who

deafened with Latin roof and God, alas,
you couldn't snap 'there are a lot of you'.

12

Tell me, what is it that makes History?
Bodies. – And Art? – A body with no head.
Take Schiller. History got it in the neck
from Schiller. You, Marie, could not have dreamt
some Jerry'd take the bit between his teeth
and bring that old affair back on the mat:
and anyway why should he be concerned
whether you slept with this man or with that?

But maybe Fred, like any Karl or Hans
himself was simply frightened of the axe.
Another thing, I'll tell you, it's beyond
(imagine this) the power of anything
but Art, to comprehend your queenliness.
History you can leave to Good Queen Bess.

13

The ram shakes out his curls (a fleece is what
they call it) and breathes in the scent of hay.
All round Glencairns, Douglases, the like
of them. These were the words they spoke that day:
'They have cut off her head. Alas!' 'Just think
how furious those Parisians will be.'
'The French? Annoyed about a woman's head?
Now if they'd aimed a bit above the knee . . .'
'She's not a man though. Came out in her shift.'
'What of it? That's no reason.' 'Shameless woman.
wearing a see-through dress!' 'And what of it?
Perhaps she had no other to put on.'
'Russians are luckier: take Ivanov – it
sounds like a lass whatever case it's in.'

14

Love is more powerful than separation,
but not so long. The more magnificent

the stone, the more we note the absence there
of cheeks and so on. And of smell and sound.
Maybe you can't kick up your legs to heaven:
that is the way stone is (how it must hurt),
and passion, powerful as six-armed Shiva –
is powerless – stone won't exempt the skirt.

Not because so much water, so much blood
(oh, if it only had been blue!) has flowed,
but out of grief at being left alone,
Marie, I would have hoisted up not stone,
but glass, the incarnation of goodbye,
the image of the penetrating eye.

15

Marie, believe me, you were not brought low
because your lovers on the battlefield
summoned no joiners to raise high a roof;
the fault was not your mixing 'you' and 'thou';
not someone's coded messages; and not
that behind seven seals Elizabeth
loved England with a greater love than you
loved Scotland (though incidentally I have to note
that's how it was); and it was not that song,
the dirge you chanted in your lonely cell's
confinement to your nightingale of Spain.
They did the dirty on you for one crime,
Something they saw no end to at that time:
they killed you for the beauty of your face.

16

Corners are softened by the dark, they say.
A square may easily become a ball,
and with its doused fire staring into night,
the crimson wood with all its pores of bark
silently listens to the curlew's cry.
A setter, nervous of a stray dead leaf,
barks to the seven stars in the sky
that look down on the folds of winter wheat.

How little that human tears were wooed by then
has managed to survive transition to
the humus' shade. And now the fountain pen
of all the things that occupy the view
can only trace the ever-circling year,
sing 'Melancholy Days' in harmony.

17

The thing that dragged from English mouths a shout
of wonderment, and that impels
my own mouth with its taste for rouge
to blasphemy, that could compel
Philip to tear his face from Art
and order an Armada to set sail,
it was – I can't complet the big
build-up of phrases – well, your wig,
lying fallen from your fallen head
(evil eternity), it seemed
your one and only bow, and though
it may not have provoked a fight
among spectators, even so
it brought your enemies to their feet.

18

To one whose mouth has said farewell to you
and not just anyone, is it not all the same
whatever tasteless muck he has to chew
in years to come. I'll wager you became
accustomed to the lack of do-re-mi.
If something's wrong though, don't be cross with me:
rat-like the tongue goes scurrying through a mound
of rubbish, looking what oddments it can find.

Forgive me them, fair statue in the park.
Yes, separation is no fool (although
it often seems a hole): between us lies
eternity – and ocean. Literally.
And Russian censorship. They have the knack.
They could have done the job without an axe.

19

The Scots, Marie, have wool now (and it all
looks spick and span, like freshly laundered clothes).
At six o'clock life judders to a halt,
leaving no mark upon the sun's round O.
The lakes – unnumbered as in days gone by –
have spawned strange monsters (serpentine and frisky),
and soon they'll have their private oil supply,
Scotch oil, to go in bottles meant for whisky.

Scotland, you see, can get along without you.
And England too, or so it seems. How far
it is from this your Gallic garden statue
to her who turned the heads of boys and men.
There may be ladies now we might prefer,
they're not like you, whether in flesh or stone.

20

With simple soul and not rebellious pen
I have sung this meeting in a foreign park
with her who in '48 on a white screen
taught me the lessons of a tender heart.
And readers, judges, you can now consider
a) if I learned my lessons well from her,
b) a new setting for a Russian writer,
c) my soft spot for playing games with words.

The capital of Nepal is Katmandu.

Chance, which is really called necessity
lends us a hand in everything we do.

Leading the life I lead, I am grateful to
all those originally snow-white leaves
of writing paper twisted to a flute.

7
'Polden' v komnate'
Gerald S. Smith

Polden' v komnate (PK) is one of the most substantial texts in Brodsky's sixth major collection, U, where it occupies pp. 20–26. It is undated in this publication. The poem first appeared in the journal *Vestnik russkogo khristianskogo dvizheniya*, 126 (1978), pp. 47–52, in a version that differs significantly from the collected text. We will take the latter as definitive. No comparison of the variants will be undertaken here, even though some of them are very interesting. And, recognising that we may be ignoring what matters most, we will not attempt to deal with the linguistic texture of the poem. It is manifestly the work of an original, refined, and mature master of Russian verse technique; as always with Brodsky, it exhibits great metrical and rhythmical ingenuity and some arresting manipulation of phonetic resources. We will set aside examination of these features and attempt simply to construe the poem's arguments and themes.

The two nouns in the title of PK relate to the dimensions of time and space respectively. Time is mentioned first, suggesting that it might be the principal topic of the poem. We soon discover that an important way in which the poem deals with time is articulated by tense in its verbs: the tenses turn out to organise the text and correlate with its principal subjects. The bearers of Indo-European languages verbalise time in three tenses: past, present, and future. In PK, Brodsky keeps these tenses largely separate. They are associated with and help to delineate three major subjects in the poem. The first of them concerns time, space, number, and perception, and is initiated by the poet's contemplation of his room at mid-day; these thoughts are expressed in the present tense. The other two subjects are not hinted at in the title. The second concerns the poet's native city; it is presented in the imperfective past tense. The third subject mainly concerns the nature of what could be called 'the city of the future'; inescapably, this theme is presented in the future tense, and it employs both perfective and imperfective aspects.

Broadly speaking, the present tense and the first subject dominate the first third of the poem, increasingly interrupted by the past tense and the second; and then the future tense and with it the third subject dominate the final part. The first subject accounts for lines 1–24, 29–32, 35–6, 49–60, 73–84, 97–108, 133–44, and 161–68; the second, for lines 25–28, 33–4, 37–48, 61–72, 85–96, 109–32; and the third, for lines 145–92. It may be seen that seven of these fifteen segments are twelve lines long; they coincide to a certain extent, but by no means consistently or absolutely, with the twelve-line units of three quatrains each, and numbered in sequence with Roman numerals, which are the major compositional elements of the poem. It may also be seen that the three subjects are not equally weighted if they are reckoned in terms of the number of lines each may claim; in fact, they diminish in a pleasingly regular sequence: 86–66–48.

Some difficulty arises from the way Brodsky switches between the first two subjects. After the first two sections of the poem, which present subject 1, subject 2 abruptly appears at line 25. This is the first line of a twelve-line section (III); first time through, the reader is taken aback, and then assumes that subject 2 will continue for at least the remaining eight lines of the section. But it does not. Instead, subject 1 reappears for one quatrain (lines 29–32); subject 2 comes back at 33–34; and then, for the last two lines in the section, subject 1 returns. (The grammatical parallelism between the first and second couplets of this stanza is a false trail!) The next section (IV) begins insouciantly by referring back to 25–8 as if there had been no interruption.

We shall see in greater detail later that the divisions between the three subjects are not as cut and dried as the list of lines we have given would suggest; there are some important cross-references that hold them together. But it is still perfectly possible at least preliminarily to disentangle the three subjects and examine each one separately.

Easily the most accessible of the poem's three subjects is the second. This is partly because Brodsky seems to deal here in the coin of common humanity, which as a self-proclaimed elitist is not often his concern: '. . . art "imitates" death rather than life; i.e. it imitates that realm of which life supplies no notion: realising its own brevity, art tries to domesticate the longest possible version of time' (L: 104). The stanza in which subject 2 is introduced is one of the plainest statements Brodsky has ever permitted himself ('I was born in a big country,/at the mouth of a river. In winter/it always froze. I/won't be going back home', 25–8).[1] This manner is maintained throughout the treatment of the second subject. Also, Brodsky helps the reader by flagging the appearance of subject 2 with anaphora, the repeated phrase 'In that place there was' (*tam byl*).

There is another, extrinsic, reason for the accessibility of subject 2: Brodsky has published three essays that deal with it, and the parallels are worth pointing out. First, we find the probable reason why Brodsky does not actually name Leningrad in PK: 'I abhor this name for the city which long ago the ordinary people nicknamed simply "Peter" . . . as a word, "Leningrad" to a Russian ear already sounds as neutral as the word "construction" or "sausage" . . . A survivor cannot be named after Lenin' (L: 4); and again: 'this . . . city has two names, maiden and alias, and by and large its inhabitants tend to use neither' (L: 70–1).

Other parallels concern internal and external settings in the native city at the mouth of a big river, and some of them are very close. Lines 37–40 of PK say: 'In that place was a city, where, thanks to/the precision of the perspectives,/it was pointless to rush off in pursuit,/if you missed something'; and, from 'A Guide to a Renamed City': 'The geometry of this city's architectural perspectives is perfect for losing things forever' (L: 47). Lines 65–8 of PK: 'Like a reversed ray, the needle anesthetised/the contents of the clouds'; in English prose we find the double meaning of the Russian *igla* spelt out and the particular needle identified: 'And always in the distance, the golden needle of the Admiralty's spire tries, like a reversed ray, to anesthetize the contents of the clouds' (L: 90).[2] Further, straying into the domain of subject 3, there is PK 157–60: 'Or, like the city, whose beauty,/whose uniqueness/was sated by its own reflection,/like Narcissus in the stream', and: 'The . . . Neva . . . provides this city with such a quantity of mirrors that narcissism becomes inevitable . . .' (L: 77; we shall meet some more mirrors later). And then there is PK 61–4: 'In that place there were rows of columns,/that had found their way into those snows,/like men taken into captivity,/and stripped naked', which chimes with 'those naked columns with their Doric hairdos, captured as though driven into this merciless cold, into this knee high snow' (L: 90). But, alas, we get no help with one enigmatic aspect of the Leningrad scene: PK 41–5 speaks of 'A bridge over the frozen river in [one's] mind/with the steel of its cartilages/ engendered thoughts of another winter/that is, the winter of things,//where no traces are to be met', whereas for the young Brodsky on his way to school 'The wide river lay white and frozen like a continent's tongue lapsed into silence, and the big bridge arched against the blue sky like an iron palate' (L: 32). In these images, we find a familiar tendency in the literary interpretation of the city: having a malign personality of its own, it menaces and subjugates human beings, continuing to exact the sacrifices that were made in its foundation and construction.

In section VIII of the poem, subject 2 moves indoors. Here, prefaced by the 'In that place there was' that has signalled subject 2 before, we find some rooms, in which restricted space generates clutter, enhancing the appeal of the ceiling; piles of books; and more mirrors, these particular ones gathering dust. These details, enigmatic and capricious in isolation, may be found in closely contextualised detail in Brodsky's essay 'In a Room and a Half', his memoir (L: 447–501) of a coddled upbringing as the only child of cultured middle-class Jewish parents, and of the psychological torture of not being permitted to meet them again after the poet emigrated in 1972.

It would be wrong to suggest that these parts of the poem need the prose parallels in order to be understood. They do not. The parallels interestingly confirm and amplify the poem's text, which as always in Brodsky is maximally taut and economical, and they convert the general into the specific in a uniquely authoritative way.

We pointed out earlier that subject 2 uses the imperfective past. It therefore presents events that happened more than once, and this element of habit and duration is important in the Leningrad theme. There, despite the cold hostility of the city's exterior aspect, the poet used to be 'at home', as we infer from the opening statement of the theme. There was a routine to the day; it was at mid-day that the Admiralty spire behaved (imperfective) like a hypodermic; at six it got dark, at eight one wanted to go to bed (129–30; these numbers echo the 6 and 8 that appear in the last stanza of II). Most important of all is the autobiographical confession that begins in section X of the poem (line 109), where Brodsky says that in Leningrad he was 'a sound rather than a ray', and that he 'spent nights [imperfective] within the convolutions of the ear' (113–14). This statement engages an important aspect of the poem as a whole, and of Brodsky's outlook in general, where the properties of hearing versus vision are of great concern. This formulation of Brodsky's view of his past self is essentially pessimistic; as we shall see, he believes that sound perishes, while sight (the ray) remains.

Let us turn now to the first subject and attempt to elucidate its principal ideas. Subject 1 is connected to subject 2 by certain common elements. The rooms of PK 86 echo the room of the title from which the poem starts; and the dust that used to accumulate on the Leningrad mirrors (91) recalls the dust that accumulates on the author's facial pores in 9. And we have already pointed out that mid-day used to be needle time in Leningrad. What happens in the room of theme 1 at mid-day falls into two sections, the first dealing with effects of light and therefore vision (1–20, 97–108) and the second with air (21–4, 49–60, 73–84). The key quality of both is stasis. In contrast to the habitual actions in the past of Leningrad, the present tense in the poem indicates immobility. The height of the sun at the zenith – the present is summer, as opposed to the winter (always immensely preferable in Brodsky) of Leningrad – solidifies things that had been insubstantial, such as shadows. The shadow in its turn converts words into figures, which are more easily perceived by the air (21–40). The air is 'nothing', a definition amplified in a stream of metaphors (73–6).[3] In the reappearance of subject 1 at section IX (line 97), we find a contest between sound and light that has relevance to the poet's judgement on his past self in Leningrad. He tells us here that light is superior to sound not in speed, but 'in things', which are comprehensible in any state. Both, though, can degenerate – sound into silence, and light into dark, which is, ominously, a conversion into words. But light and sound 'are happy only outside the body. Far from us' (108–9). Sight is superior to sound because the visual object can still be perceived when it is motionless or reduced; 'turned to stone' (*okamenev*, 99) anticipates the caryatids at 121–32.

Subject 1 is a series of observations on the nature of things concrete and abstract, full of bewildering transformations and hierarchies which are said to occur between entities that common sense would consider to belong to unlike realms and therefore be incommensurate; however, we have perhaps learned to expect these speculations from Brodsky. As we said before, the principal categories involved are light, air, sound and number. The final appearance of subject 1 in section XII closes out the thoughts about number with what appears to be a reference to the genetic code (the cellular 'tsifir'', 133–6); the next stanza (137–40) says that this numerical entity impels the thinker to thoughts of the future. No link between these two stanzas is made. The idea seems to be that the genetic code encapsulates the notion of past and present in their sequence and therefore implies the future. But the thought of the future is repudiated (141–4) on the grounds that 'a body full-face is in itself a magnitude'. This idea recalls the statements in the earliest appearance of the theme about the solidification of profiles at mid-day.

The concept of number reappears and dominates with the arrival of subject 3 at XIII (line 145). Central is the idea of multiplication ('In the future . . .' 145, and the following string of parallels). For the first characteristic of the future is that in it, numbers 'will disperse the gloom'; this idea evidently stems from the idea of the genetic code that has been touched on before; it guarantees the future. Numbers are immortal. They will expand language. In this same way, there will be expansion through the multiplication of images, just as the Narcissus-like city admires its reflections in the waves. In the same way (tak), says Brodsky, a grown man deliberately treads in puddles so that his reflections will add more images (or, perhaps, to destroy them in order to prove his corporeality).

Closing out section XIV, and connected by an enigmatic 'thus', comes one of Brodsky's boldest personifications, where 'your today' is said, 'like a blind man scratching the convex face of memory with all five [fingers/senses]' to 'recognise itself'. The idea that the present is entirely contained in the past and uncovers it is not, however, all that outrageous or unfamiliar.

So far (line 168) it has not been too difficult to follow Brodsky's train of thought in his third subject; he has been elaborating the general idea that the future will produce an expansion of analytical/representational tools; in fact, there will be more of everything. That is, the future belongs to the mass; the future is bigger than the past in many senses.

It is the final two sections of the poem (XV, XVI) that present the greatest difficulty for simple comprehension. The difficulty arises partly from the manner of expression, because the syntax is convoluted to a degree, and partly from the conceptual fields involved, because here Brodsky makes no concessions whatsoever to received concepts. Let us attempt to read stanza by stanza.

Stanza 169–72 contains two cruxes. The first of them resides in the use of the word 'sut'': is it a verb form, or is it being used as a substantive ('the essence')? Whatever may be the grammatical explanation, the sense of the phrase seems to be 'what matters is . . .'. The second obscurity derives from the absence of punctuation at the end of the second line of the stanza (1.170). There seems to be no printing error here: the passage is identical in the original publication, and the next line begins with a lower case letter. Therefore, 'v otrazhennom' must mean 'the essence is in what was reflected yesterday'. It is more likely, though, that 'vchera' is being used as an indeclinable noun, and the phrase therefore means 'the essence is in the reflected yesterday'. Lines 171–2 are straightforward; and if read as a continuation from the opening phrase, 'in the future' (v budushchem), they simply assert that in the future there will still be changing seasons, and the process of reproduction will continue in nature, since the bees will continue to buzz in summer.

What, though, to go back to 170, is 'that which is reflected yesterday'? Whatever entity is referred to here stands in parallel to the 'amalgam' of 169. Now, amalgam is a substance of which Brodsky is rather fond. In other poems of U we find it twice. Addressing Tomas Venclova, Brodsky says (58): 'For one another we are [sut'] the two-sided bottom of a pool of amalgam, incapable of shining'. And in the first of the two Venice poems in the collection Brodsky concludes by saying he feels drawn to 'undress and press [himself] to the living bone, as to a hot mirror, from whose amalgam one cannot scratch the tenderness with a finger' (104). And in the essay on Leningrad that has been quoted before, we find the following observation about the Neva: 'Reflected every second by thousands of square feet of running silver amalgam, it's as if the city were constantly being filmed by its river' (L: 77). It may be deduced from these passages that Brodsky thinks of amalgam as a substance that reflects and also – disconcertingly – as a substance that is dull and does not reflect. The explanation is that when Brodsky wishes his amalgam to be capable of reflection he means by metonymy a mirror; the amalgam applied to the back of the glass is what makes it reflect rather than being transparent. So, in 169 he seems to be saying that the essence of the future is in amalgam because mirrors' backings are capable of storing the images the mirror reflects, perhaps unknown to those who observe themselves; and the 'child' who 'will scrape us off the amalgam' using his fingernail (178–80), may thereby bring us back to life, or prevent us from dying (177). We thus end up with a version of the immortality theme, expressed with formidable opacity. However, we see even more clearly that the 'mirror theme' in Brodsky is one that would repay intensive investigation; it is, of course, an obsessive image in the work of his patroness Akhmatova, and is one of the few concrete parallels there are between the work of the two poets.

The connection between on the one hand stanzas 169–72 and 177–80, which speak about amalgam and the future, and on the other the stanza that comes between them (173–6) is not easy to see; but as we discovered earlier when discussing the introduction of theme 2, we should not necessarily expect that Brodsky will work in a linear way on one theme at a time. Line 173 begins with 'in that place' (tam), recalling the statements that were made in theme 2 about the city; but in contrast with the past tenses that followed them, we now have a future. So that this 'tam' would seem to be ironic in its recalling of the city of the past; but it does, like them, precede a cityscape, if the presence of squares is anything to go by: this is the city of the future. But the 'echo' in this place, exceeding the sound by a hundred times – the stimulus that generated them – takes us away from the cityscape of theme 2 and back into the problems of light and sound that were so prominent in theme 1. We are told now that this characteristic of the sounds of the future, that the cause will be dwarfed by the effect, is going to be the same in the case of vision ('the eye', 176).

Now we arrive at XVI, the final section of the poem, lines 181–92. The first of the three stanzas asserts a thought that is familiar in Brodsky's work: that in all categories, material and non-material, the individual remains the individual and (picking up an echo of the same verb in 175) nothing can bring about a repetition of it, no matter how great the multiplication that the future might bring.

The last eight lines of the poem consist of one single sentence. Its main clause is in the final stanza. Here, it is asserted that 'eyes' will begin to send back everything they have absorbed. This process of transmission is qualified by two present gerunds; they state that the eye (vision) will outstrip and go further than the body, and imply that the process of sending back its stored images will begin when it 'emerges in front'. Behind this idea we may perhaps suspect the impact of the technology and physics of deep space probes, which may be thought of as eyes that have outstripped the body of the human race; the signals they transmit back to Earth when received are already of considerable antiquity, and hence may be thought of as a future that is already past. This cosmological dimension is supported by the penultimate stanza of the poem. Here, the eye of the last stanza (or its glance) is compared to a star across a thousand years (i.e., the 'cherez' means 'physically across', not 'in 1000 years' time') which is of no use to anyone since it does not so much radiate light as swallow dark.

Now, what is the 'everything' that this projectile, exploring eye will transmit back? Brodsky does not tell us. The poem ends with what it is tempting to regard as a proclamation of self-sufficiency on behalf of the foregoing text; the text means, literally, 'everything it takes into itself'.

The superiority of the eye as an instrument of perception over the other senses has already been asserted (175–6). It is now we realise that the end of the poem has been anticipated by the obscure passage beginning at 97; sound is inferior to light, and consequently hearing is inferior to vision. The future belongs to light and sight, not sound and hearing. Here we find ourselves in familiar territory, on the verge of the famous Brodsky idea of the endurance of the poetic word as something written, his obsession with the alphabet, with written marks.

In this way Brodsky asserts a familiar claim to immortality made by poets: that they will be immortal in their writing. No, he says, 'we will not die, when the hour comes' because some vestige will be retained in the *visual* memory of the mirror's amalgam, and this vestige can be recaptured by the finger-nail of a child of the future. A child, that is, will have the curiosity to commit this act. But the child will recognise not the individual, for the individual is unique, but some sort of collective, that 'my' and 'nas' of stanza 177–8, the only plural pronouns in the whole poem. And we are brought back to the today recognising itself like a blind man who has only memory and no visual perception for new things.

We have seen that PK deals with past, present, and future. But the three subjects are not dealt with in the same way. The treatment of the present and future is on the whole general, impersonal, ahistorical, metaphysical, and ratiocinative; that of the past is specific, autobiographical, historical, descriptive, and tinged with emotion. The contrast is fortified by the extrinsic authorial material we have cited from U. The essays on Leningrad round out the verse text; though Brodsky does not name the city in PK, our assumption that it must be Leningrad and no other is inevitable. Brodsky says himself in his essay on Tsvetaeva's prose, 'That a poet resorts to prose, which creates the illusion of a more consistent development of thought than poetry does, is in itself a kind of direct proof that the paramount spiritual experience is not so paramount; that experiences of a higher nature are possible, and that a reader can be taken by the hand by prose and delivered to where he would otherwise have to be shoved by a poem' (U: 191). But we have seen that the assistance it gives will not help by any means with all the problems PK poses; in fact, it is relevant disproportionately, bearing heavily on the second subject but not on others, and it unbalances and prejudices our receptivity.

The title of the poem, we now see, refers only to the first of its three subjects, the point in space and time from which the text takes off. Together, its two terms identify a nexus between what Brodsky might call Clio and Urania, since he prefers the abstract terminology of the ancient world to that of the modern.[4] He does so quite justifiably, because he is persistently concerned to talk about time and space in terms of myth, that is, without specifying their location within the concrete realms of History and Geography. But the intrusion of these realms in the poem's second subject creates fundamental difficulties for the success of his poem, since by contrast it alienates his abstractions even further from what with due hesitation one calls the normal referential world.

In the first subject, sitting in his room at mid-day, the hero becomes his own shadow, which in turn becomes a centaur as the sun amalgamates it with the shadow of his chair. And in the third subject, the first person has become absorbed into the plurality of human kind ('We will not die . . .' 177), presumably as just one of the images retained by the mirror. The present is wooden and inert, the future is crowded with the mass. The past is a repository of human values. But the past, where among other things the poet was valorised as an individual in relation to others, is irretrievable ('I/will not be going home'). It is this element that gives PK its profoundly elegiac quality, despite the eventual affirmation of collective immortality through the permanence of visual images. And compared with this quality, the things PK has to say about the relative merits of modes of perception are of lesser significance. In this particular report on his world, then, Brodsky suggests that in abandoning his home he has been dehumanised and depersonalised, and that he will end up in an eternal realm of the masses even more inhospitable than the one he has left behind.

Notes

1. The last sentence is expressed impersonally in Russian with a dative/infinitive construction that suggests external agency. Lines 25–8 of PK contrast touchingly with the famous lines from *Stansy*, an alternative prophecy: 'Neither country, nor graveyard/do I wish to select./To Vasilevsky Island/I will come back to die.'
2. We find the needle image echoed in the first couplet of the poem 'V okrestnostyakh Aleksandrii' (U: p. 138).
3. Here, Brodsky is offering a tour-de-force solution to a problem he identifies in his essay on W.H. Auden's '1 September, 1939': 'Every poet, as you probably know, tries to grapple with this problem: how to describe an element. Of the four, only the earth yields a handful of adjectives. It's worse with fire, desperate with water, and out of the question with air' (L: 335).
4. Lev Loseff has amicably ticked him off for this habit in his poem 'Ob obuvi'; and perhaps Brodsky was defending himself when he wrote with reference to W.H. Auden: 'Because they are so remote, the Greeks are always of an archetypal denomination to us . . . And in a didactic poem, one is more successful with one's audience if one throws it an archetype to munch' (L: p. 333).

8

A Journey from Petersburg to Istanbul

Tomas Venclova

> These days giaours praise Istanbul . . .
> *Pushkin*

> . . . that you cunningly gnaw a hole through space's cat-bag so that the silver of Europe's tears dries in the Asian wind.
> *Brodsky*

Joseph Brodsky's 'A Journey to Istanbul' is strange and idiosyncratic. First of all, it exists in two versions, Russian and English,[1] and therefore enters into two different textual spaces. By the way this is characteristic of many of Brodsky's recent works, perhaps the majority of them. The English text has been translated by Alan Myers along with the author. However one should take it on its own terms. The Russian and English versions do not fully coincide: the first is broken up into 43 sections, the second into 46. The jokes, hints and intratextual commentary all differ: the Russian reader, unlike the Anglo-American reader, needs no explanation of the name of the author's native city or who Khodasevich or Tsiolkovsky were. In the English version sometimes significant additions appear (English pp. 414–15, 419, 440–41); there is only one case of the reverse, when a not insignificant piece of the Russian version is left out of the translation (English p. 429/ Russian p. 98). What is particularly remarkable is that the two versions are oriented towards different literary subtexts. The English title, 'Flight from Byzantium', paraphrases W.B. Yeats's 'Sailing to Byzantium'. The link is underscored by the fact that the last line of Yeats famous poem ('Of what is past, or passing, or to come') is introduced in somewhat changed form into the essay's dramatic epilogue: 'to roar to a sea of heads about your detestation of the past, the present, and what is to come' (English p. 445). There are other noticeable echoes of Yeats, beginning with concrete details (the mechanical nightingale) and ending with more general motifs threaded through the entire text (the theme of old age). Brodsky, as the title indicates, constructs his entire essay as a rebuttal to Yeats. Against Yeats' splendid Byzantium, the concentrated essence of Art, Wisdom and Holiness, the Gate of Heaven, or sometimes Heaven itself, Brodsky sets sullen Istanbul, where the traveller as well as local resident is obliged to abandon all hope. This subtle play is lost on the Russian reader who is usually, alas, unacquainted with Yeats' poetry. (Just as the English-speaking reader will not detect the Pasternak quote 'what's the millennium outside?' which in the English version is replaced by the neutral 'millennium'.) The Russian title of the essay, a deliberately straightforward one, points to a different tradition – the tradition of Russian philosophical travel sketches: Mandelstam's *A Journey to Armenia*, Pushkin's *A Journey to Arzrum* and, finally, Radishchev's *A Journey from Petersburg to Moscow*.

There is one more essential difference between the Russian and English versions. Although the English text is colloquial and even slangy, the sharp stylistic relief of the Russian text is undoubtedly lost. 'A Journey to Istanbul' brims with expressions that might have been overheard in Leningrad and Moscow kitchens in conversations among intellectuals, or rather quasi-intellectuals. This language, which is stumbling, scattered, crippled by cliche bureaucratese and pseudo-scientific expressions, sometimes degenerates into idle chat and often into abuse: 'at this point in time', 'by a pair of degrees', 'he immediately exited', 'the Alexandrine tradition absorbed all this stuff and really compressed it', 'Aeneas is in essence an unprincipled jerk', 'sand flying into the kisser', 'war are [sic] an echo of the nomadic instinct', 'any ideas of anything are based on experience', 'sorry bastard', 'once again we're dealing with', etc., etc. Sometimes it is Mandelstam, rephrased in the language of a contemporary resident of Liteyny Avenue. 'One god or another can – should he take it into his billowy head – at any given moment visit a man and for a certain time period inhabit him. The hearth is no different than the amphitheatre, the stadium than the altar, the kettle than the statue' (p. 82). Sometimes it is a history discussion reminiscent of Zoshchenko's or even Averchenko's parodic histories: 'What followed is well known: the Turks came from who knows where; the answer to where they came from is not very clear; what's clear it is that it's from a long way away; what brought them to the shores of the Bosphorus – is not very clear either, but, obviously, it was horses' (p. 94).

Brodsky's devices here cannot be termed 'skaz', if only because the distance between narrator and author is hard to define. One should speak rather of a specific narrative mode. Among other things, this mode involves constantly checking with the reader or interlocutor, constantly provoking him, aiming at a dialogue that ends without having time to begin ('I foresee as well that there will be no vases, no shards, no dishes, no bespectacled man . . . that no objection will follow, that silence will fall not so much as a sign of assent but as a sign of indifference', pp. 102–3).

In any case translating such speech into English is either difficult or impossible. 'Vyblyadok' (*'whore's offshoot') is not exactly 'bastard'; 'ustervim' (*'let's make it f---ing stronger') is not quite 'let us nastify'; 'rhezat' ('to cut [throats]') pronounced with the Caucasian accent is a long way 'to massacre.' The stylistic flattening takes place when 'ikhnikh' (illiterate) is translated as 'theirs', 'dve tyshchi' (*'two grand') as 'two thousand', 'shikarny vid' (*'great view') as 'splendid panorama,' and finally, 'v protsesse vse my znaem chego' ('in the process of we all know what') as 'in the course of the Great Terror.'[2]

Brodsky's racy, even feuilletonesque, language has a special semantic potential. As some critics have already noted, Brodsky is ironic in relation to himself: the poet overcomes the Soviet era's inarticulateness by recognising and using it.[3] The mask of funnyman and quasi-intellectual occasionally drops to reveal the face of a historian and thinker. Side by side with the blatantly flippant remarks, brilliant aphorisms appear ('effects are rarely capable of looking at their causes approvingly'; p. 80), there are also phrases devoid of any parody ('In the purely structural sense the distance between the Second Rome and the Ottoman Empire is measurable only in the units of time'; p. 96). And even in the passages given in a particular mode, Brodsky manages to express his fundamental, though controversial, philosophy of history. The parade of parodies on the pages of 'A Journey to Istanbul' cancels out any elevated ceremonial and exalted attitude towards history. For Brodsky, history is something close and intimate, something physical, something in the blood (the only possible analogy here is probably late Mandelstam). The poet is a natural inhabitant of the sphere in which history unfolds, i.e. time ('Space for me is indeed less dear, and less than time. Not because, however, it is less but because it is a thing, whereas time is a thought about a thing. In choosing between a thing and a thought, say I, the latter is always preferable'; p. 102). This is precisely why Brodsky's perception of history is more tragic than that of other major Russian writers. But being a victim of history is humiliating and psychologically impossible since the poet is part of – and in command of – something bigger than history, something that encompasses history. The pressure of history is overcome by the stoic's splendid contempt.

Time is the basic theme of 'A Journey to Istanbul' – the basic theme in fact of all of Brodsky's work. In time – as opposed to space – he feels himself at home. 'Journey' interweaves, in rather complex fashion, personal time ('I lived thirty two years in the Third Rome and roughly one in the First'; p. 69' 'I'm forty years old'; p. 83) and historical time – the fifth, ninth, twentieth and many other centuries. It would be hard to find a more polychronic text in Russian literature: there is talk of Tamerlane and Suslov, of Darius and Peter the Great, of Tiberius, Dido, Leontiev. The author finds it necessary to point out his own unprofessional approach; he apologises, corrects himself, anticipates and allows objections: 'Here I would like to admit that my ideas concerning antiquity seem somewhat wild even to me. I understand polytheism in a simple and therefore, probably, erroneous way' (pp. 81–2). One constantly encounters such phrases as: 'I have no clear notion of what was going on in Judea at that time' (p. 80); 'Under Sultan Whatever-His-Redundant-Name-Was Hagia Sophia was turned into a mosque' (p. 100). Brodsky's erudition occasionally does fail him – for example, in the discussion of elegiac distichs (p. 74) which was clarified in the English version. Yet the chief impression made by 'A Journey to Istanbul' is one of broad historical and cultural horizons, freedom regarding material from very different eras, a keen eye for analogies and structural similarities between phenomena quite distant from each other on a diachronic axis. Let us add originality of thought, which is enhanced by the 'estranged' point of view of the outsider, the accidental, inexpert observer.

Byzantium, Constantinople, occupies a special place in Russia's cultural consciousness, as is well known. It is worth recalling that the earliest surviving Russian travel text – 'The Journey of Abbot Daniil' – contains remarks on 'Tsargrad' – indeed at its very start. Thus Brodsky's essay relies on an 800-year-old tradition. The semiotic connection between Constantinople and Moscow is a huge and frequently studied topic.[4] However, there is undoubtedly a semantic parallel between Constantinople and Petersburg as well (one can postulate the analogy: Moscow is to Rome as Petersburg is to Constantinople). Rome and Moscow are the older primary cities located at the centre of corresponding state-universes, moreover, both have grown up gradually, naturally, out of native soil. Constantinople and Petersburg are the younger, secondary cities, eccentric in relation to their universes, created by outstanding reformers' single act of will. Both are named for their founder (in Petersburg's case this is the name of his heavenly patron Peter – which, however, does not change matters). Moreover in both cases these names have been replaced by different ones, 'barbarian' ones. Moscow and Rome are both situated inland ('on seven hills' by a medium-sized river), Petersburg and Constantinople – on the seacoast. In Constantinople's case we are speaking of a city situated on the very border between Europe and Asia – and moreover of a city turned toward the Asia yet to be drawn into the cultural world of the Roman Empire (p. 78). In Petersburg we are dealing with an ideally reversed situation: it, as everyone knows, is 'a window on Europe' allowing Asian or half-Asian Russia to adjoin the West (we might note that in both cases these 'supertasks' have remained partly or even entirely unaccomplished). As Yu.M. Lotman has recently pointed out, in the mythology of both Petersburg and Constantinople there is a consistent eschatological motif – that of the 'non-eternal city', i.e. the city which is destined to be swept from the face of the earth by a flood – or rather, The Flood. Such is Methodius of Patar's prediction for Constantinople: 'And the Lord God will call down the fury of his wrath upon it and will send down His Archangel Michael and will mow down the city with His sickle and will smite it with His scepter and will turn it into a millstone and so will drown it and all its people in the depths of the sea and the city will perish, save for one pillar in the market square'.[5] The corresponding Petersburg myth is all too well known. We might note that these eschatological prophesies have been fulfilled, at least on a social-historical level: both cities have lost their primary status and have become cut off from world civilisation.

Many Russian artists have recognised the likeness between these two great cities.[6] Brodsky constantly keeps a whole network of comparisons between Istanbul and Leningrad in mind, pointing out, in part, that by significant coincidence they are located on practically the same meridian (Istanbul, the more Eastern in culture, is paradoxically shifted a bit westward (p. 67–8)). Eurasian Istanbul – like Eurasian Leningrad in all of Brodsky's work – appears in an apocalyptic light, symbolising a civilisation approaching the edge of cataclysm[7] – or rather, one that has already stepped over the edge. One can legitimately say that in Brodsky's work Istanbul and Leningrad oppose each other, but that on a certain level they are identical. A trip to Istanbul turns out to be a psychological and metaphysical substitute for an impossible return to Leningrad, to Russia, to the 'necropolis' of Chaadaev and Khodasevich.

'A Journey to Istanbul' breaks down into two texts not only externally but internally as well. It exists not merely in two versions – Russian and English – but each of the versions themselves is divided into two parts which, though tightly interwoven, coincide neither in genre, nor style nor semantics. In each, one can single out chapters relating the historical fate of Constantinople and mutual relations between Europe and Asia: these fit into a coherent narrative with the marks of a scholarly philosophical tract. This narrative, though larded with numerous and often fanciful digressions, does for the most part follow chronology and historical logic. Having started with Constantine, the author ends with the modern, almost totally desacralised Istanbul – a 'Third World' city, where 'there is nothing but the unenviable, third-rate present of hardworking people robbed by the intensity of this place's history' (109). On the other hand, having begun with the Roman Empire and stories about the Byzantine and Ottoman Empires, he concludes his tract with the newest incarnation of the imperial idea – namely, the Soviet Union (pre-Gorbachev). This outwardly calm (and inwardly taut) narration is interrupted by chapters of a different order. One might call them lyrical digressions (in Brodsky's favourite elegiac mode), or call them pictures, engravings, vignettes. They too fit into a unified whole – not syntagmatically but paradigmatically. Their common theme, which is turned at all possible angles, as is given in different grammatical persons or cases, is defined by the opening words of one of the first vignettes: 'The delirium and horror of the East. The dusty catastrophe of Asia' (p. 76). While the narrative part is packed with names, dates and facts, the lyrical part is dominated by metaphor and metonymy, by the ironic joke, or simply by the cry. There are chapters in which the two approaches are combined (pp. 98–100); in the center of the piece stands the meta-textual Chapter 23, where the author expresses his dissatisfaction at the fact that his notes have gotten out of hand, and speaks of his dislike for prose ('it lacks any form of discipline aside from that generated in the process' (p. 90)). However one ought to note that the two texts, superimposed one on another, 'in the process' form an expressive and disciplined composition. The vignettes interrupt the narrative like a refrain or a rhyme; the iconic analog of Greek ornament, to which Brodsky devotes an important part of his arguments, comes to mind ('Such ornament . . . is temporal. Hence its rhythm, its tendency toward symmetry, its essentially abstract character, subordinating graphic expression to a rhythmic sense . . . Its persistent – by means of rhythm, or repetition – abstracting from its unit, from that which has already been expressed. In short, its dynamism'; p. 101).

Interestingly, this device has a rather archaic antecedent in an early Russian description of a journey to the East – namely Afanasy Nikitin's.

> His expository manner might be described this way: Afanasy Nikitin carries on his exposition in calm tones, then suddenly remembers how lonely he was among the non-believers and begins to bemoan his fate, to complain, grieve, pray; then he calmly begins to further relate his tale, but later on falls into complaint and prayer once again, then again calmly takes up his tale, then later switches back to complaint and prayer and so on. In a word, Nikitin's entire *Journey* constitutes an alternation between rather long sections of calm exposition and shorter sections of religious-lyrical digression.[8]

The compositional analogy between *A Journey over Three Seas* and 'A Journey to Istanbul', by the way, can be taken even further: the narrative portion in both is circular.[9] This fact, which might be interpreted as simple coincidence, still forces one to ponder such a category as 'genre memory'.

Both parts – historico-philosophic and lyric (or syntagmatic and paradigmatic) – are not merely compositionally intertwined: they are connected by a common mythological underpinning, albeit one that acquires varying meanings depending on the context. The contemptuous and alienated tone Brodsky takes with Turkey may shock – and already has shocked – some critics, who see it as 'imperial arrogance'.[10] If that is in fact fair, then it is so only in part

('Racism? but it's just another form of misanthropy'; p. 76). Moreover, one ought always keep in mind the mythopoetic nature of this essay, and also that in it Turkey and Islam serve as metaphor (or metonymy) for other (broader) cultural-historical phenomena.

One of the archetypes integrating all of world culture shines through the picture of 'the delirium and horror of the East': we have before us a description of *katabasis, the descent into Hell, suffering after death*. This theme is directly and forcefully addressed in Chapter 18: the author wanders through the Athenian crowd that itself seems to be the other world and the only thing that convinces him that this is not eternity, in fact, is that he cannot find his dead parents. However, the lyric passages about Istanbul assert the opposite: they describe Hell itself, 'an evil infinity' (Russian mathematical term for 'undefined infinity' – *Translator*), an oppressive, entropic world, something akin to Dostoevsky's bathhouse with spiders. Here, any concrete (and factual) details can come into play. So, for example, Istanbul's special *isolation* is significant. The author visits Istanbul by plane, that is by the most modern means of transportation, which is also a sort of fairytale carpet. Moreover, it is difficult to get out of Istanbul; its space is *viscous*, clinging, 'unabandonable' (on another level this theme appears as the viscosity, the overgrowth of the text itself). Remarkable, too, is the Kafkaesque story of 'Boomerang', a company whose existence at first encourages the author, but which turns out to be a Soviet tourist agency: the word 'boomerang' connotes constant return – to Istanbul, to the USSR – or more precisely, the impossibility of leaving the world described, of overcoming the barrier between the world of the dead and the world of the living (p. 87). The first lyric excerpt (p. 70), the one that actually begins the story of Istanbul, is devoted to a dream, a distressing dream, like Ippolit's in *The Idiot*. While abstaining from psychoanalytic interpretation of this dream, let us attend to two points: in the first place, Istanbul and Petersburg are once again brought together; in the second, there is a persistent connection between sleep and katabasis in shamanism, in ritual, myth, and literature, including the *Aeneid* (Aeneas visits the underworld while awake, but leaves it by the gates of sleep – this is just as ambiguous a situation as in Brodsky's essay, wherein the borders of sleep and reality are somewhat shifted). The city is perceived not only as *a dream* to be deciphered, but as *an illness* ('I arrived in Istanbul, and left it by air, having thus isolated it in my mind like some virus under a microscope . . . I really do feel a little feverish from what I have seen, hence a certain incoherence in all that follows'; p. 69); cf. a similar concept of Petersburg in *The Bronze Horseman*, in Russian symbolist texts, in *The Egyptian Stamp*: 'He thought that Petersburg was a childhood disease and that all he had to do was wake up, come to his senses, and the delusion would disintegrate . . .'[11] Negative predicates crowd the description of Istanbul – *closeness, narrowness, the crookedness* of space, *heat* and *airlessness, stench*, the 'hellish spectrum of colors'[12] ('Ubiquitous concrete, with the texture of turd and the colour of upturned grave'; p. 76; 'brown-black rivulets . . . down the undulating arteries of this primeval kishlak'; p. 78; 'A normal hot, dusty, perspiring day in Istanbul'; p. 103; and so on, and so forth). *The dead-endedness of space* is deceptively compensated for by *the excess of time* – by a past full of innumerable generations gone to dust and by a joyless, immobile present. This world is populated by Boschian *monsters*: 'These enormous toads in frozen stone, squatting on the ground, unable to stir!' (p. 99). People in the city are presented as denizens of hell:

> The local population in a state of total stupor whiling its time away in squalid snack bars, tilting its heads as in a namaz in a reverse toward the television screen, where somebody is permanently beating somebody else up. Or else they are dealing out cards whose jacks and nines are the sole accessible abstraction, the single means of concentration (p. 76).

'This is a strange feeling – to watch an activity, which cannot be expressed in monetary terms, entirely unappraisable' (p. 94) (cf. Pushkin's 'Well we're playing not for money,/But just to kill some eternity'). *Communication* with them is *impossible*. The author does not know anyone in Istanbul (108), does not know the language ('Russian will do for me, I thought'; p. 93); he is surrounded by signs 'inaccessible to the eye' or 'beyond the reach of the mind' (103), by strange inscriptions, hieroglyphs; in this *inside-out* world the *signifier and the signified shift*, mockingly winking in sequences of sounds and letters ('Who here hears whom? Here, where *bardak* ('brothel' in Russian) means 'glass', where *durak* ('fool' in Russian) means 'stop'. *Bir bardak cay* – one glass of tea; *otobus duragi* – a bus stop'; p. 93). The whole situation is a caustic, bitter parody of the bilingualism and polylingualism of international cities.

The basic symbol of this world is *dust* (p. 78), which (especially since the beginning of this century) has long connoted diabolic essence, evil in its entropic aspect.[13] This is chaos lacking any cosmogenic or logogenic potential, infinitely distant from reason, the word. The city becomes the nothingness ('and the sound of harpers and minstrels, of flute players and trumpeters shall be heard in thee no more, and a craftsman of any craft shall be found in thee no more, and the sound of the millstone shall be heard in thee no more'; Revelations, 18:22). The only craftsman it is worthy of is the traveller, alien and attempting unsuccessfully to break loose.

This confining and cramped space, this inert and immobile milieu has its own gravitational centre and logical limit.[14] At the centre of Istanbul is the Topkapi Palace, at the centre of Topkapi is a pavilion where the relics of the Prophet are kept, and at the centre of the pavilion, under a glass canopy is his footprint. 'Size 18 shoe minimum, I thought as I stared at the exhibit. And then I shuddered: Yeti!' (p. 93). This is a mythologem of the death of Kashchei[15] – a direct incarnation of the danger, the trap and simultaneously, the inhuman essence of the given universe.

It should be said that the mythopoetic description of Istanbul is paradoxically intertwined with its demythologisation: Istanbul is a city without depth, reduced to surface, to what is visible and immediately tangible. Although the poet tries to decipher it (p. 69), it is not like a book. It lacks true ontological status and locus – and that is precisely the chief mark of a modern Hades. The true name of this city is Nowhere (p. 108). Just like the name of inaccessible Leningrad.

Chapter 39, a sample of Brodsky's high poetry, describing the Greek temple at Sounion, stands in complex counterpoint to these pictures of Istanbul. Cramped space opens up, time shifts, the ominous dust is replaced by the four classical (and, by the way, Petersburgian) elements: *water* and *air*, *earth* and *fire (light)*. The temple at Sounion – eighteen white columns latently associated with Petersburg columns – represent the origins of individuality, order, rhythm, that is, everything alien to the entropic universe of Istanbul. Istanbul and Sounion are the spatial and semantic poles of 'Journey'. The chapter on Sounion can be interpreted as an *escape from hell*, an *end to suffering*, the acquisition of ontological completeness. However it is followed by an anticlimax – the narrative returns to Istanbul, to the Third World (and the Third Rome); the entire piece ends on a bitter but stoic note – with a smile worthy of a denizen of Dante's Inferno.

The syntagmatic part of the essay is also founded on a myth deeply rooted in both Russian and Western tradition: this is a Manichean-tinged myth of East and West, of their perpetual opposition and struggle. Speaking of myth in this connection, I would not like to become the 'art historian or ethnologist' (p. 102) whose positivistic objections the author foresees and rejects. For me myth is not a value category, but simply the most convenient category for describing the structure of poetic thought. Undoubtedly, Brodsky's constructs can be criticised for their susceptibility to the influence of stereotypes, etc. However, if it is a poet's business to present a coherent and internally convincing image (*gestalt*) of culture, then Brodsky does not disappoint us. His tract is also an attempt at a poetic typology of culture and an essay on the culturogenic role of symbol, on its various possible readings, on how symbols acquire a life of their own, becoming not so much *realiora* as *realissima*.

The West in Brodsky's system is far from ideal; but Asia and the East are proffered as the negative poles of human society and human experience. First and foremost this means Islam. Here it is easy to see a subtext harking back to the Acmeists (see Nadezhda Mandelstam's memoirs):

M. thought this preference for the Muslim world was not accidental *among our people*. The people of our time were less suited by Christianity with its doctrine of free will and the inherent value of the person than by Islam with its determinism, the submerging of the individual in the army of the faithful, and *with its ornamental inscriptions on oppressive buildings*. M., to whom the Muslim world was alien ('and with shame and pain she turned away from the bearded cities of the East'), was *looking only for the continuity of Hellenic and Christian tradition.*[16]

However Brodsky goes considerably further. The Sublime Porte corresponds directly to Orthodox Byzantium, and the 'severe Byzantine spirit'[17] – to the pagan spirit of Virgil and Augustus. The three empires are semiotically isomorphic: regardless of the difference in culture and religion, each is a logical continuation of its predecessor. The Ottoman state (and after it the contemporary Soviet Union) merely take the possibilities intrinsic to Byzantium and Rome to their limit. Rockets and minarets are also isomorphic (p. 99).[18]

'A Journey to Istanbul' is an invective of rare force directed against the authoritarian spirit characteristic of Russian (and Soviet) tradition. One might say that this invective is the most remarkable of its kind since Chaadaev's *Philosophical Letters*, but Brodsky, perhaps, outdoes Chaadaev in 'scandalousness': he aims to reveal even deeper cultural strata since he perceives a dangerous authoritarian potential in Christianity as such, and all the more so – in monotheism as such.

Brodsky's historico-philosophical system ranks with those systems that deduce culture from some 'primaeval phenomenon'. The best known among these is Spengler's. Brodsky's opposition of West versus East is generally similar to the opposition between 'Apollonian' and 'magic' cultures in Spengler's *Decline of the West*. But Brodsky is suggesting a singular and apparently original criterion for a typology of culture: cultures are divided into two large classes – those *oriented towards space* and those *oriented towards time*.

'A Journey to Istanbul' draws up a largely traditional series of contrasts between West and East. The West is regarded as the source of democracy, the East as the source of autocracy ('dreading generalisations, I will add that the East means, first of all, a tradition of obedience, of hierarchy, of profit, of trade, of adaptability: a tradition, that is, drastically alien to the principles of a moral absolute, whose role – I mean the intensity of the sentiment – is fulfilled here by the idea of kinship, of family. I foresee objections, and am even willing to accept them, in whole or in part. But no matter what extreme of idealisation of the East we may entertain, we will never be able to ascribe to it the least semblance of democracy'; pp. 87–8). The West conceives of man as an individuality, while the East lacks not only respect for individuality but also the very concept of it. ('And, perhaps, *rhezat* [cutting throats] precisely because all are so much alike that there is no way to detect a loss'; p. 97). The West is dialogic, the East monologic ('Though in Athens Socrates could be judged in open court and could make whole speeches – three of them! – in his defence, in Isfahan, or, say, in Baghdad, such a Socrates would simply have been impaled on the spot, or flayed, and there the matter would be ended, there would have been no Platonic dialogues, no Neo-Platonism, nothing: as there wasn't. There would have been only the monologue of the Koran'; p. 85).[19] The West strives for legality, order, the norm; the East is the non-systemic, 'infernal' source of lawlessness and arbitrariness; in this lies one of the West's weaknesses, for it closes its eyes to man's negative potential, to his capacity for anarchic and destructive behaviour, relegating it to pathology and thereby deprives itself of the opportunity to react adequately (pp. 90–2). If there is anything positive to be found in the East, it is at best a capacity for self-absorption, for constructing private and local alternatives to the surrounding world. Such are the Samarkand mausoleums of Shakh-I-Sind: 'Like lamps in the darkness. Better: like corals in the desert' (p. 99).

This whole system of oppositions comes down to a certain constant. The West possesses a sense of time (which 'is a profoundly individualistic experience'; p. 103); the East substitutes collective bonding for uniqueness, that is replaces time with space ('everything in this life intertwines, everything is, in a sense, but a pattern in a carpet. Trodden by the foot'; p. 100). In essence this is a development of Chaadaev's idea of 'geographical fact' and 'historical motion' (*Apologia for a Madman*).

Brodsky's thought becomes brilliantly explicit in his example of Arabic and Greek ornament: the former is based on a purely spatial, visual, nonsensical use of letters, words and phrases; the latter – on rhythmic repetition of notches which establish certain parallels marking the movement of time (p. 101). By the way, in Brodsky's view, poetry, i.e. that which expresses the essence of humankind as a species, 'is based on the resemblance to each other/of the repetitious days, running into the distance' ('Verses on the Death of T.S. Eliot').

For Brodsky, space is tied to the linear principle (manifested in Virgil's epic, in the expansion of Roman Empire, in the treks of nomads and in monotheism); time – to the ordering principle, to the cycle, to repetition, return (manifested most clearly in Greek culture and in the similar culture of the Roman elegiac poets: 'the Greeks should not be idealised overmuch, but one cannot deny them in their cosmic principle, informing celestial bodies and kitchen utensils alike'; p. 75). The linear principle, according to 'A Journey to Istanbul', is ideally expressed in the symbol of the *cross*, which is not only – and perhaps not so much – a holy Christian sign, as it is a plan for a Roman settlement. Within the essay's text one can isolate a fanciful *étude* on the semiotics of the cross; it probably seems blasphemous to many, although it is characterised by an internal logic and some refreshing estrangement. The theme of the cross in various twists and turns runs through the entire essay: the cross appears in either very concrete incarnations (as a sign on a cupola, p. 84; a crucifix in an Istanbul bazaar, p. 110); or else in extremely abstract ones (geographical latitude and longitude, p. 67; the movement of civilisations from South to North and of nomads from East to West, p. 98). In the final analysis it acquires, perhaps, a particular, definitive and irrevocable meaning: it is a sign *crossing out* our civilisation, a *sign on the grave* of our era. For the linear principle, having exhausted itself, has not led to the restoration of the cosmic cycle. The world's centre and sense are irretrievably lost; civilisation is plunging irreversibly into entropy and chaos; there is no salvation from dehumanisation, from 'rot'. The triumph of linearity comes down to the fact that man in general and the poet in particular are torn away from their own roots, from their place in the world. ('Misanthropy? Despair? Yet what else could be expected from one who has outlived the apotheosis of the linear principle? From a man who has nowhere to go back to?' (p. 76) The linear, spatial East, the dust and ashes of the East prevail over the West, swallow it up. Neither walls nor the sea save Constantinople from the onset of the East. The last phrase of the essay unambiguously lets the reader know that nothing will save Western democracy from the onset of the newly-born totalitarian Third Rome (p. 111).

One can – and probably should – disagree with Brodsky. We will not speak of the fact that the Third Rome, as is now fortunately becoming obvious, has proved unfit to carry out its apocalyptic role. For me the main refutation of the thesis that the East is hopeless tyranny and entropic 'black hole', is in the very phenomenon of this poet, in all his work of course, not just in 'A Journey to Istanbul'. 'I think that a country and a people have already justified their existence if they have created just one entirely free person'.[20]

Notes

1. 'Puteshestvie v Stambul', *Kontinent* No. 46 (1985), pp. 67–111; 'Flight from Byzantium', in Joseph Brodsky, *Less than One: Selected Essays*, New York: Farrar, Straus, Giroux, 1986, pp. 393–446. Numbers in parentheses signify page numbers in *Kontinent* (if not marked otherwise). Our own translations sometimes substitute the classical English translation.
2. Translations marked (*) are included here to suggest to readers who do not know Russian the degree of slanginess of certain expressions used by Brodsky. It should be noted, however, that these vulgar

interpolations are quite normal in informal conversational Russian.
3. Cf. [Anonym], 'Pis'mo o russkoy poezii' in *Poetika Brodskogo*, Lev Loseff (ed.), (New Jersey: Hermitage, 1986), pp. 16–37.
4. Among recent publications see S.S. Averintsev, 'Vizantiia i Rus': dva tipa dukhovnosti', *Novy mir* No. 7, pp. 210–20, and No. 9 pp. 227–39 (1988).
5. Quoted in Yu.M. Lotman, 'Simvolika Peterburga i problemy semiotiki goroda', *Trudy po znakovym sistemam*, 18 (*Uchenye zapiski Tartuskogo gosudarstvennogo universiteta*, 664), pp. 31–2.
6. Cf. this author's *Neustoychivoe ravnovesie: vosem' russkikh poeticheskikh tekstov* (Yale Russian and East European Publications, No. 9), 1986, pp. 160–1.
7. Cf. Z.G. Mints, M.V. Bezrodny, A.A. Danilevsky, '"Petersburgskiy tekst" i russkiy simvolizm', *Trudy po znakovym sistemam*, 18, p. 87.
8. N. Trubetskoy, '"Khozhdenie za tri morya" Afonasia Nikitina kak literaturniy pamyatnik', *Versty* (Paris) No. 1 (1926), pp. 166–7.
9. Ibid., p. 171.
10. Cf. Rafal Grupinski, 'Ci wspaniali mezczyzni od podstawowych wartosci . . .', *Kultura* (Paris), No. 9 (1988), pp. 13–23.
11. Osip Mandelstam, *Sobranie sochineniy v trekh tomakh*, t.2. New York: Mezhdunarodnoe literaturnoe sodruzhestvo, 1971, p. 37.
12. Cf. numerous works of V.N. Toporov on 'Petersburg text'.
13. For a broader discussion of this problem see this author's 'K demonologii russkogo simvolizma' (in preparation).
14. Cf. V.N. Toporov, '*Gospodin Prokharchin*': *k analizu peterburgskoy povesti Dostoevskogo*, Jerusalem: The Magnes Press, 1982, pp. 49, 69.
15. The evil king of Russian folklore; his usual nickname is 'The Immortal'. The Hero-Knight has to find his castle in which there is a secret room in which there is a chest in which there is hidden an egg in which there is a needle which must be broken to kill Kashchey.
16. Nadezhda Mandelstam, *Hope Against Hope: A Memoir*, New York: Atheneum (1983), p. 250. (The italicised parts, which had been translated incorrectly, are corrected here. *Editors*)
17. Anna Akhmatova's words from 'Kogda v toske samoubiystva . . .' (Anna Akhmatova, *Sochineniia*, t.1, New York: Inter-Language Literary Associates (1965), p. 185.
18. A possible subtext here: 'minaret bayonets' in Vyazemskiy's poem 'Pozdravit' s Paskhoy vas speshu ya . . .' (1853).
19. Here Brodsky almost literally repeats Averintsev (see Sergey Averintsev, *Religiya i literatura*, Ann Arbor: Hermitage, 1981, p. 43); this, probably, should be regarded not as a borrowing but as a coincidence.
20. Osip Mandelstam, op. cit., p. 291.

Translated by Jane Miller

9
Similarity in Disparity
Valentina Polukhina

> Reason respects the differences and
> imagination the similitudes of things.
>   Shelley

This article is mainly an attempt to understand the nature of disparity in Brodsky's similes. It will explore the structural, semantic, poetic and conceptual aspects of his similes.

It has been noticed that some of Brodsky's similes either include adventurous imagery, or are created out of predominantly intellectual material which overshadows visual images. When a concrete object is violently juxtaposed with an abstract category the image is subordinated to the logic. By far the most striking feature of Brodsky's poetics is the maze of analogy that exists between the most heterogeneous objects/phenomena: смех / громко скрипел, оставляя следы, /как снег, / опушавший изморосью, точно хвою, края / местоимений и превращавший я / – в кристалл laughter/squeaked loudly, leaving its traces, like snow,/covered with sleet, like pine-needles, the edges/of pronouns and transforming 'I'/into crystal (N: 139). The common predicate 'squeaked' sanctions the comparison between laughter and the snow, which freezes both laughter and speech ('edges of pronouns') and transforms the 'I' into crystal; the 'I' here is simultaneously a part of speech (a pronoun) and a person. This simile is a bold amalgamation of man, nature and speech. Such associations might be analysed in terms of logic, since the principle of similarity gives way to the principle of association by proximity, despite the fact that they all are expressed by the grammatical structure of a simile.

It would be interesting to trace which grammatical structures of simile allow such a conflict of grammar and semantics, in other words, allow the creation of analogies which are governed by disparity, incongruity and disproportionality. The mere fact that there are in Russian a great variety of grammatical structures by which similes are expressed, impels the investigator to give a systematic description of their use in the poetic language in order to establish the poet's preferences and to understand his motivations. For this purpose all Brodsky's similes from his six collections have been catalogued according to their grammatical structure. A grammatical approach has proved to be very fruitful for establishing the correlation between the grammar and the semantics of this figure of speech.

It is on the level of semantics that the disparity in similes is most noticeable. Is there any pattern in their incongruity? Some of Brodsky's similes bring into collision a dazzling chain of images; others are charged more with an intellectual concept than with sensuous perception; still others are no more than intellectual abstractions. To what extent can the grammar of a simile promote or prevent incompatible combinations between the subject and the object of a simile?[1] Do all grammatical structures possess equal transformative power?

The relations between the two components of a simile seem to fluctuate between associations by similarity and total identity, through contrast and parallelism. Which grammatical structures lend themselves more than others the expression of certain relationships between the subject and the object of a simile?

On the level of semantics we can reconstruct quite a reliable picture of the denotative basis of all Brodsky's similes. Despite the seemingly arbitrary choice of the components of similes, we cannot fail to notice a certain thematic consistency either among the subjects or among the objects of his similes. It is precisely the presence of numerous lexical doublets that leads us to the semantic centres and indicates the enormous significance of similes to the principle themes of Brodsky's poetry. The theme itself sometimes requires similes which are based not on visual resemblance but on logical argument. At this level the simile's function is either to illuminate the theme or to develop it, as for instance, in the poem 'Otkazom ot skorbnogo perechnia' (O: 87–8).[2] We can see how well Brodsky's similes are adapted to his major themes.

Because of their lack of metaphorical ambiguity, similes express the author's perception of reality more directly than do tropes. Therefore, a systematic study of all the poet's similes can either increase our understanding of his poetic world or make us question our interpretation of it by other means. At the least, it can reveal the peculiarity of his poetic style.

THE GRAMMATICAL STRUCTURE OF SIMILES

The fact that a simile has a more definite grammatical structure than most tropes, simplifies its identification within the text. The principle constructive element of a simile is a conjunction. The most widely used Russian conjuctions are: 'kak' (as, like), 'budto' (as if), 'kak budto' (as though), 'slovno' (as if, like), 'tochno' (as though, as if), 'chto' (as, like), 'chto tvoi' (like yours), etc. The choice of conjunction is usually determined by the genre or individual style. Nevertheless, it is accepted that the conjunction *kak* is the most stylistically neutral and expresses undifferentiated comparative relations. This, perhaps, explains the frequency of its occurrence in the works of every author, as has been noticed by many scholars.[3] Among Brodsky's conjunctive similes the dominating presence of *kak* is only too obvious: it makes up 85 per cent, while *tochno* – has only 7 per cent, *slovno* – 5 per cent, the rest account for 1 per cent each. In toto they generate 54 per cent of all Brodsky's similes.

Since comparison can imply various degrees of analogy, such as pure resemblance, correspondence, correlation, parallelism, affinity, equivalence, even identity which conjunctions are unable to express, other parts of speech act as conjunction substitutes. Brodsky's poetry reveals the following set of prepositions, adverbs, adjectives, nouns and verbs which are used as conjunctions: 'skhozhii, pokhozh, skhodstvo' (similar, like, resembling, likeness) – 35 per cent; 'podobnyi, napodobye, podobye, upodobliatsia' (like, similar, semblance, become like) – 20 per cent; 'napominavshii, napominat'' (resemble) – 9.5 per cent; 'vrode' (like, not unlike) – 6 per cent; 'srodni' (akin) – 6 per cent; 'na maner' (in the manner of) – 4 per cent; 'kazat'sia, chuditsia' (seem, appear) – 4 per cent; 'v vide' (in the form of) – 3 per cent; 'sravnimyi, sravni' (by comparison, compare) – 3 per cent; 'prevzoidiot' (excel, surpass) – 2 per cent; 'podstat' (match for) – 1.5 per cent; 'vygliadit' (look like) – 1.5 per cent; 'obshchee' (in common) – 1.5 per cent; 'vpriam'' (really, indeed) – 0.5 per cent; adverbs with the suffix 'ski' – 0.5 per cent; 'ekvivalent' (equivalent) – 0.5. per cent; 'vylityi' (the very image of) – 0.5 per cent; 'smakhivaya' (resemble, look like) – 0.5 per cent; 'povtoriat'' (repeat) – 0.5 per cent. In total these similes constitute 10 per cent of all Brodsky's similes.

These two groups of conjunctive links are used to express a

'pure' simile which is a part of a simple sentence. But a simile can also be expressed by a whole compound sentence with a comparative subordinate clause introduced by the same conjunctions as 'pure' similes. Such comparisons differ from 'pure' similes in two ways: they can accommodate more than one pair of analogies and they contain predicational relations: Человек размышляет о собственной жизни, как ночь о лампе. – Man ponders over his own life like night about a lamp (C: 107). This simile expresses the analogy between man and night,[4] between human life and a lamp. By sharing the same predicate, 'ponder', one abstract notion, 'night', receives a breath of life, while the other – life itself – is reduced to a concrete object, 'a lamp'.

In this grammatical structure similarity can be established through logic and the figurative aspect of a simile undermined. This is partly due to the dominant role of the predicate in such similes. The dominant role of the predicate is also typical of Brodsky's 'pure' similes. The following statistics show the frequency of similes with the conjunction 'kak' with the objects depending on the predicate: S (1965) – 65 per cent; O (1970) – 70 per cent; K (1971) – 45 per cent; C (1976) – 55 per cent; N (various years) – 75 per cent; U (1986) – 60 per cent. However, we should not make too much of this, because the second type of grammatical constructions make up only 7 per cent of all Brodsky's similes. As in the first type, the conjunction 'kak' holds the leading position, it totals 41 per cent; 'budto, kak budto' – 31 per cent; while 'tochno' – 14 per cent; 'slovno' – 10 per cent and 'vsio ravno chto' (the same as) – only 4 per cent. The increasing frequency of 'budto' and 'kak budto' can be explained by their ability to convey weak semantic relations between the subject and the object of a simile.[5] Brodsky readily uses this comparative construction and often isolates the subordinate clause in an independent sentence: вези меня по родине такси. / Как будто бы я адрес забываю. – Take me, taxi, through my motherland./As if I'm forgetting the address (S: 102). Such practice can be traced throughout his poetry and it embraces other conjunctions, especially 'kak': Они умрут. / Все. Я тоже умру. / Это бесплодный труд. / Как писать на ветру. – They will die. /All of them. I too wil die./ It is fruitless work./ Like writing on the wind (K: 109).

A certain tendency can be observed in such practice. It occurs when the subject of the simile contains an idiom or a cliché as in the above example. It also occurs when Brodsky creates a chain of similes, as in one of his early poems 'Byl chernyi nebosvod svetlei tekh nog . . .' (S: 94–5). This process can be motivated by actual dialogue, as in the poem 'Gorbunov and Gorchakov': 'Стоит огромный сумасшедший дом'. / 'Как вакуум внутри миропорядка'. 'A huge madhouse stands'./'Like a vacuum inside the universe'. (O: 204); or by inner dialogue: 'Как ты жил в эти годы?' – 'Как буква 'г' в 'ого'. – 'How did you live in these years?' – 'Like the letter "g" in "ogo"' (C: 47).

Since Brodsky has also extended this practice to the first grammatical type of similes we can assume that this enforced severence of the objects of 'pure' similes into independent sentences is dictated either by the demands of meter and rhymes or by the widely employed technique of estrangement: Видать не рассчитал. Как квадратуру круга. – It looks as if I've miscalculated. Like squaring the circle (U: 12).

More or less the same motivations can be provided for the phenomena of inversion in Brodsky's similes. Due to the flexibility of grammar, the subjects and objects of a simile can change places without any distortion of the semantics: Как тень людей, неуязвимо зло. – Like the shadow of people, evil is invulnerable (S: 167). 24.5 per cent of all objects of the first grammatical structure are situated in the pre-position of the simile. The distribution of the conjunctions is as follows: 'slovno' – 55.5 per cent; 'kak' – 23 per cent; 'budto' – 16 per cent; 'tochno' – 11 per cent. In the case of the similes expressed by a compound sentence the conjunction *kak* begins the comparison in S – 16.5 per cent; O – 8 per cent; K – 10 per cent; C – 5 per cent; N – 19 per cent; U – 9 per cent.

By the persistent use of this practice the poet can solve several problems simultaneously. He can overcome the predictability of a conventional image: Как пиво, пространство бежит по усам. – Like beer, space runs along my moustache (O: 150). Inversion can also provide an unexpected angle of observation, Подобие алфавита, тепло есть знак размноженья вида / за горизонт – Like the alphabet,/ warmth is a symbol of the multiplication of the species beyond the horizon (U: 126).

The third grammatical type of simile is expressed by the conjunction *tak* (thus). Vinogradov has termed such similes as 'joined equivalence'[6] since they are logically related to the preceding statement. It is one of Brodsky's favourite devices for making an analogy between seemingly unrelated phenomena, but in fact this conjunction organises the similes through the logic of reason which takes all points of view into account:

> Когда снег заметает море и скрип сосны
> оставляет в воздухе след глубже, чем санный полоз,
> до какой синевы могут дойти глаза? до какой тишины
> может упасть безучастный голос?
> пропадая без вести и́з виду, мир во вне
> сводит счёты с лицом, как с заложником Мамелюка.
> ... *так* моллюск фосфоресцирует на океанском дне,
> *так* молчанье в себя вбирает всю скорость звука,
> *так* довольно спички, чтобы разжечь плиту,
> *так* стенные часы, сердцебиенью вторя,
> остановившись по эту, продолжают идти по ту
> сторону моря. (U: 17)

> When a blizzard powders the harbour, when the creaking pine
> leaves in the air an imprint deeper than a sled's steel runner,
> what degree of blueness can be gained by an eye? What sign
> language can sprout from a chary manner?
> Falling out of sight, the outside world
> makes a face its hostage: pale, plain, snowbound.
> *Thus* a mollusc stays phosphorescent at the ocean floor
> and *thus* silence absorbs all speeds of sound.
> *Thus* a match is enough to set a stove aglow;
> *thus* a grandfather clock, a heartbeat's brother,
> having stopped this side of the sea, still tick-tocks to show
> time at the other.[7]

Significantly, every new analogy, which is so different from the previous one, is separated only by a comma, and not by a full stop as in the case of the much more closely related components of the types of similes discussed above. But here, too, all the subjects of the analogies have something in common: snow, universe, mollusc, silence, clock stand for time; others: eye, voice, face are its victims. This grammatical structure outlines the parallel relations in simile. And it provides the opportunity for a wide range of possible associations for the poet who is seeking a true similarity based on causal and temporal relations, and not only on external resemblances. Hence, similes with the conjunction *tak* are usually abstractions of the logical discourse, and as such they begin and end a stanza or a whole poem.[8] However, despite their striking novelty and Brodsky's frequent use of them, they constitute only 5.5 per cent of all his similes.

The next type of grammatical structure of the simile is asyndetic. It is expressed by the instrumental case of a noun: И январём его залив вдаётся / в ту сушу дней, где остаёмся мы. – And his gulf as January strikes/ the dry land where we remain (O: 140). This simile reminds us that T.S. Eliot died in January, and also implies that he has entered the ocean of time. This type of simile has often been a subject of disagreement and misunderstanding among the students of Russian tropes and figures of speech. It tends to be confused with metaphor expressed by the same syntactic means.[9] Since the choice of case is dictated by a verb, every time a verb is used metaphorically, it affects both the subject and the object of the sentence: И пространство торчит прейскурантом. – And space sticks out like a price list (K: 59). Apart from metaphor these similes allow intrusion by metonymy: и воздух входит в комнату квадратом – and air enters the room like a square (C: 9), because it penetrates the room through rectangular windows.

Not all similes expressed by the instrumental case are metaphorically coloured. Most of them lack semantic ambiguity and preserve the nominative meanings of the structural components. Arutiunova has suggested differentiating metaphor and simile of this type by 'the presence/absence of identification of objects and by the permanent/temporary character of the sign' of analogy.[10] A simple grammatical criterion can be offered: the instrumental-metaphor tends to be a part of the nominative predicate: Я памятником лжи согласен стать. – I am ready to become a monument to lies (O: 211); А её любовь / была лишь рыбой. – And her love/ was only a fish (O: 99). The instrumental-simile usually joins a semantically independent verb: Бился льдинкой в стакане мой мозг в забытьи – My brain was rattling in oblivion like an ice-cube in a glass (N: 9).

The total number of instrumental-similes amounts to 5 per cent of all Brodsky's similes.

The fifth grammatical type of simile to be described is expressed by both morphological and syntactical means. It is the comparative, which makes up 18 per cent of all Brodsky's similes. 33.5 per cent of this type employ the comparative degree of the adjective and adverb with the genitive case of a noun: правота разделяет беспощадней греха. – rightness separates more mercilessly than sin (O: 94). 66.5 per cent is made up by the comparative with the conjunction 'chem' (than): По мне, уже само движенье губ / существенней, чем правда и неправда – To me, the very movement of lips/ is more essential than truth or falsehood (K: 46).

The comparative, by its very nature, preserves a large degree of metonymy. And Brodsky uses it sometimes to convey relations of temporal succession and causality:

> Спи. Земля не кругла. Она
> просто длинна: бугорки, лощины.
> А длинней земли – океан: волна
> набегает порой, как на лоб морщины,
> на песок. А земли и волны длинней
> лишь вереница дней.
>
> И ночей. А дальше – туман густой:
> рай, где есть ангелы, ад, где черти.
> Но длинней стократ вереницы той
> мысли о жизни и мысль о смерти.
> Этой последней длинней в сто раз
> мысль о Ничто; (С: 110)

(Sleep. The earth isn't round. It's/ merely long: hillocks, hollows./And longer than the earth is the ocean: a wave/ runs at times up into the sand like wrinkles/ on the brow. And longer than earth and waves/ is only the chain of days./And of nights. Beyond that – thick mist:/ paradise, with angels, hell with devils./ But a hundred times longer than that chain of days/ are thoughts of life and the thought of death./ And a hundred times longer than this last,/ the thought of Nothingness.)

All of these similes are of a particularly discursive nature. The associations by similarity are almost totally diminished by the associations of contiguity. They appear to be a succession of quantitative conclusions based on an axiom. Or must we look more deeply for the bases of comparison of the length of the earth and ocean with the chain of days and nights, which are in turn compared with the thoughts of life and death and, further still, with the thought of Nothingness? All these similes are involved in the argument of the poem 'Lullaby of Cape Cod' and they combine higher unities on the thematic level. Sea and ocean in Brodsky's poetry are usually associated with space, while days and nights metonymically represent time. Thus, here we are dealing with the opposition between, rather than the similarity, of two universal concepts: space and time.

Considering that time is the paramount theme in Brodsky's poetry, it is precisely on the thematic level that we can reconstruct the logic of associations in his similes.

The amalgamation of the comparative with metonymy is sometimes based on the relation of the material and the product which is made of that material: Почему-то всё больше бумаги, всё меньше риса. – For some reason, there is more and more paper, but less and less rice (U: 88). In the comparative when the subject and object of the analogy change places the effect of a mirror reflection is created: Любовь сильней разлуки, / но разлука длинней любви. – Love is more powerful than separation,/ but the separation is more lasting than love (C: 57).

This grammatical type, as can be seen from the given examples, readily absorbs two abstract notions and thus allows the poet not only to compare, but also place in opposition to or even to identify the most distantly related phenomena of reality and ideas:

> ...свободы.
> Она послаще
> любви, привязанности, веры
> (креста, овала)
> поскольку и до нашей эры
> существовала.

(It [freedom] is sweeter/ than love, attachment, faith/ (cross, oval)/ in as much before Christ/ it existed.) (U: 95)

In spite of the presence of two concrete objects: cross and oval, the imagery aspect of this comparison is overwhelmed by the abstract nouns: freedom, love, attachment, faith. And the use of the conjunction 'in as much' indicates that these similes appeal more to the reason than to the senses.

The last, and the least significant, grammatical type (given its limited quantity less than 0.5 per cent) is the so called negative simile. The components of such similes are joined by conjuctions or conjunction substitutes: 'ne to chto' (unlike); 'ne v primer' (unlike); 'ne khuzhe' (not worse than), 'ne cheta' (there is no comparison); 'otlichaet' (differs); Позвоночник чтит вечность. Не то, что локон. – The backbone honours eternity. Unlike a ringlet (U: 99).

Thus, Brodsky employs a large variety of grammatical structures to create his similes. As we see, some of them more than others allow the figurative aspect to be subordinated to a thought-provoking discourse.

THE SEMANTICS OF SIMILES

Needless to say, the most obvious cases of disparity occur on the semantic level when a simile attempts to blend irreconcilable oppositions, such as for instance, eternity with the phrase 'I/he/ said' (O: 205). In order to trace some tendency or to identify a system in the sphere of semantics, three types of relationship between the subjects and objects of similes were taken into consideration: (1) the relations between semantic classes which indicate their denotative correlation, such as man, nature, things, etc.; (2) the relations from the sphere of language as a system, specifically, those which include various combinations of 'abstract/concrete';[11] (3) the relations between the real world and the poetic world which indicate the type of transformation of meanings, namely, the transformation of spiritual and human characteristics to the entire non-human world (nature, animal world, things and abstract concepts) or the reverse.

In every type of relationship we can identify some tendencies peculiar to Brodsky's poetic system. Thus, in the first type, apart from the predictable semantic and thematic classes mentioned above: spirit, man, nature, animal world, things, one cannot fail to notice a persistent semantic field, in which many subjects and objects of similes are rooted, namely, language in all the forms of its existence: sounds, letters, words, linguistic and poetic terminology, etc: На площадях, как 'прощай', широких, / в улицах узких, как звук 'люблю'. – On squares broad as the word 'farewell',/ in streets narrow like 'I love' (C: 42); и чернеет, что твой Седов, 'прощай' – 'Farewell' grows black like Sedov (C: 78); наколов на буквы пером слова, / как сложенные в штабеля дрова – chopping words from letters with a pen/ like firewood laid up in piles (C: 91); Как тридцать третья буква, / я пячусь всю жизнь вперёд. – Like the thirty-third letter,/ all my life, I am advancing backwards (N: 111).[12] I could go on. Words and letters are presented in physical terms, as objects and thus lose their signifying content. In such similes the poet endows language with the qualities both of man and of things. Even grammatical categories are used as components of a simile: За сегодняшним днём неподвижно стоит завтра, / как сказуемое за подлежащим. – Beyond this day motionlessly stands tomorrow/ like predicate after subject (C: 82).

The next unconventional sphere of analogy which cannot be ignored, without running the risk of distorting Brodsky's poetic world is that of figures and mathematical terminology. Even in one of his early poems (1963) we come across the comparison of time and zero: И вечер делит сутки пополам, / как ножницы восьмёрку на нули. – And evening divides the day/ like the scissors divide the figure eight into zeroes (N: 31). The 'mathematical' similes occur sporadically but throughout his poetry: сумма слагаемых при перемене мест / неузнаваемее нуля. – the sum of items at the change of places/ is more unrecognisable than zero (C: 90). Both 'linguistic' and 'mathematical' similes embody his conception of time. I will return to this subject in more detail.

Parts of the human body are another source for Brodsky's novel similes. The technique of *pars pro toto* as a metonymical depiction of man has become a vehicle for Brodsky's conceptual and poetic development: Твой мозг сейчас, как туча, застит мрак. – Your brain now like a cloud overshadows darkness (S: 148); И в мозгу, как в лесу, / оседание наста. – In my brain as in the wood,/ the snow-crust is settling (O: 136); Под ней, как мозг отдельный туча. – Under it [the moon] a cloud is like a separate brain (C: 10). The most inalienable parts of man are alienated in such similes: brain, consciousness, memory: И крутится сознание, как лопасть, / вокруг своей негнущейся оси. – And consciousness twists like a blade,/ around its unbending axis (O: 143).

It came as no surprise to find that many of Brodsky's similes cluster in a set of universal semantic classes by virtue of the unobtrusive recurrence of either the subjects or objects of similes. The following list is by no means exhaustive, but it does provide a useful basis for classification of his similes on the semantic level. This classification involves some simplification since, in order to make it compact and manageable for analysis, I lump together in every semantic class notions, objects, actions and features that would need to be distinguished in a close reading of the poem. I will first deal with the subject of the similes.

Similarity in Disparity

The following statistics give us an idea of the distribution of the semantic classes in each of Brodsky's collections:

Semantic classes (%)	S	O	K	C	N	U
1. Spirit	2.5	2.5	3.5	2	–	0.5
2. man	14	20.5	25	16	19.5	9.5
3. parts of the body	4	9.5	8	12	14.3	14
4. nature	19.5	14.5	13.5	13	14.3	21
5. animal world	8.5	2.5	3	7	5	6.5
6. things	16.5	17.5	15.5	16.5	14.5	26
7. abstract	24.5	26.5	27.5	27.5	30.5	16
8. language	10.5	6	3	4	2	4.5
9. numbers	–	0.5	0.5	2	–	2

The first class is not very representative. It comprises soul, angels, paradise, hell, the devil himself, and all places of worship. The second class embraces man in all positions in life and society. Such collective nouns as tribe, army, population etc. are also included in this class. In all Brodsky's collections man is represented first of all by the lyrical 'I' and the addressee 'you'. But alienated man is also depicted in his similes: Тень. Человек в тени, / словно рыба в сети. – Shadow. A man in shadow/ like a fish in a net (K: 111); Человек страшней, чем его скелет. – A man is more frightening than his skeleton (C: 80); Человек выживает, как фиш на песке. – Man survives like a fish on the sand (C: 106); туда, где стоит Стена. / На фоне её человек уродлив и страшен, как иероглиф; / как любые другие неразборчивые письмена. – there where the Wall stands./ On its background man is as ugly and as frightening as a hieroglyph;/ as any other illegible scripture. (U: 88).

This degree of alienation is extended to the parts of the human body. All kinds of previously invisible connections between the human body and its environment are linked in the similes. Many of them contain contrived images which reinforce the associations with the world of things: и глазами по наволочке лицо / растекается, как по сковороде яйцо – the face spills its eyes over the pillow-case like an egg in the frying pan (N: 144). Others are even more impersonal, but both types are full of bold and violent incongruities: глаз, мигая, заглатывает, погружаясь в сырые / сумерки, как таблетки от памяти, фонари; the eye blinking, gulps, sinking into damp/ dusk, streetlamps, like pills for oblivion; (C: 111). One of the most evocative and persistent images is the image of the estranged human body itself, which can be found in abundance throughout the six collections: тело похоже на свернутую в рулон трёхверстку – The body resembles a rolled-up map (C: 99); Как хорошее зеркало, тело стоит во тьме – Like a fine mirror, the body stands in darkness (C: 109); Тело, застыв, продлевает стул. / Выглядит, как кентавр. – The body, having grown stiff, is extending the chair./ It resembles a centaur (U: 20).

However, even in such similes a substantive reference can be suppressed when a subject is involved in a conceptual argument. Often Brodsky looks for an analogy beyond those which are available to our five senses, or he deliberately 'confuses' their functions: И голосу, подробнее чем взор, / знакомому с ландшафтом неуспеха, / сподручней выбрать большее из зол... – For the voice, acquainted better with the landscape of failure than the sight, it is easier to choose the greater evil . . . (U: 175). The voice here is the voice of the poet himself.

The fourth and the fifth semantic classes, nature and animals, are the most conventional. They produce a vast array of doublets, incorporating all of Brodsky's favourite animals and insects, such as lions, birds, butterflies, flies, moths, fish, mice. The repetition of many of the subjects of the similes taken from nature is motivated either by the theme of the poem or by the central theme of his work, e.g. foliage and grass usually stand for the masses; sea and the ocean – for space; water in general – for time.

The world of things constitutes the sixth semantic class and it is the most heterogeneous since it comprises all kinds of concrete nouns. Its counterpart, the seventh class (which is the largest), includes abstract notions, categories, conditions. The most persistent ones are: life, death, time, emptiness, darkness, silence, thought, freedom, nothingness. As the subjects of similes, they are often violently juxtaposed with concrete objects and thus, create disparity by fusing the intellectual with the visual: И пространство пятилось, точно рак, / пропуская время вперёд. И время / шло на запад, точно к себе домой, / выпачкав платье тьмой. – And space was backing up like a crab,/ letting time go ahead. And time/ was moving westward, as if it was its own home,/ soiling its dress with darkness (C: 100).

Brodsky assigns concrete qualities to abstract concepts either by personification or reification. (More will be said about this later.) Language and numbers constitute the last two classes which have been discussed briefly above. The full thematic implication of these classes is dealt with below. We must bear in mind that each semantic unit entails different couplings with the objects of similes.

The same classification is applicable to the objects of similes. The picture is significantly different in relation to the semantics and poetics of the subjects.

Semantic classes (%)	S	O	K	C	N	U
1. Spirit	2	3.5	1.5	4.5	1	2
2. man	14.5	20	18	11	13	16
3. parts of the body	6.5	8	11	10	7	10.5
4. nature	20	14.5	10	8	18	11.5
5. animal world	12	13	10.5	11	11	8.5
6. things	23.5	23	25.5	35	29.5	28.5
7. abstract	17	13	16.5	12.5	17	14.5
8. language	2.5	5	5	6	3	5
9. numbers	1.5	–	1.5	2	–	3

Although the class of man has only slightly decreased, it is precisely in this class that a large number of common similes can be found: man as a sinner, like a child, like an old man, like a thief, like everybody, like a gypsy, etc. It also includes traditional poetic phraseology, such as cultural clichés, analogies with mythical, religious and historical figures such as: like Ulysses, like Abraham, like Theseus, like friend Narcissus, like Aristotle, like Bonaparte on Elba, as if a new Christ, etc. He renovates these either by placing them into a new context: Вдохновлены травой, делаемся, как все. – Inspired by grass/ we become like the rest (N. 16);[13] or by mixing them with tropes, especially with metaphors. He is also very fond of creating a chain of objects for the same subject where a flat image is surrounded by resourceful original images.

One of Brodsky's typical devices, that of including an echo with another writer or a literary work in a simile which uses the simple demonstrative pronoun 'that': от тебя оставались лишь губы, как от того кота. – of you have remained only lips, like that cat (N: 138). This simile contains a reference to Lewis Carroll's Cheshire cat.

The comparison of the brain with a 'thing which has emerged from obedience, like/ that moment' echoes Goethe's *Faust: Verweile doch, du bist so schön*. There are several such similes which paraphrase Russian literature, particularly Pushkin and *Igor's Tale*.

Turning to the more conventional similes, it is not easy to establish exact percentages since there are no dictionaries of the similes of individual authors. The following statistics contain well-worn images, including renewed poetic phraseology: S – 24 per cent; O – 23 per cent; K – 32 per cent; C – 24 per cent; N – 15 per cent; U – 8 per cent.

It is significant that in both components of the simile the least represented class is spirit. It appears that Brodsky practises what he preaches. According to him, in our time it is no longer possible to speak to God and love in open text.[14] Love, however, does appear under its own name more often than God, who is represented by His voice, or His angels and other Celestial beings.

As with subjects, so with objects, every semantic class contains a considerable number of lexical doublets: like the brain; as in my brain; like the body, that has rotted before its shroud; a body's concession to a soul; like the father's shadow; like my shadow, emulating the heavens; like people's shadow; like a mouse; worse than a mouse; like a mouse in the ashes; like a soul; like a soul in relation to the flesh; as the souls of those who lived before us, etc. 50 per cent of all the objects of similes used in Brodsky's first collection contain an image of a bird, which has a traditional association with the soul, while his moths, flies and butterflies are settled on the edge of existence and nothingness.

A large proportion of the objects of similes are generated from the class of things. It, too, produces certain persistent images. The most powerful of them are mirrors and scissors. The image of scissors occurs for the first time in Brodsky's early poem 'A Guest': как посвист ножниц – музыка шагов – like the whistling of scissors – the music of footsteps (S: 120). It gains further significance in the poem of 1964 as 'beak-like scissors' (O: 103). It reappears in the poem '1972', and again in 'Twenty Sonnets to Mary Stuart', where we hear 'the clanking of scissors' (C: 56). This image of scissors cutting through emptiness is associated with time with particular clarity in the poem 'Lullaby of Cape Cod': Часы на кирпичной башне / лязгают ножницами – The clock on a brick tower/ clanks like scissors (C: 99).

By this technique of recurrence and variation of both components of the simile Brodsky involves this figure of analogy in the development of his principle theme and makes the simile functional.

The network of associations in the domain of things is affected by tropological relations. Apart from metaphor and metonymy, some of Brodsky's similes include litotes: Там схож закат с прорезом – The sunset there resembles a cut (U: 71); or hyperbole: Я, прячущий во рту / развалины почище Парфенона – I, who hide in my mouth/ ruins comparable with the Parthenon (С: 28); others reproduce oxymoron: Мрамор белокур, / как наизнанку вывернутый уголь, – The marble is blondish/ like a coal turned inside out (U: 174).

The amalgamation of simile with tropes creates an additional aspect of disparity as well as renovating poetic stereotypes. Such well-worn images as star, moon, sea, night are juxtaposed in Brodsky's similes with deliberately prosaic, everyday vocabulary: Но и звезда над морем – / что есть она как не ...мозоль, / натёртая в пространстве светом? – Even a star above the sea/ – what is it but . . . a corn/ in space, from rubbing against the light (K: 81). This intentional mingling of the low with the high could be seen as the de-romanticisation of traditional poetic imagery.

In relations which comprise 'abstract/concrete' combinations the following tendency can be observed. It is usually the combination of an abstract subject and a concrete object that creates visual similarity. The reverse creates a speculative analogy of which Brodsky is particularly fond. By constantly comparing of the world of things, animals and man with abstract concepts he tends to highlight the image and thus conceal the motive for analogy:

> Ты лучше, чем Ничто.
> Верней: ты ближе
> и зримее. Внутри же
> на все на сто
> ты родственна ему.
> В твоём полёте
> оно достигло плоти;
> и потому
> ты в сутолке дневной
> достойна взгляда
> как лёгкая преграда
> меж ним и мной.

(You [the butterfly] are better than Nothingness./ Or to be more precise, you're nearer/ and more visible. But inside,/ you're a hundred per cent/ an equivalent to it./ In your flight/ it is fleshed out;/ and for that reason/ amidst the bustle of daily grind/ you are worthy of my gaze,/ being a frail barrier/ between it and me. (C: 38).

Brodsky moves from the particular [the butterfly] to the general (nothingness) throughout the poem: the butterfly is also compared with days, with the form of time, with thought itself. Brodsky blends the abstract with the concrete in all possible ways, including the coupling of two abstract notions in one simile: время, сильно упавшее ниже / нуля – time, falling heavily lower than/zero (U: 120); физики 'вектор' изобрели. / Нечто бесплотное, как душа. – Physicists discovered 'vector'. /Something fleshless, like the soul (O: 148).

It appears on first reading that Brodsky in his speculative similes goes beyond the bounds of logic. But the motive for rational analogies is usually provided on the thematic and conceptual levels. And it is our task to establish such motivation even in similes which appear to be no more than poetic generalisations. To make sure that it is not merely a fault of style but a well thought-out device Brodsky includes in such 'abstract' similes additional speculative categories: form of; thought of; idea of; concession to; a hint at: Ибо незримость / входит в моду с годами – как тело уступка душе, / как намёк на грядущее, как масхалат / Рая, как затянувшийся минус. – For invisibility/ becomes fashionable with the years as a body's concession to the soul,/ as a hint at the future, as a camouflage of/ Paradise, as a delayed minus (U: 61). This simile is highly generalised and impersonal. The selection of its objects is based not so much on their actual similarity as on the assumed identity between such abstract concepts as invisibility, and no less abstract speculations as to the future conversion of body into soul, a camouflage of Paradise, a minus which we delay to put before our life. In other words, all the objects of this simile are mere paraphrases of death and time; the latter is depicted metonymically in the subject of this simile through its essential feature, invisibility. By conventional standards, this simile falls short of perfection since it is tautological by design.

The last two, small but significant, semantic classes are explicitly involved in considerable philosophical speculation on the nature of time and language. If the semantic class of language is very often found in thematic opposition to time, then numbers provide a conceptual embodiment of time.

THE THEMATIC AND CONCEPTUAL FUNCTIONS OF SIMILES

It is time, the paramount theme of Brodsky's work, that moulds his similes and motivates their incongruity. By his own admission, Brodsky writes 'exclusively about one thing: about time and what time does to man'.[15] By comparing man and his physical and intellectual activity with the world of things, he de-animates human life, as if though imitating time's merciless effect on us.

The reification of the living world is found itself in direct opposition to the traditional personification of the world around us. These two principles of transformation govern both the semantic and thematic aspects of similes. Since they have a close affinity with the two way traffic of transforming meaning by means of metaphors[16] they might be considered as the unifying principles of associations which run through the entire system of Brodsky's tropes and figures of speech. Personification is most clearly exemplified by the objects of similes which are taken from the class of spirit and man, while reification manifests itself in the classes of things, language, and numbers. Brodsky's extension of this process of transfering meaning onto language and numbers violates the conventional means of representing reality in poetry. It is also partially responsible for the disparity in his similes.

If personification is a depiction of the world basically from man's point of view, reification is a more detached and impersonal look at the world as if 'from the point of view of time' (N: 140). In the face of time, the generally accepted hierarchy of things appears to be defective and is replaced by the principle of relativity which is persistently stated in many poems: от всякой великой веры / остаются, как правило, только мощи. – of any great faith,/as a rule, only holy relics remain (O: 173); от лица остаётся всего лишь профиль. – of the face there only remains the profile (K: 103); От всего человека вам остаётся часть / речи. – What remains of a man is a part/of speech (C: 95); От великих вещей остаются слова языка – Of great things, the words of language remain (C: 109); от великой любви остаётся лишь равенства знак – of great love, only a sign of equality remains (U: 18).

The process of reification comprises not only man but the whole universe. Time unleashes a whole chain of unstoppable transformations: since 'man is his own end and runs into time' (C: 109), he ends up with 'a featureless face like a Cycladean thing' (N: 109); a thing, in turn, also 'loses its profile' and 'having received a name, straightaway/becomes a part of speech' (O: 204). Being 'devoured by words' (O: 205), both, man and things are further reduced to the level of a sign, whether that be ancient cuneiform, a hieroglyph, a letter, a number or a punctuation mark.[17]

The inclusion of words and numbers into the similarity and opposition of spiritual and material, abstract and concrete, living and inanimate allows Brodsky to remove the boundaries of established conceptual orders, to reinterpret some of the most fundamental existential situations.

The supremacy of language in the transformation of the real world into the poetic world is explicitly stated in many of Brodsky's writings.[18] The word's forceful and mediating role in the system of his similes, cannot be overestimated. The word in Brodsky's poetic world is twofold. On the one hand, the word as an alienated part of speech links man with numbers. 'The reduction of man to things', he has said, 'to a hieroglyph, to numbers is a vector into nothingness'.[19] At a certain level of abstraction, any semantic class can be reduced to a sign: Полицейский на перекрёстке / машет руками, как буква 'ж', ни вниз, ни / вверх; – The policeman on the crossing/waves his arms like the letter 'zh' neither down, nor/up (C: 113); Сад густ, как тесно набранное 'ж'. – The garden is as dense as the tightly printed letter 'zh' (C: 61); На мягкий в профиль смахивая знак / и 'восемь', но квадратное в анфас, / стоит он в центре комнаты – The chair at the centre of the room/resembles a soft sign in profile/and the figure 'eight', but squared in full face (U: 12). The denotants of some objects of Brodsky's similes are totally supplanted by the formula of their chemical compounds, i.e., water in the following simile is replaced by H_2O: Вещь, помещённой будучи, как в Аш- / два-О, в пространство, презирая риск, / пространство жаждет вытеснить; – A thing, being placed in space, as in H_2O/ necessitates forcing space out, / despising risk (U: 11).

On the other hand, the word is no less frequently identified with Spirit and thus, links man with God. References to the spiritual aspect of language in Brodsky are so considerable that they form a kind of theology of language. In talking of the 'all-seeing eye of words' (K: 80–1), Brodsky has in mind not ubiquitous universal reason, but the hypostasis of God in the word. He ascribes to a Russian letter (to a letter of any language, for that matter) far more power to foresee than the Sybil ever had:

> кириллица, грешным делом,
> разбредаясь по прописи вкривь ли, вкось ли,
> знает больше, чем та сивилла,
> о грядущем. О том, как чернеть на белом,
> покуда белое есть и после.

cyrillic, a sinful matter, / roaming over writing whether randomly or not, / knows more than that Sybil / about the future. About how to put black on white, / as long as white remains, and after) (U: 123).

Such an ending of the 'Fourth Eclogue' of a poet with a Christian world-view is its own kind of answer to the pre-Christian author of the 'Fourth Eclogue'.

In Brodsky's 'linguistic' tropes and similes, two extreme views of language coalesce: 'language is only language' and 'language is all'.[20] According to the former, a word can be compared or even identified with a number, just as a sign with a sign. According to the latter, language is something mystical, of immense significance and, perhaps, the only weapon for securing victory over time. It is the word, both with a small and a capital letter, that makes a transformation of meaning in Brodsky's tropological system reversible: associations move backward and forward between all classes. Taken in this context, it is understandable why the opposition of 'word/number' is either highlighted or neutralised as can be seen from the poem 'Midday in the room': Воздух, в котором ни встать, ни сесть, / ни, тем более, лечь, / воспринимает 'четыре', 'шесть', / 'восемь' лучше, чем речь. – air, in which you can't stand or sit/or, what's more, lie down / perceives 'four', 'six', / 'eight' more readily than speech (U: 20). The air is, in turn, identified with nothingness and zero (U: 21); while sound and light, 'being petrified in things' (U: 23), are 'transformed into words' (U: 23). Petrification is also setting in on man who has lost his speech (U: 24). In this terrifying process of time's victorious march only numbers have a touch of immortality.

Numbers, unlike any other semantic class, lack denotees, they are fleshless abstractions, perhaps, embodiments of time by the very virtue of their metonymical association: В будущем цифры рассеют мрак. / Цифры не умира. / Только меняют порядок, как / телефонные номера. – In the future figures will disperse the gloom. / Figures don't die. / They only change order like / telephone numbers (U: 25). The daring truncation of the verb 'umira' (die) demands motivation. Even if we assume that Brodsky, who knows all Russian rhymes by heart, did not want to repeat Mandelstam's rhyme from the poem 'I return to my city': Петербург, я ещё не хочу умирать: / у тебя телефонов моих номера (Petersburg, I don't want to die yet:/You have my telephone numbers), the unexpected severence of the suffix of an infinitive hints at the mortality of a part of speech. It is significant that this verb has already been used as a substitute for the name of a dead friend: 'as if your name was "died"' (K: 27).

Although the immortality of numbers is stated explicitly, it is illusory by virtue of the appearance in tropes. Like things, which can be seen as an intermediate stage of man's transition from the Word-Spirit to a word-sign and further to an asemantic sign as such, numbers, once included in a trope, become the essence of something else. For instance, zero stands for different referents in Brodsky's 'mathematical' tropes and figures of speech: as a metaphor of substitution for death: нуль открывает перечень утратам. – zero opens the list of losses (C: 9); for time: И вечер делит сутки пополам, / как ножницы восьмёрку на нули – And evening divides the day by half/like the scissors divide the figure eight into zeroes (N: 31); for exile: сумма мелких слагаемых при перемене мест / неузнаваемее нуля. – the sum of small items at the change of places/is more unrecognisable than zero (C: 90); finally, for the absurdity which has already infected the words: и зараза бессмысленности со слова / перекидывается на цифры; особенно на ноли. – and the infection of meaninglessness is transferred from the words onto the figures; especially the zeroes (U: 88).

In conclusion, we can assume that Brodsky's poetic world as it is seen through his similes may well be construed in accordance with his conception of time and language. They have a widespread influence on the structure and semantics of his similes. These two central themes impel the poet to introduce two additional semantic groups, word and figures, which are treated as equal to the traditional semantic classes in order to typify his major themes.

Having increased the number of semantic classes, Brodsky has simultaneously solved several problems. At the poetic level, the introduction of linguistic and mathematical terminology has extended the boundaries of poetic language. Like Khlebnikov before him, Brodsky tends to 'scientificise' his lyrics, force it to take the form of logical discourse. This, in turn, affects his imagery since associations by similarity sometimes are substituted by a set of associations by contiguity. The relationship between the subject and the object of the simile can fluctuate between the diverging principles since much of Brodsky's reasoning takes the form of drawing analogy by simile. Thus, his similes seek to define rather than to compare and to show.

At the conceptual level, in his search for hidden correspondences between the material and the spiritual, Brodsky continuously changes the point of observation. His piercing eye does not miss much. In order to ensure neutrality of perception his radius of vision is never limited. Perhaps, of great significance is the fact that, in striving towards neutrality in order to comprehend 'the idea that lies behind the thing',[21] Brodsky has failed to rid himself of the typically Russian obsession of going to extremes. He tirelessly reminds us that we must not be afraid to think things through, 'to take everything to its logical end – and further'.[22] To feed this obsession he employs 'linguistic' and 'mathematical' analogies to invoke a further abstraction of both the material and the spiritual.

There exists a coherent system underlying the relations between all semantic classes. Personification and reification are two consistent principles for the ordering the poetic world. The prominence and recurrence of the latter as a means of perceiving man's position in the world shows a great capacity for accommodating the poet's imagination and insight. It is also the main factor which chiefly determines the nature of disparity in his similes.

Discrepancy and disparity in Brodsky's similes convey the antinomical nature of human existence. The degree of conflict at the conceptual and thematical levels has a direct effect on the degree of incongruity in Brodsky's figure of speech. In addition to what language offers him Brodsky deploys a wide variety of grammatical, semantic and poetic means which can accommodate a vast range of disparate material.

The reader is presented with a sufficient amount of clues to grasp the underlying associations in this diverse material. They intricately link the major themes of his poetry. Through his similes Brodsky either highlights the antinomy of matter and spirit, or attempts to reconcile it by means of synthesis. The moving force behind this synthesis is language. The conceptualisation of time in many ways is balanced by the conceptualisation of language.

Notes

1. Preference is given to the terminology used by Russian students of simile: what is compared is called the subject of simile (in Genette's terminology it is *comparé*); the term 'objectis' taken to signify that to which it is compared (Genette called it *comparant*), while his term *modalisataeur* is simply called conjunction. However, I have borrowed his fourth term *motif* since the Russian term 'priznak' (sign, indication) for the basis of comparison (*tertium comparitionis*) is too ambivalent. The term 'simile' is used for the whole comparative construction. See, G. Genette, *Figures of Literary Discourse*, Alan Sheridan (tr.) (Oxford: Blackwell, 1982); *Yazykovye protsessy sovremennoi russkoi khudozhestvennoi literatury. Poezia*, A.D. Grigoryeva (ed.) (Moskva: Nauka, 1977), p. 241; M.A. Baskina, E.A. Nekrasova, *Evoliutsiya poeticheskoi rechi XIX–XXvv. Perifraza. Sravnenie.* (Moskva, Nauka, 1986), p. 89.
2. A detailed analysis of this poem is given in my book *Joseph Brodsky: A Poet for Our Time* (Cambridge: The Cambridge University Press, forthcoming), ch. III.
3. See V.I. Dyakov, 'Sravneniya Turgeneva in *Turgenev i ego vremia*,' N.L. Brodsky (ed.) (Moskva, 1923), pp. 77–141; C. Proffer, *The Simile and Gogol's 'Dead Souls'* (Paris: Mouton, The Hague, 1967).
4. Loseff has noticed the same unusual analogy between man and night in Wallace Stevens' poem 'The House was Quiet and the World was Calm'. 'The reader became the book; and summer night/Was like the conscious being of the book'. See Loseff's article 'Zhizn' kak metafora' in Mikhail Eriomin, *Stikhotvoreniya* (Tenafly: Hermitage, 1986), pp. 137–51.
5. 'In many cases', writes V.V. Vinogradov, 'the jointed syntagma have the character of free associant coupling without any direct grammatical dependence on the main syntactic group. Hence, both parts of the comparative combination can easily be separated and exist as adjacent syntactic units'. V.V. Vinogradov, *Russkii yazyk*, 2nd edn (Moskva: Nauka, 1972), p. 555.
6. V.V. Vinogradov, *Stil' Pushkina*, (Moskva, 1941), p. 218.
7. Translated by Brodsky, *The New York Review*, 18 February 1988, p. 16.
8. Several examples of similes with *tak* can be found in 'Strofy' (stanzas XVI, XXIV) (N: 108–16); 'Gorenie' (N: 134–6); 'Sidia v teni' (U: 155–6).
9. The reference here is to B. Eikhenbaum, *Anna Akhmatova* (Petrograd, 1923); N.A. Kuzmina, 'Probivayas' moguchim potokom', *Russkaya rech*, 1977, No. 2; E.A. Nekrasova, 'Stravneniya v stikhotvornykh tekstakh', *Yazykovye protsessy v sovremennoi ruskoi poezii* (Moskva: Nauka, 1982). I have dealt with this problem in my article 'Grammatika metafory i khudozhestvennyi smysl', *Poetika Brodskogo*, edn, L. Loseff, (Tenafly: Hermitage, 1986), pp. 70, 93–4.
10. N.D. Arutiunova, 'Yazykovaya metafora (Sintaksis i leksika)', *Lingvistika i poetika* (Moskva: Nauka, 1979), p. 158.
11. The classification of subjects and objects of simile according to 'abstract/concrete' is not without problems since there is no clear-cut linguistic criterion for their differentiation. In general terms, concrete

nouns denote the material world, the rest is made up by abstract ideas, conditions and intangible things.
12. I am only too painfully aware of the inadequacy of my translation. David McDuff and Brodsky have translated this metaphorical simile as follows: 'Like our thirty-third letter/I jib all my life ahead' (Brodsky, *A Part of Speech*, OUP, 1980, p. 140). Their translation doesn't convey the real meaning of this figure either. As Loseff has pointed out to me, the Russian letter "Я", which is the last letter of the alphabet, looks like a man moving from right to left, while Russian writing moves in the opposite direction. Therefore, this image hints at Brodsky's position in relation to Russian letters. I would also like to think that this simile sheds light on several essential features of Brodsky's poetics as regards his use of metaphor and metonymy, meter and syntax, lyricism and anti-lyricism, to name but a few. Roy Fisher has offered two other English versions: 'All my life like the thirty-third letter I face backwards as I go ahead'; 'I am an "I" like the thirty-third letter/that moves through time facing backwards'.
13. Brodsky often provides an interpretation of his own imagery in his prose: 'but leaves . . . This I suppose is where the concept of majority came from' *Marbles*, Tr. by Alan Myers with Brodsky *Comparative Criticism*, v. 7 (Cambridge University Press, 1985), p. 221.
14. From a private conversation with Brodsky.
15. Brodsky interviewed by the author, 10 April 1980, Ann Arbor.
16. For a more extensive discussion of transformation of meaning by metaphor see my article 'A study of Metaphor in Progress: The Poetry of Joseph Brodsky', *Wiener Slawistischer Almanach*, Band 17, 1987, pp. 149–85.
17. A few examples of how a comparison of a concrete object with a sign invokes the abstraction of the latter: И те же фонари горят над нами, / как восклицательные знаки ночи. – And the same streetlamps burn above us,/like the exclamation marks of night (S: 68); фонари обрываются, как белое многоточье – the streetlamps stop suddenly like white dots (U: 82).
18. See Brodsky's essays on Tsvetaeva, W.H. Auden, on Russian writers in *Less than One* (London: Penguin, 1986), pp. 176–383.
19. Brodsky interviewed by the author, 10 April 1980, Ann Arbor.
20. M. Mamardashvili, A. Piatigorsky, *Simvol i soznanie* (Jerusalem: Maler, 1982), p. 100.
21. Brodsky, *Marbles*, p. 211.
22. Ibid., p. 214.

APPENDIX: THE GRAMMATICAL STRUCTURE OF BRODSKY'S SIMILES (%)

Table 1

Brodsky's collections:	S	O	K	C	N	U	Average
I. The 'pure' similes							
a. with conjunctions:							
kak (as, like)	86	86	88	76	88.5	87	85
tochno (as though, like)	1	1.5	1.5	13	10	11.5	7
slovno (as if, like)	10	10	9	2	1.5	1	5
budto, kak budto (as if, as though)	3	2.5	–	–	–	0.3	1
chto (as, like)	–	–	1.5	4.5	–	–	1
chto tvoi (like yours)	–	–	–	4.5	–	0.3	1
b. with conjunction substitutes							
skhozhii, pokhozh, skhodstvo (similar, like, likeness)	61	23	10	36	67	23	35
podobnyi, napodobye, upodobliatsia (like, similar, become like)	18	40	10	7	11	16	20
napominat' (resemble)	3.5	13	30	21.5	11	7	9.5
vrode (like, not unlike)	–	10	20	–	–	7	6
srodni (akin)	11	3.5	–	–	–	9	6
na maner (in the manner)	–	–	–	21.5	–	5.5	4
kazat'sia (seem, appear)	3.5	3.5	–	7	–	5	4
v vide (in the form)	–	–	–	–	–	7	3
sravnit' (compare)	–	3.5	20	7	–	–	3
prevzoidiot (excel)	–	–	–	–	11	3.5	2
podstat' (match for)	–	–	–	–	–	3.5	1.5
vygliadit (look alike)	–	–	–	–	–	2	1.5
obshchee (in common)	–	–	–	–	–	3.5	1.5
vpriam' (really)	3	–	–	–	–	–	0.5
adverbs with the suffix -ski-	–	3.5	–	–	–	–	0.5
ekvivalent (equivalent)	–	–	–	–	–	2	0.5
vylityi (the very image of)	–	–	10	–	–	–	0.5
smakhivaya (resemble)	–	–	–	–	–	2	0.5
povtoriat' (repeat)	–	–	–	–	–	2	0.5

II. Compound sentences with conjunctions:

kak (as, like)	17	44	33	55	67	58	41
budto, kak budto (as if, as though)	60	31	40	11	–	11	31
tochno (as though, like)	–	–	13.5	22.5	33	28	14
slovno (as if, like)	23	19	7	–	–	–	10
vsio ravno chto (the same as)	–	6	7	11	–	3	4
III. Sentences with the conjunction:							
tak (thus)	5	4	1	9	21	60	100
IV. The instrumental case	24.5	17	10	11	10	27	99.9
V. The comparative							
a. The comparative + chem (than)	53.5	60.5	57	62	81.5	75.5	66.5
b. The comparative + the genitive case	46.5	39.5	43	38	18.5	24.5	33.5
VI. The negative similes	–	–	12.5	–	25	62.5	100
Average (S – U)	16.5	16.5	9	15	9	34	100

Table 2

I. The 'pure' similes	
(a) with conjunctions	54
(b) with conjunction substitutes	10
II. Compound sentences with conjunctions	7
III. Sentences with the conjunction *tak*	5.5
IV. The instrumental case	5
V. The comparative	18
VI. The negative similes	0.5

10
Beginning at the End: Rhyme and Enjambment in Brodsky's Poetry
Barry P. Scherr

Poets sometime rhyme the end of one line with the beginning of the next, create rhyme at the caesura, or employ some other form of the phenomenon generally known as internal rhyme. End-rhyme, however, occurs much more frequently and is what people normally have in mind when they use the word rhyme. Similarly, enjambment, while it may bridge a caesura within the line, principally involves line endings. Yet, even though the two devices are commonly associated with the same position in the line, they are rarely discussed together. This reluctance is understandable, for the chief functions usually assigned to them are diametrically opposed. As Zhirmunsky once stated, rhyme, broadly speaking, represents an aspect of the poem's 'sound instrumentation' – that is, the way in which sound similarities and identities are introduced to create an aesthetic effect.[1] To the extent that rhyme joins groups of lines together, and in particular creates recurrent clusters (stanzas), it also helps structure the work. Enjambment belongs to the realm of poetic syntax rather than sound. More importantly, it is in one sense 'anti-structural': when enjambment occurs, that syntactic unit (the phrase or sentence) does not come to an end with the rhythmic unit (the colon, the line, or the stanza), but instead is carried over to the next.[2] Thus if end-rhyme calls attention to line boundaries and can impart particular emphasis to words in the final position,[3] then enjambment at least has the potential for obscuring the boundaries. Joseph Brodsky, writing on Marina Tsvetaeva's long poem 'Novogodnee', has pointed out that the enjambment running from lines two through four diverts attention from the commonplace quality of the rhyme *krovom/*

novom in the first two lines (L: 215). Enjambment may, then, serve as an antipode, or perhaps an antidote, to rhyme. A minimum or an absence of enjambment in a rhymed poem will by default emphasise line endings, while the regular use of enjambment can vary the way in which the boundaries are perceived.

This model, while no doubt applicable to many poets, seems less valid for the work of those twentieth-century Russian poets whose enjambments have been most original and striking. Perhaps the most radical poet in this regard, as in so many others, is Tsvetaeva.[4] In her case enjambment becomes, *inter alia*, one of several means for shifting attention from the end of the line to the beginning. She does not so much obscure the boundaries between lines as create boundaries in unexpected places; most notably, she often sets off the beginning of a line from what follows. In Brodsky, as in Tsvetaeva, enjambment greatly expands the expressive range of the verse. Startling disjunctions between rhythmic and syntactic units may make the diction more prosaic than poetic, or, at the opposite extreme, heighten the emotional tone of a passage. Brodsky's rhyming practice, while it exhibits certain distinct traits, is on the whole not unusual for a modern poet; entire poems may be written with rhymes every bit as exact as those found in nineteenth-century Russian poetry, while most of his approximate rhymes still exhibit a great deal of sound similarity. However, his more extreme instances of enjambment lead to some highly original rhymes that do distinguish him from his contemporaries. Of more general significance, enjambment and rhyme are not opposed in Brodsky but work in harmony. Enjambment, especially when it leads to innovative rhymes, does not necessarily efface line boundaries but can just as well emphasise them. What is more, the enjambment in Brodsky's verse bears a strong resemblance to the practice of English and American poets whom he is known to have read and admired. Thus one of his major contributions to the Russian poetic tradition would appear to be the manner in which he has borrowed certain characteristics of English verse and made those part of the repertoire for Russian poetry. Consequently, any study of Brodsky's line endings must also touch, at least in passing, on his relationship to the English verse tradition.

In order to gain a full appreciation of Brodsky's enjambment, it is necessary to begin with a survey of his rhyme practice against the background of contemporary Russian rhyme in general. The situation in Russian poetry is roughly analogous to that in English, where two different poles can be found. For English poets one end is represented by rhyme, the other by 'rhymelessness'.[5] In Russian, where unrhymed verse remains a relatively minor part of the tradition, the choice is more between exact and approximate rhyme.[6] Some poets – Voznesensky, Slutsky, Evtushenko, and others – have on occasion carried approximate rhyme to an extreme, where only the stressed vowels are the same (ugol/umnyy).[7] One critic has coined the term pre-tonic rhyme to specify sound rhymes where the sound similarities are concentrated *before* the stressed vowels (vozdúshnykh/sdúet, blagodarén'em/derévnya).[8] M.L. Gasparov, one of the most prominent scholars working on Russian verse, agrees that, after a hiatus of some years, experiments with rhyme again come to the fore during the 1950s and 1960s; however, he cautions against assigning too much significance to pre-tonic rhyme.[9] Indeed, for all that many of today's rhymes seem highly irregular when viewed against the 'traditional' rhymes of the nineteenth century, some poets, such as Kushner and Tarkovsky, largely avoid the more radical forms of rhyme. None the less, nearly all modern poets have come to pay greater attention to the sounds that occur before the stressed vowel, the phenomenon known as enriched rhyme (or deep rhyme, when the sound similarities extend back for a syllable or more).[10]

Thus Russian poets are faced with a situation in which a great deal of care is paid to rhyme at the same time that a wide degree of latitude is allowed. Just as some poets use the more modern (and less regular) meters, such as the 'dol'nik' and accentual verse, quite regularly, while others prefer to rely more on the meters that came into the Russian poetry during the eighteenth century (the iamb, anapest, etc.), so do poets vary in the degree to which they use approximate rather than exact rhyme. Further, as with meters, a poet's preferences for modern as opposed to traditional rhymes may vary from one poet to the next or may evolve over the years. Yet, since both poles now exist, a poet who insists on traditional rhymes is making just as strong a statement as one who fills his verse with approximate rhymes.[11] Also, while it is true that rhyme practice shows a great deal of variety, a few general tendencies can be discerned. In contemporary Russian verse on the whole, about twenty to 25 per cent of the rhymes are approximate. Whereas earlier in the century a clear majority of the approximate rhymes involved the presence of one or more consonants in only one member of a rhyme pair (truncation), today's poets prefer to substitute one sound for another (that is, rhymes of the type 'neudóbnyy/dóbryy' are now more common than the type 'smérti/svéte'). Also, many rhymes are based on a sufficiently complex series of sound and, ultimately, lexical associations that it becomes appropriate to speak of 'word rhyme' – to consider the rhyme to be comprised of entire words or groups of words rather than just sound correspondences.[12]

Where does Brodsky fit into this picture? At first glance his rhymes over the years may simply appear to be adhering to the general traits of modern Russian verse in general. And such a conclusion would not be entirely wrong. Still, some evolution has taken place in his rhyming, and certain of its features are quite distinctive. To establish some benchmarks for his rhymes, three sets of poems were examined in particular detail: the sixteen poems (582 lines) that comprise the section 'Anno Domini' (O: 77–100), the twenty poems (244 lines) in the cycle 'Chast' rechi' (C: 77–96), and the seventeen poems (636 lines) grouped under the heading 'Zhizn' v rasseyannom svete' (U: 161–89). The first set of poems dates from the 1960s, the second from 1975–76, and the third, while containing a number of undated poems, belongs primarily or perhaps entirely to the 1980s. Where relevant, though, examples have been drawn from the rest of Brodsky's poetry as well.

The earliest group happens to include four unrhymed poems with 94 lines. Brodsky, like nearly all Russian poets, has written some unrhymed verse. In his case it appears most often along with the iambic pentameter and thus is closely connected with the most common type of blank verse in Russian since the nineteenth century.[13] However, the great majority of Brodsky's verse contains rhyme. In the section 'Anno Domino' the 488 rhymed lines form 244 rhymes, only 24 (10 per cent) of which are approximate.[14] Not only is the frequency of approximate rhymes low for a contemporary poet, but most of the differences involve closely related consonants: 'Al'kazáre/v zále, grýzli/mýsli' (O: 89). To be sure, in a few instances the distinctions are sharper: 'redkolés'yu/bolézn'yu' (O: 91), 'nezabúdki/búnte' (O: 83). In the first case both truncation (of the *n*) and substitution (s/z) occur, and in the second a double substitution takes place (dk/nt). Once in a while substitutions also occur among the post-tonic vowels: 'pustómu/dóma'. Such combinations were of greater import in the nineteenth century than they are in the twentieth, where approximate rhyming is essentially based on differences between the post-tonic consonants.[15] The phonetic differences are quite tame by standards of the twentieth-century. In addition, the approximate rhymes are all feminine; the masculine rhymes, where any differences would be felt more strongly since they would occur in the stressed syllable, are all exact.

By the time of 'Chast' rechi' Brodsky's rhyme practice has matured. Evident earlier, but now even more characteristic, is the tendency to write poems exclusively in masculine or feminine rhyme. Since the eighteenth century, alternating masculine and feminine rhyme has been favored by Russian poets. While it is by no means rare to find poems that employ just one kind of ending, it is less common to find an entire cycle such as 'Chast' rechi', where over half the poems contain exclusively masculine or exclusively feminine rhyme. By now Brodsky has also come to employ approximate rhyme more often; it appears in twenty-six of the 122 rhymes, or 21 per cent – a figure that is within the norms for contemporary poetry. As before his masculine rhymes are nearly always exact, and the approximations still tend to involve substitutions among closely related consonants. Thus 'lésa/zheléza, otsyúda/vsyú-to' (C: 91). Sometimes the approximate rhymes within a given short poem may be quite varied: 'lyutsérnoy/ bestsénnoy' (truncation of the 'r'), 'stropíla/chto býlo' (substitution of 'p/b'), and 'prilip/priliv' (substitution in a masculine rhyme) (C: 86). Still, the differences are hardly extreme.

More significantly for his rhyme practice, Brodsky comes to pay greater care than before to the pre-tonic position. His enriched and deep rhymes become more complex and at times extend the sound similarities into preceding words. Note 'shkól'noy kárte/na kárpe' (C: 85), where the minor difference between the post-tonic phonemes (t/p) is more than compensated for not just by the identity of the pre-tonic 'k', but also by the way in which *na* echoes the final syllable of 'shkol'noy'. Of course, exact rhymes may also be enriched; note the following examples, all from a single poem (C: 79): 'travú/tatarvú, potolkú/polkú, yazýk vo rtú/yarlýk v Ordú'. In the first rhyme pair, both the first and second syllables of the second word echo the first syllable of the previous word. In the second pair the first word contains an extra syllable that 'interrupts' the enrichment by separating the 'p' and 'l'. The third pair shows just how far back into the line Brodsky may extend his sound similarities; indeed, the rhyme vowels play only a relatively minor role amidst the array of sound harmonies. A similar effect occurs in the oft-cited 'oktyabryá/okh ty blyá' (C: 91). Enrichment also embellishes many of Brodsky's compound rhymes, which will be discussed below in connection with enjambment. For now, it may be sufficient to point to such pairs as 'nevázhno/ne vásh, no' (C: 77), 'zá dva/závtra' (C: 82), and 'vitrinakh/vnutri nikh' (C: 92). Particularly when resorting to alternating rhyme, Brodsky will sometimes employ enrichment in such a way that all the rhyme words are linked, not just those that rhyme with each other. Consider the four rhyme words in the first stanza of 'Eto – ryad nablyudeniy' (C: 80). The rhyme scheme is clearly abab: 'tepló, sléd, stekló, skelét'. Enrichment occurs within the rhyme pairs: 'sled/skelet, teplo/steklo'. But the 'l' of sled also echoes the 'l' in 'teplo', while 'sled' and 'steklo' share both 's' and 'l'. The strongest similarity, however, is between *steklo* and *skelet*. Even though they do not rhyme, they share five of their six phonemes – all except the stressed vowels. Brodsky happens to create a particularly complex sound harmony throughout the stanza; for instance, the combination 'st' occurs several times over the last three lines. However, the striking echoes among the rhyme words not only draw attention to the line endings, but also, within the context of the poem, suggest semantic affinities among these words as well.

In this cycle, to a greater extent than in his poetry as a whole, Brodsky shows a definite predilection for 'open' masculine rhymes (in which the stressed vowel is the last letter of the line). Examples include the first poem ('Niotkuda s lyubov'yu', C: 77), where all four of the masculine rhyme pairs are open, and 'Uznayu etot veter' (C: 79) where five of the six rhyme pairs are based on open vowels (and in four cases the rhyming vowel is 'u', usually one of the least frequent vowel sounds). Since masculine rhymes by definition lack any trailing syllables, the sound harmonies cluster around the stressed vowel. But when the rhymes are open, all the supporting sound similarities must be pre-tonic. Hence the especially well-developed enrichment in several of the poem's rhyme pairs, as described earlier, is a logical consequence.

Nouns predominate among the rhyme words throughout the cycle and for that matter in most of Brodsky's poetry. In the poems on C: 79 and C: 85 eleven of the twelve rhyme words are nouns, and in the latter case the one other is a pronoun. For the cycle as a whole, over 70 per cent of the rhyme words are nouns. Verbs and verbal adverbs (gerunds) together account for only fourteen of the 244 rhyme words. The preferred 'part of speech' in this regard is clearly the noun. The early Esenin showed a similar proclivity toward nouns and avoidance of verbs,[16] though it is worth keeping in mind that a relative paucity of verbal rhymes is typical of modern poetry. This represents another stage in the move away from grammatical rhyme. During the early nineteenth century, verbs, whose grammatical endings made it easy to come up with exact (if relatively uninteresting) rhymes, were employed quite frequently. When Brodsky does use a verb or verbal adverb, he prefers to rhyme it with a different part of speech, thus avoiding obvious rhymes: 'kráya/povtoryáya' (C: 77), 'mysh'/spish'' (C: 86). Of course, it is also possible to rhyme the grammatical endings of nouns, but Brodsky again seeks more original combinations: noun rhymes such as S 'mýsa/smýsla' (C: 82) and 'iney/liniy' (C: 89), noun/adjective combinations such as 'orávoy/dyryávoy' (C: 95), conjunction plus noun (ésli/krésle, C: 84), and almost anything else imaginable (pódle/pó dve (C: 83), botvú/búkvu 'ú' (C: 92)). As W.K. Wimsatt has stated, 'the greater the difference in meaning between rhyme words the more marked and the more appropriate will be the binding effect'.[17] The effort to rhyme words from different grammatical categories or from different parts of the lexicon may help explain the acceptance of approximate rhyme in modern Russian poetry, for by its very nature it brings together words whose relationship is not immediately obvious (v báne/ zubámi (C: 82), krépko/klérka (C: 93)). Particularly in combination with approximate rhyme, enrichment intensifies the connection and often results in what is sometimes called 'paronymous attraction' – the tendency for a semantic tie to be perceived between etymologically unrelated words that sound alike.[18] In this way modern rhyme gives further significance to the end of the line by creating surprising sound harmonies that in turn lead to complex resonances on the level of meaning.

The three features discussed so far – approximate rhyme, enrichment, and compound rhyme – are all quite common in Russian poetry. Brodsky sometimes resorts to less familiar forms of rhyme. In a few cases he uses a subcategory of approximate rhyme known as consonance, where the stressed vowels differ and the consonants carry the rhyme. Interestingly, when consonance appears at all in a poem by him it generally affects more than one rhyme pair. Thus in 'K Evgeniyu' he rhymes 'piramídy/gromády, poddélke/krivotólki, and pobédakh/razbítykh' (C: 70). While consonance has appeared on occasion in Russian poetry since the days of Blok and Khlebnikov, two pioneers of this device, it is still sufficiently uncommon in Russian poetry to be noticeable. The similar or identical phonemes sometimes appear on both sides of the stressed vowels (cf. the first and third examples here) but just as often appear only in the post-tonic position, as though the rhyme were regular: 'móshchi/véshchi, vlásti/grústi' (N: 59). If such is the case in a masculine rhyme (pech'/luch, N: 59) the similarity between the two words can be reduced to an absolute minimum. Consonance represents some of Brodsky's most radical rhyming; perhaps this is the very reason why he prefers to group his consonant rhymes, since a single such rhyme, out of context, could well be jarring. He also makes sparing use of repetend rhyme (when the same word appears twice in a rhyme pair – e.g., *sluchilos'* at the end of 'K Evgeniyu') and homonym rhyme, where the rhyme words contain the same phonemes but have different lexical or grammatical meanings. Several intriguing homonym rhymes appear in his most recent collection: 'dam' (from dama)/ 'dam' (from dat') (U: 15); 'naz.' (the abbreviation(!) of 'nazyvaemom')/'nas' (U: 18). Finally, while most rhymes involve pairs of words, Brodsky employs larger rhyme sets with some regularity. Even a non-stanzaic poem such as 'Fontan' (O: 132–33) may employ a moderately complex repeating pattern such as aBBaBa that does not vary until the last few lines of the poem.[19] Perhaps his most notable work in this regard is the 1399-line poem 'Gorbunov i Gorchakov', in which most of the stanzas exhibit the rhyme scheme aBaBaBaBaB – that is, each of the two rhymes appears five times. More characteristic of Brodsky, though, are triplets: three rhyming words in adjacent lines. Examples include the AAABCCCB stanzas of 'Rech' o prolitom moloke' (K: 6–17), the AAABBBCCC stanzas of 'Dekabr' vo Florentsii' (C: 111–13), and the AAABBB stanzas of 'Ekloga 5-ya: letnyaya' (U: 124–31). Note that the large rhyme sets appear most often in poems that are at least moderately long. While such rhymes might at first seem harder to sustain than the usual pairs, Brodsky appears to enjoy the challenge of adhering to a more difficult pattern over a significant number of stanzas. Until *Uraniya* Brodsky employed three-line stanzas only once, but in this collection he uses stanzas based on triple adjacent rhymes both for a section within a longer poem (U: 44, with rhymes aaa) and for the entirety of the 96-line 'Pyataya godovshchina (4 iyunya

1977)' (U: 70–73, rhyming AAA). The juxtapositions of rhyme words in the triplets are often particularly original: note, for instance, the dactylic rhymes 'brátie/rádi ya/ rádio' and 'súffiksy/ súzdal'skim/súzilsya' (C: 26).

In the most recent works Brodsky's rhymes have not changed drastically since the previous decade, but they, like all other aspects of his writing, are constantly evolving. Of the 318 rhyme pairs in the seventeen poems that make up the final section of *Uraniya*, 72, or 23 per cent, are approximate. Thus the frequency of approximate rhyme is about what it was in the previous decade. Within this group feminine rhymes are by far the most common, partly since 'Mukha', with its 252 lines making it by far the longest of the seventeen poems, is written exclusively in feminine rhyme. The totals are 247 feminine rhymes, 66 masculine, and 5 dactylic. Four of the five dactylic rhymes are approximate, as are just five of the 66 masculine – both statistics are typical for Brodsky, who makes most of his dactylic rhymes approximate but only a handful of his masculine rhymes. The masculine approximate rhymes still sound quite similar; Brodsky nearly always substitutes one closely related consonant for another and supports the rhyme with enrichment: 'zhir/zhil, pozhár/sbezhál' (U: 180). As before, such substitution also forms the basis for much of his feminine approximate rhyme. He continues his practice of writing many poems with exclusively masculine or exclusively feminine rhyme – in this case, ten of the seventeen poems employ just one type of clausula. Now, though, he is inclined to use feminine rhyme more often. Even if 'Mukha', which admittedly distorts the picture, is omitted from consideration, he still has nearly twice as many feminine rhymes as masculine.

Some new characteristics of his rhyme practice have emerged. While the poems written entirely in masculine rhyme strongly favor exact rhyming and those in feminine rhyme contain much approximate rhyming, those with alternating masculine and feminine endings exhibit almost no approximate rhyming. There is no intrinsic reason why the feminine rhymes in this last group should not be approximate as often as those in poems that utilise just feminine rhymes. Brodsky seems to be narrowing the instances when he turns to approximate rhyme but then relying on it more heavily in individual poems. In other words, he appears to be employing two distinct kinds of rhyming. Some poems are entirely or almost entirely composed with exact rhymes, while in others the approximate rhymes are a regular occurrence. Thus half of the sixteen rhymes in 'Zhizn' v rasseyannom svete' are approximate as are nearly all the rhymes in 'Ty uznaesh' menya po pocherku'. Even at this point in his career Brodsky employs pre-tonic rhyme only rarely (e.g. 'tsárstve/tsátski'). He much prefers to provide a variety of sound similarities both before and after the stressed vowels ('nómer/sekonómil,' both U: 179). His exact rhymes show ever more imaginative forms of enrichment. Thus the first poem of the series has eight exact rhymes, all of which with similarities in the pre-tonic position: cf. 'okolótku/lódku, sirotá/Izo rtá' (U: 161). This last ending resonates not only with the other half of the rhyme pair, but also with the preceding words in its own line: 'ni shar', ni cherta. Izo rta – ' The *rta* cluster appears twice, while both 'a' and 'r' occur three times. It is as though the line plays with the sounds of the first word in the rhyme pair, preparing for the appearance of 'rta' at the end.

Brodsky's rhymes are neither so unusual in their sound relationships nor so frequent as to set him apart. Rather, their distinctive qualities consist of the care with which the great majority are constructed, the broad repertoire of devices that come into play, and the surprising ways in which normally unrelated words are joined together within rhyme sets. Many of the instances in which he resorts to enjambment, though, are highly unusual in of themselves, and in certain poems enjambment becomes the rule rather than the exception. One result for his poetry is the creation of some highly original rhymes. His compound rhymes sometimes include words that are not normally found at the end of the line, and, in a related phenomenon, he not infrequently has a rhyme word that is unstressed – thereby breaking one of the most unbreakable of rules of Russian prosody. Ever since the time of Lomonosov it has been necessary to stress the final ictus on each line. A handful of contemporary poets have violated this law on rare occasion, but Brodsky does so with some frequency. The abundance of enjambment in certain poems also creates a strong tension between the syntactic and rhythmic movements. The resulting effect, while not uncommon in English poetry, imparts a unique sound to his Russian verse.

Brodsky's attitude towards enjambment marks a major advance from the days of Nikolay Ostolopov, in whose three-volume dictionary of poetic terms enjambment is characterised as a fault. It is something to be used only in light or humorous verse; enjambment in serious poetry is said to make the line weak and prosaic.[20] Despite Ostolopov's strictures, enjambment has been an important feature of Russian verse since the time of Pushkin. To be sure, enjambment may indeed cause a passage to sound prosaic, but that is often the point: the poet uses the disjunction between syntax and rhythm to create a special tone or diction. Zhirmunsky has claimed that enjambment can be perceived only against a background in which rhythmic and syntactic boundaries normally do coincide.[21] That is, he treats enjambment as essentially a break in the work's basic pattern. For the interruption to take place, it is necessary for an expectation to be established in the first place. It would be wrong, though, to conclude that enjambment necessarily loses its effect if it is used often throughout a poem. The expectation of a syntactic break at line boundaries is determined not so much by the individual poem as by the weight of poetic tradition. A series of enjambments, or a poem in which enjambment prevails throughout, can call still greater attention to the device. Similarly, while enjambment itself provides a kind of 'anti-closure', the end to a consecutive run of lines with enjambment can signal closure quite effectively.[22]

Kiril Taranovsky has suggested that the juncture between lines can be marked in one of six ways. In only one of these – when the line boundary coincides with the end of a sentence – is enjambment impossible. When the line boundary divides a word, separates a proclitic or enclitic from the main word, or when it divides a syntagm (a minimal syntactic unit), then enjambment is always present. In the remaining two cases – when inversion causes part of a syntagm to appear in the next line even though the boundary itself does not divide a syntagm, and when the boundary simply comes between two different syntagms – enjambment will occur only when the intonational break within one of the lines is stronger than that at the boundary.[23] The three instances that always result in enjambment might be termed absolute enjambment; the two that may employ the device can be characterised as conditional enjambment.

Brodsky's use of enjambment, like his rhyme, appears to have matured during the 1970s and then been subject to further experimentation in the years since. Not that enjambment is rare in his earlier poetry; the first eight poems in 'Anno Domini' have 240 lines or 232 line boundaries. Of the latter, 64, or about 28 per cent, exhibit enjambment. For the entire cycle 'Chast' rechi' enjambment occurs at 74 of 224 line boundaries, or 33 per cent. Thus the frequency is greater in the 1970s, but not by a statistically significant amount. The more important change involves the nature of the enjambment, which is more often 'absolute'. The strongest type of enjambment, the division of a word between lines, remains quite rare in Brodsky's verse. The total number of appearances is too low to speak confidently of any trend, yet in his latest collection examples are not difficult to find. Thus 'za-' [za-piski]/sleza' (U: 87) and 'verto-' [verto-grad]/nichto' (U: 156) comprise rhymes in which the first word is split over two lines. Similarly, a hyphenated compound may be spread over two lines: 'menazh-//a-trua' (U: 10; '//' indicates a line boundary) or 'Ash-//dva-O'. More critical for Brodsky's poetics, though, is the frequent appearance of prepositions, conjunctions, and articles at the syllable that bears the rhyme, so that unstressed rhyme, an extraordinarily rare phenomenon in Russian poetry, becomes a favourite device. Take the thirty lines that comprise the fourth section of 'Lullaby of Cape Cod' ('Kolybel'naya Treskovogo Mysa', C: 102). Twenty of the twenty-nine line boundaries involve enjambment, and in three instances a rhyming vowel occurs within a preposition: 'na/oná, glazá/za, peró/pro'. What is more, the third type of strong enjambment, division of a syntagm by the word boundary, also appears several times in the same section: 'iz vsex//vnutrennostey, iznanki//zhizni'. In particular, subjects and predicates are often separated: 'glaza//sokhranyayut, ryba//dremlet, pero//rvyotsya'. Brodsky also uses conditional enjambments, but in this section of the poem they account for less than half the total.

Enjambment, it will be recalled, may also occur between stanzas, where it is especially perceptible since stanzas generally form self-contained semantic (as well as syntactic and rhythmic) units. In this particular section of the poem all four of the stanza boundaries have enjambment; for the work as a whole it occurs at fourteen of the 48 boundaries. Often, the enjambment at stanza boundaries is quite strong: 'iz//spinok' (C: 101), '. . . Ni treska, ni//sel'd'' (C: 103), 'navyk//nagoty' (C: 107). In some poems Brodsky does prefer to maintain the integrity of the stanza even though he may have frequent enjambment between lines within each stanza. An example is '1972 god' (C: 24–27), where there is no enjambment between any of the sixteen stanzas. At the opposite extreme stands 'Mukha', with three four-line stanzas in each of its twenty-one sections. Not only does enjambment between stanzas occur regularly, but twice Brodsky even has enjambment between the different sections of the poem. Perhaps the most unusual case of enjambment occurs in 'i pri slove' from 'Chast' rechi', where enjambment could be said to take place at the 'boundary' *before* the first line, which begins in the middle of a sentence (C: 95).

The absolute enjambments create the most unusual types of rhyme in Brodsky. Sometimes compound rhymes include a word that consists of a single-consonant preposition: 'góru s/gólos' (C: 82), 'slov/chisló v' (U: 20). Other compound rhymes are equally striking: 'Témze/tém zhe' (C: 46), 'nichéy, no/znachén'ya' (U: 178), or the triple rhyme 'veká, na/vulkána/kulaká: no'. The unstressed rhymes are as original as these compound rhymes, and, as indicated above, they possess the added quality of flaunting a basic law of Russian verse. Thus within a single poem Brodsky rhymes 'nulyá/dlya, vniz/iz, oná/na, vovné/ne, and no/pyatnó' (U: 49–52). In all these cases enjambment does not so much efface the line boundary as call attention to it. Since the rhymes create a sound echo at the ends of the lines, words that would usually play a subordinate role are suddenly given prominence. The coherence of the syntagm is disrupted, and the perception of both the syntactic and rhythmic units becomes less automatic. Rhyme words are, it has been suggested, given a particular emphasis in the poem because of their position in the line and the sound relationships between rhyme pairs. By placing usually unstressed words in that position Brodsky defeats expectations and thus heightens awareness of the endings. Furthermore, the rhythmic structure of Brodsky's lines often points to the end as well. As G.S. Smith has pointed out in his study of the poem 'Kellomäki', in Brodsky's unusual type of dol'nik the intervals between stresses are generally two syllables over most of the line, but the last interval usually has just one syllable.[24] Rhythm, rhyme, and enjambment all focus on the end, where it all begins.

As strange as Brodsky's line endings may seem within the context of the Russian verse tradition, they may not strike the English ear as extraordinary. Brodsky, who while still in the Soviet Union translated English poetry into Russian and after leaving has begun to translate his own poems into English, has an intimate knowledge of the English language along with both American and English poetry. Two of the poets whose work he knows well are W.H. Auden and Richard Wilbur. Consider this stanza from Auden's 'Mundus et Infans':

> Therefore we love him because his judgments are so
> Frankly subjective that his abuse carries no
>   Personal sting. We should
> Never dare offer our helplessness as a good
>   Bargain, without at least
> Promising to overcome a misfortune we blame
> History or Banks or the Weather for: but this beast
>   Dares to Exist without shame.

and the opening few lines of Wilbur's 'Lightness':

>   A birdsnest built on the palm of the high-
> Most bough of an elm, this morning as I came by
>   A brute gust lifted-and-left in the midst of the air;
>   Whereat the leaves went quiet, and there
>   Was a moment of silence in honor of
> The sweetness of danger. The chalice now bobbing above, . . .

Three aspects of these excerpts are of special relevance for the topics being treated here. First, both poems are highly organised. Each displays a regular pattern of rhyme (in the case of Auden, creating stanzas with the scheme aabbcdcd), and each contains a mixture of one- and two-syllable intervals between stresses – not unlike the type of 'dol'nik' line that Brodsky favors in much of his mature poetry.[25] Second, since Brodsky's own poetry is most often both rhymed and metrical, he would feel a natural affinity for such poetry in English, rather than for the free verse that at various times in the twentieth century has been so prominent within the English verse tradition. Third, Brodsky's use of enjambment bears great similarity to that of Auden and Wilbur. Both the passages quoted here happen to use enjambment freely, and in 'Lightness' as a whole about two-thirds of the line boundaries are marked by enjambment. For all that Brodsky relies heavily on enjambment, he does not use it quite that often in most of his works, but in the 36-line poem 'Elegiya' ('Do sikh por, vspominaya tvoy golos . . .', U: 90) not a single line ends with a period and all but four of the boundaries feature enjambment. Further, while a lone enjambment often appears in his poems, he usually creates clusters of several consecutive lines with enjambment, a feature that is quite common in English poetry. Many of the enjambments in both passages are absolute: 'so//Frankly, good//Bargain, high-//Most, there//was'. In some instances the rhyme words are no more than weakly stressed: cf. both *by* and *of* in the Wilbur poem.

It is instructive to see how Brodsky's experiments come across in English. The English translation of the following poem from the cycle 'Chast' rechi' was done by Brodsky himself:

> . . . i pri slove 'gryadushchee' iz russkogo yazyka
> vybegayut myshi i vsey oravoy
> otgryzayut ot lakomogo kuska
> pamyati, chto tvoy syr dyryavoy.
> Posle stol'kikh zim uzhe bezrazlichno, chto
> ili kto stoit v uglu u okna za shtoroy,
> i v mozgu razdayotsya ne nezemnoe 'do',
> no eyo shurshanie. Zhizn', kotoroy,
> kak darenoy veshchi, ne smotryat v past',
> obnazhaet zuby pri kazhdoy vstreche.
> Ot vsego cheloveka vam ostayotsya chast'
> rechi. Chast' rechi voobshche. Chast' rechi. (C. 95)

> (. . . and when 'the future' is uttered, swarms of mice
> rush out of the Russian language and gnaw a piece
> of ripened memory which is twice
> as hole-ridden as real cheese.
> After all these years it hardly matters who
> or what stands in the corner, hidden by heavy drapes,
> and your mind resounds not with a seraphic 'doh',
> only their rustle. Life, that no one dares
> to appraise, like that gift horse's mouth,
> bares its teeth in a grin at each
> encounter. What gets left of a man amounts
> to a part. To his spoken part. To a part of speech.) (PS. 105)

In keeping with the theme of this paper, Brodsky places the beginning of the poem, the unstated title, at the very end in both the English and the Russian. Not surprisingly for a poet so sensitive to the formal aspects of poetry, he takes great care to convey both the rhyme and enjambment of the original in his translation. Indeed, now that he is translating more of his poetry himself, it is easy to find further evidence of his concern that English renderings maintain the form as well as the sense of the Russian.[26] Here he maintains the alternating rhyme, though he does make all the rhyme masculine (which, by the way, is more typical for English poetry, though in other translations Brodsky frequently does try to find feminine rhymes in English to match those in Russian). While some of his English rhymes are exact, others are approximate: piece/cheese, drapes/dares, mouth/amounts. Approximations are not at all unusual in English; at various places in 'Mundus et Infans' Auden rhymes Us/does, impossible/all, other/over. To a large degree, then, not only are Brodsky's rhymes in the original broadly typical of Russian poetry, but the rhymes he uses in his translation show a familiarity with the English tradition. However, an influence of the Russian on his English rhymes appears, first of all, in those instances when he does employ feminine rhyme regularly. English poets only rarely maintain feminine rhyme, and in most instances the distinction between feminine and masculine rhyme plays no role in determining the structure of a stanza. Thus to a Russian poet (and, it would seem, to Brodsky whether he is writing in English or in Russian) the stanza AbAb, with feminine rhymes in the odd lines, differs from aBaB. For English poets the stanza is likely to be thought of as simply abab and there would be no particular effort to place feminine rhymes in the same position in each stanza. Brodsky's approximate rhyming in his translation would also seem to owe something to his Russian background. More often than Auden or most English poets Brodsky compensates for the approximation by various forms of enrichment. Note the 'd' and the transposition of the 'r' in drapes/dares, or the 'm' in mouth/amounts.

If his rhymes sound quite natural in Russian and perhaps a little unusual in English, then the exact opposite could be said of enjambment in the two versions. The Russian has a lot of enjambment, some of it quite strong. The English translation maintains the series of enjambments after the first three lines (a typical 'run' of enjambments for Brodsky) and maintains the split 'who//or what' at the end of line 5 (the order in Russian is 'what//or who'). Both have enjambment after the penultimate line, though the effect is more interesting in the Russian, where the last two words (*chast'*, *rechi*) appear both horizontally and vertically (the ends of lines 11 and 12). The English has more enjambment than the Russian, though since modern English poetry employs enjambment more freely, that is perhaps to be expected. The key point is that the amount and kind of enjambment appears striking in the original, while in the English it is no more extreme than what is found in the Auden and Wilbur passages quoted above.

Thus Brodsky's use of rhyme and enjambment is significant not just for the way in which he brings weight to bear on his line endings, but also for the way in which he creates cross-borrowings between two poetic traditions. The enjambment in his Russian poems at least in part reflects his reading of English poetry; it is one of several ways in which Brodsky has come to infuse Russian poetry with new formal possibilities. Conversely, his English translations reveal a definite influence of Russian rhyme. Only time can tell whether Brodsky's translations (and the original verse he writes in English) will come to have an impact on English prosody to match that which his poems have had on Russian.

Notes

1. V. M. Zhirmunsky, *Rifma: Ee istoriya i teoriya*. Reprinted in his *Teoriya stikha* (Leningrad: Sovetskiy pisatel', 1975), pp. 245–53.
2. B. M. Eikhenbaum, *O poezii* (Leningrad: Sovetskiy pisatel', 1969), p. 329.
3. On the significance of rhyme words for the poem as a whole, see V. V. Mayakovskiy, *Polnoe sobranie sochineniy v trinadtsati tomakh*, 12 (Moscow: GIKhL, 1959), 100–6.
4. On enjambment in Tsvetaeva's poetry, see Lev Loseff, 'Znachenie perenosa u Tsvetaevoy', in the forthcoming collection of articles from the International Symposium on Tsveaeva held in 1982 at Lausanne.
5. Donald Wesling, *The Chances of Rhyme* (Berkeley: The University of California Press, 1980), pp. 50–51.
6. On the traditions of exact and approximate rhyme in Russian see Barry P. Scherr, *Russian Poetry: Meter, Rhythm, and Rhyme* (Berkeley: The University of California Press, 1986), pp. 197–208.
7. A. L. Zhovtis, 'Russkaya rifma 1960–1970-x godov (zametki i razmyshleniya)' *Russkaya literatura*, 24, no. 3 (1981), 78–9.
8. Yu. I. Mineralov, 'Fonologicheskoe tozhdestvo v russkom yazyke i tipologiya russkoy rifmy', *Uchenye zapiski Tartuskogo gosudarstvennogo universiteta*, p. 396: *Studia metrica et poetica* 1 (1976), pp. 63–64, 67–76.
9. M. L. Gasparov, *Ocherk istorii russkogo stikha: Metrika, ritmika, rifma, strofika* (Moscow: Nauka, 1984), pp. 289–90.
10. Enrichment, of course, is not limited to modern poets; the first major study of the topic, written by Bryusov in 1928, was devoted to Pushkin: 'Levizna Pushkina v rifmakh', in Bryusov's *Sobranie sochineniy v semi tomakh*, vol. 7 (Moscow: Khudozhestvennaya literatura, 1975), pp. 148–63.
11. D. S. Samoylov, *Kniga o russkoy rifme*, 2nd edn. enl. (Moscow: Khudozhestvennaya literatura, 1982), p. 298.
12. This list is based on Samoylov, *Kniga*, p. 348.

13. Scherr, *Russian Poetry*, pp. 222–23.
14. Here and elsewhere I reserve the term approximate for rhymes that would not have been part of the nineteenth-century canon. Thus a feminine rhyme such as *beznadézhnoy / nézhno*, while not strictly speaking 'exact', would none the less have been regarded as acceptable by nearly all nineteenth-century poets.
15. Cf. the classifications given by Samoylov, *Kniga*, pp. 36–52.
16. Samoylov, *Kniga*, pp. 282–3.
17. W. K. Wimsatt, Jr. *The Verbal Icon: Studies in the Meaning of Poetry* (Lexington, Ky.: University of Kentucky Press, 1964), p. 164.
18. V. P. Grigor'ev, 'Paronimicheskaya attraktsiya v russkoy poezii XX v.', *Sbornik dokladov i soobshcheniy Lingvisticheskogo obshchestva Kalininskogo gosudarstvennogo universiteta*, 5 (1975), 131–64.
19. In a table accompanying an earlier article on Brodsky I mistakenly indicated that this poem is freely rhymed. See 'Strofika Brodskogo', in Lev Loseff (ed.) *Poetika Brodskogo* (Tenafly, NJ: Hermitage, 1986), p. 117.
20. *Slovar' drevney i novoy poezii* (St Petersburg: Tipografiya Imperatorskoy Rossiyskoy akademii, 1821), 2, pp. 364–66.
21. Zhirmunsky, *Kompozitsiya liricheskikh stikhotvoreniy*, in *Teoriya stikha* (Leningrad: Sovetskiy pisatel', 1975), p. 440.
22. Barbara Herrnstein Smith, *Poetic Closure: A Study of How Poems End* (Chicago: University of Chicago Press, 1968), p. 72.
23. Kiril Taranovsky, 'Some Problems of Enjambment in Slavic and Western European Verse', *International Journal of Slavic Linguistics and Poetics*, 7 (1963), 83–84.
24. G. S. Smith, 'Versifikatsiya v stikhotvorenii I. Brodskogo "Kellomyaki"', in Lev Loseff (ed.) *Poetika Brodskogo*, (Tenafly, NJ: Hermitage, 1986), pp. 144–8.
25. For an attempt to describe the use of what are essentially *dol'niki* in English verse, see James Bailey, 'Linguistic Givens and Their Metrical Realization in a Poem by Yeats', *Language and Style*, 8 (1975), no. 1, 21–33.
26. Note for instance the English translation of 'Polonez: variatsiya' (U 100–1) in *The New Yorker*, 21 September 1987, p. 40, where the rhyme scheme (including the alternation of masculine and feminine rhyme) and the enjambment of the original are closely followed.

11

An Interview With Bella Akhmadulina
Valentina Polukhina

VP Bella Akhatovna, it seems to me that you are one of the few Russian poets who does not suffer from a 'Brodsky complex'. How do you explain this apparent complex? Do you feel other poets suffer from it, or is it just my own fantasy?[1]

BA Valya, my dear, I don't quite understand what you mean. Do you think that some poets feel themselves somehow shrunken in stature before Brodsky, or are you talking of his influence?

VP I'm not talking about his influence in any positive way, nor how his stature and greatness is comprehended, but about how these poets all, without exception, somehow want to diminish his stature, to wound Brodsky personally.

BA Goodness! I don't know of any such poets.

VP I myself have personally met such poets, both here in the West and among those who have arrived from the Soviet Union.

BA I don't mix with such poets. Besides, Joseph is perfection.

VP How does his presence make itself felt?

BA I talked of this only yesterday on the BBC Russian Service, but I can repeat it. The presence of any great poet in the world creates a marked effect on human existence. Even among those who haven't yet read Brodsky . . . There are such who haven't read him. For suddenly, I myself can notice this very effect on the young poets I know. They bring their poems to me and I ask them 'so you've read a lot of Brodsky then?' and they answer 'But where can we get hold of him?' and I say 'But you've clearly read him'. His influence is just so noticeable, so widespread. I think that his presence has in some way influenced the development of minds and especially the methodology of versification among poets who are living in Russia.

VP Could you be more specific here, how exactly do you feel Brodsky influences their poems?
BA Well, among those poets I know, it is evident in their lines, rhythm, and intonation. They have read less Brodsky than myself, yet they so love Brodsky. It's as if he is something guessed of in advance. His influence reveals itself in a certain structure, it could be said in a structure of a line. Well, you know, it's as if Brodsky has a method, I don't really think of it as a method as such, more as a correlation of word with word, and a transition from one line to another. It simply didn't exist before in Russian versification.
VP But surely it has. Such a quality is detectable in Khlebnikov, Tsvetaeva . . .
BA But what I'm talking about I've only seen in Brodsky alone. This is a far stranger alignment of word with word, line with line . . . But in the end, the most important thing is Brodsky's perfection, a perfection of harmony. I'm talking now only about poetry, you understand. It is an absolute perfection, his words seem to be held in some sort of formula. If something is taken out or shifted then the whole thing collapses: the line, the formula, this whole universe falls apart. Nowadays Americans and English people tell me that Brodsky's English is itself his very own personal creation, his own unique and entirely personal form of English. And while we suffer in Russia Brodsky is elsewhere. I think that this has been useful to him. In other words he has none of the negative qualities of narrow mindedness, pettiness, parochialism. He is a world-wide phenomenon. Indeed, his sense of world culture, of language in general, it seems to me, reveals itself in his poetics.
VP As regards this, do you then think that he has derived something positive from his exile which is of use to Russian literature?
BA I have no doubt of it.
VP Even at the price of fifteen years of emotional torment, at the cost of his health?
VP I have no doubt about it, even at the cost of his own health. Let's touch wood. As to his life in Russia . . . It was for him . . . at the price of such suffering, of such terror. But even so, it is the noblest, purest path. But, of course, without a doubt, exile is far better than putting in an appearance at the Luzhniki stadium.
VP What do you think about the fact that Brodsky has to some extent been mythologising language, creating a solid ground for

himself in exile? I know that it distresses him deeply that he has been torn away from the living Russian language, and is therefore not able to follow its idiom.

BA Yes, indeed, his colloquialisms are very strange.

VP But then, Bella, isn't yours? Could you not say your everyday language is a little 'pre-Turgenev'?

BA My locutions and Joseph's are quite different. His are far simpler than mine, and therefore much closer to everyday Russian speech, even in its vulgarisms.

VP So do you then consider his fears to be ungrounded?

BA He has nothing to fear. If we're dealing with someone of such exceptional talent as Joseph and I don't compare him with anyone else; each person is entirely different, unique and alone. But in exceptional cases, as with Bunin, with Nabokov, then we are talking of people who have taken with them something that became . . . as if they procreate the Russian language inside themselves, and they succeed entirely. He doesn't need to hear Russian spoken around him, he himself becomes a force that is ripe. He himself is now the garden and the gardener. And he has taken with him something within himself so that he is no longer a victim of his own absence, of his separation from living speech. He becomes a rich soil for the Russian language to take root. I said this at some time to Nabokov. He asked me to reply 'Do you like my language?' and I answered 'Your Russian, it's the best', and he said 'But it seems to me that it is like frozen strawberries''.[2] And whatever fate does . . . Well, with such people what is fate? Here, they seem to coincide, one with the other. For that matter, he himself procreates the language.

VP Your opinion of Brodsky is so high. How would you defend him from those writers and critics who accuse Brodsky of coldness, that he has only written a few love poems, and that he looks down on the reader?

BA I have neither listened to, nor have I met such fools.

VP Do you think that he is a cold poet?

BA Goodness! No! How could that be said. He's written a great many poems about love. I've read every one that he's written.

VP So then, you think such criticism should be ignored and brushed aside?

BA Of course it should! How could such criticism have been made of him? Certainly, as must be the case, he stimulates all sorts

of attitudes from people, but why should we talk about complete fools?
VP Fair enough, but let me ask you, if I may, to defend Brodsky from one particular poet, who you know, Krivulin. He wrote two articles about Brodsky, and stated that when Brodsky appeared Anna Andreevna repeatedly said that a new blossoming had occurred in Russian poetry.
BA She was quite right.
VP But he goes on to state that now, Brodsky has matured, his presence in Russian poetry is evidence of its impasse, a 'condition of extended crisis', and not of blossoming.[3]
BA I didn't know that he set himself up as an arbitrator of poetry. Brodsky is, without doubt, the only proof of this blossoming in Russian poetry.
VP How would you explain the fact that, despite the long friendship that existed between Brodsky and Akhmatova, almost nothing of her style is reflected in the idiom of his? How is it that despite her great spiritual and cultural influence on him he is in fact closer stylistically to Khlebnikov and Tsvetaeva, than to her?
BA What is important here is this. We have in Brodsky one whose greatest feature in his innate ability to take on board the culture of the whole world. Taking into account the kind of education he had it is a personal triumph. It is Fate that has so prescribed . . . His correspondence is to the whole universe, to its cultural treasures, classical, Biblical, and more contemporary. It is indeed his very personal victory. He is the only person, who I know, who absorbs into himself everything that is the best. The poverty of life is not evident in his work. As to the influence of Anna Andreevna Akhmatova, there are two happy proofs: her perfection and the perfection of Brodsky. She immediately understood the nature of the miracle we now talk about. I believe, that stylistically, too, she has influenced him. But it would be a fruitless search to locate it and what would it prove anyway? This man borrows everywhere for himself. But the most important think of all is his ability to comprehend the essence of life, our debt to it.
VP But, alas, for a researcher of Brodsky's work, seeking to establish his Russian roots, we must try and arrive at something more concrete. As well as Krivulin, I would like to quote from Karabchievsky. In his book *The Resurrection of Mayakovsky*, he established a link between Mayakovsky and Tsvetaeva, which is

not difficult. But he also maintained that there is a link between Mayakovsky and Brodsky, insisting that Mayakovsky has been resurrected and is alive within Brodsky.[4] Perhaps we can say Karabchievsky has not read all of Brodsky?

BA I have read Karabchievsky's book, but I don't remember this bit. Besides, I think that even taking into account Mayakovsky's talent and his tragic fate, Mayakovsky and Brodsky strike me as being absolutely opposites, the antithesis of each other. Mayakovsky was a tragically unfulfilled man but Brodsky is tragically fulfilled. If they can be compared in any way it is only in their utter opposition to one another.

VP Bella, I would like to ask you about your own personal connection with Brodsky, with his poetry. Having recently read your poems very carefully I noticed that two particular themes appear to dominate in your work: a theme of time and that of language. The themes that are themselves most dominant in Brodsky's work. He sometimes speaks with time itself, addressing it in its 'pure form'. Is this thematic similarity between you both entirely coincidental?

BA My particular relationship to Brodsky can be described quite simply: uncritical. It's adoration. I myself have stated somewhere in connection with Akhmatova 'Of all calamities adoration is the worst'. An admirer can never expect his adoration to be returned. And I am sure, that Joseph . . I never think about myself when I think about him. And even when they said to me 'you know, what Brodsky thinks of you!' (Thumb downward). As he pleases. But it is my business to talk about him with thumbs up.

VP This is not true at all. I have spoken to him about you.

BA I have nothing but tenderness. And it's just as I stated only yesterday, that when I heard about the Nobel Prize . . . By the way I always knew that Brodsky would receive it. I only thought that I wouldn't live to see it. If we can call it the highest recognition as such, then I interpret it as a sort of personal triumph of my own. It coincides with my feeling of tenderness towards Brodsky, with my friendship with him, how I understand him. Such rejoicing! As if it were my own achievement. My happiness was that I had lived to see it. Whatever happens after that only one thing is important, his good health. Later all the specialists, many learned men will study his work in order to understand his contribution to Russian literature. I am sure that there will be much research done and much written about him. For me he is the confirmation that Russian poetry is alive and has not dried up.

VP All the same, I don't want to allow you to move off the question. So I put it to you more concretely. You have written a poem entitled 'The Butterfly', which has something in common with Brodsky's poem 'The Butterfly' not only in name, but also thematically.

BA Mine is far simpler. It was indeed the 16th October and there was really a butterfly trapped between the window panes. Probably it was proclaiming itself, but only despairingly. Even now I remember this actual butterfly, 'October, the sixteenth, Tuesday – And the day of resurrection of my butterfly'.[5]

VP What is most noticeable is that your butterfly and Brodsky's butterfly both raise common thoughts between you about life, death, existence and nonexistence.

BA Brodsky is closer to me than any contemporary writer or poet. As for his thoughts concerning life and death, they are quite remarkable. His perception of eternity is so very real that it is sad to read it, as though he touches non-existence.

VP Bella, I want to put to you one more question. It is a question concerning the future, but all the same I'll ask you now: Pushkin and Brodsky. For some it is a blasphemous comparison, for others an entirely real one.

BA But why should it be? In the first case, we all of us follow somehow in Pushkin's footsteps. Pushkin is what we are all about, and we all kneel before Pushkin . . . Perhaps Brodsky is the second coming of Pushkin. Perfection and perfection. In the second place, Brodsky less than anyone else is guilty before Pushkin. Before his harmony.

VP But this comparison is made still more complicated because behind all of you stand 'the magnificent seven': Blok, Khlebnikov, Mayakovsky, Mandelstam, Akhmatova, Tsvetaeva and Pasternak. They are still so close to you, that you turn towards them, whether you like it or not, you can feel their breath on your back. And here we compare one of you over their heads with Pushkin. Surely, a contemporary of Brodsky cannot accept such a comparison.

BA Why not? I can, because there is no poet at the moment who is better than Brodsky in the world.

VP Even including those who don't write in Russina?

BA Well, perhaps there are. I don't read much. In this sense they coincide.

VP Does it ever occur to you that the role of Pushkin falls on Brodsky not only by virtue of his talent and fate, but also by the very demands of the Russian language?

BA Could you make yourself a little clearer?

VP In the last seventy years of the Soviet state such changes have occurred in the Russian language that a poet was needed who could record all these changes in the most perfect poetic form and also endow his verse with the eternal problems of existence.

BA But clearly Pasternak and Akhmatova lived in this period. And they too preserved the Russian language.

VP But they didn't permit such democracy in their poetic language which we can observe as being the case in Brodsky. It's all there in his poetry.

BA It is a miracle. An absolute miracle. And indeed in this sense we can compare Brodsky with Pushkin. It is accepted that our poetic language begins with Pushkin. It's absolutely characteristic of Brodsky. His language is unprecedented, unheard of before. It's entirely his own discovery. In this sense he is fated to be a poet for a new age. Such a grandiloquent and at the same time colloquial style! It's simply remarkable! There is absolutely nothing like it. And everything is included in it. But I'm not a scholar . . . It seems to me, though, as if he is a completion of something and . . .

VP What you perhaps mean is that if for us he represents the pinnacle of Russian poetry, its highest point, for the future generation he will be a new point of departure. A new beginning of something.

BA I have no doubt that he will.

VP You have already spoken a little à propos his links with world and European culture. Do you consider him to be one of our most European poets?

BA Yes, certainly I do.

VP Even more European than Mandelstam?

BA But we must bear in mind when Mandelstam was born and when Brodsky was. His communion with the whole world, with world culture is something that was very true of Mandelstam also. We've already talked about this. It only goes to show of course, that it seems to be just one feature of genius.

VP Do you think that Brodsky's poetry would be different if he had remained living in Russia?

BA You know of course that hypothetical speculation is always

utterly fruitless. We can never know the answer to such a question. Would he have been able to survive there?
VP   I have asked him the very same question. Brodsky said that what would have happened to him personally, if he had remained in Russia is not an important question.⁶
BA   Fate also will not admit hypothetical speculations. But it seems to me that the tragedy of Brodsky's separation from Russia is not so much a personal tragedy for him as a tragedy for the people who live there. But all the same his poetry will remain. It will always exist. I think that Brodsky even in the geographical outcome that his fate has imposed on him can consider himself lucky. Everything has turned out for the best.
VP   'All will be as it should', said Woland to Margarita; 'that is how the world is made'. What is the essence of Brodsky's conflict with the Soviet state? Why is he so unacceptable to them?
BA   It's quite simple really, they perceive him differently. In what way is Brodsky at odds with the state? It is simply there is no . . . On the contrary . . . Well, generally a poet and the state can never get on. They have no particular reproaches against him. We must hope, though that he will be published there.⁷
VP   But the conflict still remains. What do you think is the real source of this conflict? Clearly none of Brodsky's other 'famous contemporaries' have and never have had such a conflict.
BA   It is and always will be the same conflict. As it was with Pushkin, so it is with Brodsky. At least, as far as my knowledge of the official opinion of the Soviet Union now goes, they have nothing against Brodsky. But all this so petty in comparison to Brodsky's talent. So why talk about it. It is not a question of the official view, but a comprehension of his talent. This kind of conflict always has existed and always will in Russia. How could it be otherwise? A poet is a poet, a state is a state. And no-one gains any satisfaction or comfort from this state of affairs.
VP   Fine, but returning to poetry. The fact is that Brodsky is separated from the Russian reader, and more importantly, Russian readers are separated from Brodsky . . .
BA   No, there is only one relevant point here and it is that Brodsky is distressed because of this separation. At any rate, Brodsky's poems are the best we have now in Russian poetry.
VP   Yes, but his poetry is not accessible to the majority of Russian readers.
BA   Yes, true, it is not accessible. But we cannot have everything

at once. If we already have a great Russian poet in the world we can't be capricious and demand that all must be as it should. Yes, we can't read him now, but we will eventually be able to.

VP   I really wonder, though, if Soviet readers are ready to understand Brodsky's poetry.

BA   They are ready, quite ready.

VP   But do you really think that if all his work were to be published tomorrow he would be popular?

BA   You couldn't get your hands on a copy for a start!

VP   Is this perhaps because he was banned.

BA   That's not the point.

VP   But clearly he is a difficult poet to understand.

BA   Difficult, yes, but there are a large number of people in Russia who can think, you couldn't get your hands on it. Despite the complexity of his poetry he has plenty of admirers. I see this from the historical perspective: we can't read him today, but we can read him tomorrow. What's the difference?

VP   But you and I, we have already read him.

BA   And if Brodsky is going to or hopes to return, and . . .

VP   Do you think he will return?

BA   I don't know, you should ask him.

VP   Since he has already answered this question during one of his interviews I can quote him. He said that he would return to Russia on one condition only, that everything he has written be published there.[8]

BA   Well then, in reality that means never. Fate cannot accept a change twice. But if he wants to visit . . . It makes me weak all over to think of it, his appearing in Leningrad.

VP   How would he be received there?

BA   With devotion, adoration. With utter adoration.

VP   There is still one more theme which I would like to discuss. One in fact of importance to Brodsky. He seems to think that we are standing at the threshold of a post-Christian era if indeed we have not already crossed into it. This is something which he has expressed fully in his poem 'A Halt in the Wilderness' which was written in 1966, and more recently in his play 'The Marbles'. Could you comment on this theme. Are his fears justified? Does this idea of the end disturb you?

BA   Yes, indeed, Brodsky has expressed this idea very strongly. I think, that if everything has died for a certain period then it will be reborn once again, so it will exist. There are no other possibilities.

Unless of course everything turns to dust. Because it is harmony, and harmony is such that it can never be destroyed by artificial powers. It can be disturbed, frustrated, but destroyed forever? That is impossible. Incidentally, Brodsky's poems are . . . I don't know what to call it, thoughts about God? A poet always address himself only to God, the rest . . .

VP In this sense then, do you agree with the idea that a poet can never in reality be an unbeliever?

BA Yes, I do. Returning to Pushkin, we can say that he was an atheist. And he suffered for it. But who conformed to the traits of Christian behaviour and ethics more than Pushkin? His goodness, pity for others . . .

VP Do you think then that the term 'Christian' poet is a redundant one?

BA Yes. The gift is the grace of God. It may coincide with a religious idea, but it's undoubtedly so.

VP Bella, could you say a little about yourself? What is the very thing which you cannot help but write about in your poetry?

BA Well, what is there to say? You've read my books, you know me well enough. I can only say that in all these years I have been able to help those who live in Russia. They needed me. Look, Brodsky is elsewhere, but I am there, on the spot. I managed in some way to comfort them. Brodsky is superior to me, but he is a long way away.

VP Bella, this is just your innate modesty. But let me now tell you this from my conversation with Brodsky, so as to prove to you that the gesture which someone showed to you does not have any justification with what he said about you. He said that Bella is one of the few Russian poets living in Russia who by some miracle has succeeded in preserving her purity, conscience and independence. That is, that you have not turned towards compromise, like several others, that you have resisted the temptation of topicality to which so many others have succumbed.[9] How have you succeeded?

BA Well, that means something is lacking in those people. I always, when talking about Brodsky, repeat that fortunately for him there were no petty and vulger temptations offered to him, such huge audiences and stadiums. And I had all this. How did I succeed . . . Well, I think a person has some sort of star watching over him. Without doubt something or someone looks after us from on high. But you must also carefully guard yourself. Sometimes I suddenly hear a voice saying 'Do this' or 'Don't do that!'

and I listen to it. And somehow a pardon is granted to me. And I can then write. But this guardian is not enough. We must still look out for ourselves, examine our conscience. But let us not forget, let's not comfort ourselves that everything is ordained. Although this is the case. That's it I think.

VP Thank you very much.

Notes

1. Bella Akhmadulina was in London for two weeks with the Mayakovsky Threatre. She gave two poetry readings together with an Armenian poet Gevorg Amin at the Littleton Theatre on the 29 and 30 October 1987. The interview took place at the West Morland Hotel where she was staying with her husband, the artist, Boris Messerer on 31 October 1987.
2. Akhmadulina visited Vladimir Nabokov in Switzerland in March 1977. She had written to him from Paris where she was staying at the time with Vladimir Vysotsky and Marina Vladi as their guest. Nabokov had replied and allowed her to go and see him. He was already very weak, almost transparent, as Akhmadulina put it. The audience lasted about fifty minutes. She told me about this meeting in great detail during her previous visit to England in April 1977.
3. Krivulin's articles were published in the West under the psuedonim Aleksandr Kalomirov: 'Iosif Brodskii (Mesto)', *Vestnik Russkogo Khristianskogo Dvizheniya* (Paris, 1977), pp. 140–50; Reprinted in *Poetika Brodskogo*, L. Loseff (ed.)(Tenafly: Hermitage, 1986), pp. 219–29; 'Dvadtsat' let Noveishei russkoi poezii', *Russkaya Mysl'*, December 1985' 'Literaturnoe prilozhenie', No. 2, pp. VI–VII.
4. Yuri Karabchievsky, *Voskresinie Mayakovskogo* (Munchen: Strana i mir, 1985), pp. 272–9.
5. B. Akhmadulina, *Taina* (Moskva: Sovetskii pisatel', 1983), pp. 88–9.
6. Brodsky interviewed by the present author, April 1980, Ann Arbor, unpublished.
7. Since this interview some of Brodsky's poems have been published in *Novy Mir*, No. 12, 1987, pp. 160–8; in *Neva*, No. 3, 1988, pp. 106–9; in *Ogoniok*, No. 31, 1988, pp. 28–9; in *Literaturnoye Obozreniye*, No. 8, 1988, pp. 55–64.
8. Brodsky interviewed by D. Savitsky, January 1983, New York, *Emois*, 10, April 1988, pp. 62–3.
9. From a private conversation with Brodsky, April 1980, Ann Arbor.

Translated by James Lipsett

Index

INDEX TO WORKS BY BRODSKY DISCUSSED OR NOTED IN THE TEXT; TITLES IN RUSSIAN

'*Anno Domini*', 179, 186

'Babochka', 17, 23, 24–7, 199
'Biust Tiberiya', 89, 90
'Bol'shaya elegiya Dzhonu Donnu', 35, 95
'Byl chernyi nebosvod', 16, 24
'Chast' rechi, 84n.12
'*Chast' rechi*', 179, 180, 186, 188, 190

'Dekabr' vo Florentsii', 65, 71–3, 81, 183
'Dvadtsat' sonetov k Marii Stiuart', 53n.8, 71–4, 98–123, 164

'Ekloga 5-ya: letniaya', 183
'Ekloga 4-ya: zimniaya', 96–7, 169
'Elegiya', 189
'Eto – ryad nablyudeniy', 181

'Fontan', 183

'Gorbunov i Gorchakov', 67–8, 183
'Gorenie', 172n.8
'Gost'', 164

'Kellomiaki', 188
'K Evgeniyu', 182
'Kolybel'naya Treskovogo mysa', 30n.23, 80, 92, 96, 157, 164, 187
'Konets prekrasnoi epokhi', 34, 47, 51–2, 53n.2
'*Konets prekrasnoi epokhi*', 53n.2, 53n.6
'K Uranii', 96

'Laguna', 70

Mramor, 16, 29n.14, 89, 173n.13, n.21, 202
'Mukha', 184, 187

'Na smert' Zhukova', 71, 74–6, 81
'Natiurmort', 14, 17–24, 31n.27, 31n.32, 44
'Niotkuda s lyubov'yu', 181
'Novye stansy k Avguste', 59–60
'*Novye stansy k Avguste*', 110

'Odissei Telemaku', 58, 65
'Ostanovka v pustyne', 34, 38–41, 48, 53n.2, 106, 202
'Otkazom ot skorbnogo perechnia', 151

'Pamiati T.B.', 29n.15, 54n.15
'Pesnia nevinnosti, ona zhe opyta', 58
'Pis'ma rimskomu drugu', 58, 63–4
'Pis'mo generalu Z', 34, 46–50, 53n.2
'Pochti elegiya', 103
'Poet i proza', 33n.45
'Pokhorony Bobo', 58, 71
'Polden' v komnate', 124–133, 169
'Polonez: variatsiya', 193n.26
'*Post aetatem nostram*', 53n.6, 62, 90
'Posviashchaetsia Yalte', 17
'Proshchai, madmuazel' Veronika', 47–8, 54n.20
'Puteshestviye v Stambul', 54n.12, 135–149
'Pyataya godovshchina', 183

'Razgovor s nebozhitelem', 78–9
'Razvivaya Platona', 78–9, 81
'Rech o prolitom moloke', 34,

41–5, 52, 53n.2, n.3, 54n.20, 183
'Rimskie elegii', 80, 89, 91–5
'Rozhdestvo', 39

'Sad', 15
'Sadovnik v vatnike', 58
'Shestviye', 52, 58, 68–9
'Sidia v teni', 172n.8
'Sreten'ye', 39, 58, 68–9
'Stikhi na smert' T.S.Eliota', 35, 147
Stikhotvoreniya i poemy, 55n.31
'Strofy', 172n.8

'Temza v Chelsi', 94
'Tors', 90
'Ty uznaesh menya po pocherku', 185

Uraniya, 97n.1, n.8, 114n.10, 183
'Uznayu etot veter', 181

'Velikiy Gektor', 106
'V okrestnostiakh Aleksandrii', 134n.2
'V ozernom krayu', 58, 66–7

'Ya vkhodil vmesto dikogo zveria', 80

'Zhizn' v rasseyannom svete', 179, 185

'1 Janvaria 1965 goda', 78–9, 81
'1972 god', 57, 67, 69, 70, 81, 112, 164, 187

INDEX TO WORKS BY BRODSKY DISCUSSED OR NOTED IN THE TEXT; TITLES IN ENGLISH TRANSLATION

'Adieu, Mademoiselle Véronique', 47–8, 54n.20
'Almost an Elegy', 103
'Anno Domini', 178, 186

'Black night sky . . . , The', 16, 24
'Burning', 172n.8
'Bust of Tiberius, The', 80, 90
'Butterfly, The', 17, 23, 24–7, 199

'Catastrophes in the Air', 13, 28n.3
'Child of Civilization, The', 13, 29n.16
'Christmas', 39
'Condition We Call Exile', 84n.4
'Conversation with an Angel', 78–9

'December in Florence', 65, 71–3, 81, 183

'Elaborating Plato', 76–8, 81
'Eclogue IV: Winter', 96–7, 169
'Eclogue V: Summer', 183
'Elegy', 189

End of a Beautiful Epoch, The, 53n.2, n.6
'End of the Belle Epoque, The', 34, 47, 51–2, 53n.2

'Fifth Anniversary, The', 183
'Flight from Bysantium', 54n.12, 135–149
'Fly, The', 184, 187
'Fountain, The', 183
'From Nowhere with Love', 181
'Funeral of Bobo, The', 58, 71

'Garden, The', 15
'Gorbunov and Gorchakov', 67–8, 183
'Great Elegy to John Donne, The', 35, 95
'Great Hector, The', 106
'Guest, A', 164
'Guide to a Renamed City, A', 126

'Homage to Yalta', 17

'In a Room and a Half', 127
'In the Lake District', 58, 66–7

Index

'I recognize this wind', 181

'Kellomäki', 188

'Lagoon', 79
Less Than One, 15, 25, 28n.3, 84n.2, 113n.5, 148n.1
'Letter in a Bottle, A', 34, 36–9, 53n.2, 60–2
'Letter to the General Z, A', 34, 46–50, 53n.2
'Letters to a Roman Friend', 58, 63–4
'Life in the Diffused Light', 179, 185
'Lullaby of Cape Cod', 30n.23, 80, 92, 96, 157, 164, 187

Marbrls, 16, 29n.14, 89, 92, 173n.13, n.21, 202
'May 24, 1980', 80
'Midday in the Room', 124–133, 169

'Nature Morte', 14, 17–24, 31n.27, n.32, 44
'Near Alexandria', 134n.2
'New Stanzas to Augusta', 59–60
New Stanzas to Augusta, 110
'Nunc Dimittis', 39, 58, 68–9

'Odysseus to Telemachus', 58, 65
'On the Death of Zhukov', 71, 74–6, 81
'Part of Speech, A', 179, 180, 186, 188, 190
Part of Speech, A, 84n.5, n.12, 87n.37, 173n.12
'Poet and Prose', 33n.45
'Polonaise: A Variation', 193n.26
'Power of the Element, The', 28n.3

'*Post aetatem nostram*', 53n.6, 62, 90
'Procession, The', 52, 58, 68–9

'Quilt-jacketed, a tree-surgent', 58

'Refusing to catalogue all of one's woes', 151
'Roman Elegies', 80, 89, 91–5

Short and Long Poems, 55n.31
'Sitting in the Shadow', 172n.8
'Song of Innocence and Experience', 58
'Speech on Spilt Milk, A', 34, 41–5, 52, 53n.2, n.3, 54n.20, 183
Stop in the Desert, A, 53n.2, 106
'Strophes', 172n.8

'Thames at Chelsea, The', 94
'This is a series of observations', 181
'Torso', 90
'To Eugeny', 182
'To Please a Shadow', 113n.5
'To the Memory of T.B.', 29n.15, 54n.15
'To Urania', 96
To Urania, 97n.1, n.8, 114n.10, 183
'Twenty Sonnets to Mary Stuart', 53n.8, 71, 73–4, 98–123, 164

'Verses on the Death of T.S. Eliot', 35, 147

'You recognize me', 185

'1 January 1965', 78–9, 81
'1972', 57, 67, 69–70, 81, 112, 164, 187

GENERAL INDEX

Acmeism, 14, 17, 33n.46
Acmeist, 16, 17, 29n.10
Adorno, Th.W., 9

aesthetics, 4, 5, 96
affinity, 12–13, 152, 167, 189
allegory, 31n.36, 46

allusion, 102, 105, 111
Akhmadulina, B.A., 51, 194–204
Akhmatova, A.A., 1, 2, 50, 80, 87n.36, 92, 102, 105, 131, 149n.17, 156, 172n.9, 188–9, 197–200
Amin, Gevorg, 204n.1
analogy, 32n.39, 138, 141, 150, 152–8, 160, 163, 165–6, 171
anagram, 41, 54n.10
anaphora, 126
Apraksin, F.M., Admiral, 84n.8
Archimedes, 38
Aristotle, 163
Arnold, Matthew, 5
Arutiunova, N.D., 156, 172n.10
Auden, W.H., 1, 11, 41, 103, 134n.3, n.4, 173n.18
Augustus, 145
avant-garde, 35
Averintsev, S.S., 149n.4, n.19

Bailey, James, 193n.25
Bakhtin, M., 105
Bal'mont, K., 106
Bal'zak, Honoré, de, 8
Baratynsky, E., 3
baroque, 35
Baskina, M.A., 172n.1
Baudelaire, C., 103
Beatles, The, 36
Beckett, S., 98
Bennefoy, Y., 114
Berdiaev, N., 43
Bezrodny, M.V., 149n.7
Birkert, S., 115
Blok, A., 22, 45, 50, 54n.16, 55n.29, 102, 183, 199
Bloom, Harold, 13, 28n.4
Bothwell, Earl of, 113n.6
Boyle, Robert, 38
Brezhnev, L.I., 46, 48, 51
Brodsky, Joseph, *passim*
Brodsky, N.L., 172n.3
Briusov, V., 192n.10
Brown, C., 29n.10
Buddhism, 43
Bulgakov, S., 42–3, 54n.14
Bunin, I., 196

Burnett, L., 12, 28n.9, 29n.15, 31n.33, 32n.39
Buttafava, Giovanni, 84n.1
Byron, Lord G., 84n.6, 110

caesura, 176, 184
Catullus, Gaius Valerius, 33, 93
Carrol, Lewis, 163
Chaadaev, Piotr, 140, 146–7
Christ, 22, 93, 96–7, 158, 163
Chuang Chou, 31n.37
conceit, 25, 37
Conrad, J., 83
copula, 148

Danilevsky, A.A., 149n.7
Dante, A., 10, 19, 65, 71–3, 81, 86n.24, 100, 102, 144
Darius, 138
Darwin, C., 38
Derzhavin, G., 76, 86n.28, n.30
Dickens, Ch., 7, 8
Dido, 110, 138
Dietrich, Marlene, 111
distich, 138
dol'nik, 178, 188–9, 193n.25
Donne, John, 12, 35, 95, 106
Dostoevsky, F., 7, 8, 28n.3, 142
Dyakov, V.I., 172n.3

Eastern Orthodox Christianity, 50
echo, 13, 25, 30n, 23, 86n.28, 87n.36, 105, 127, 131, 136, 188
Edison, Thomas, 38
Eikhenbaum, B., 172n.9, 192n.2
Einstein, Albert, 38
Elizabeth I, Queen, 71, 74, 103
English, Maurice, 65, 72–3
enjambment, 176–7, 181, 185–92
Epelbouin, Annie, 95
epithet, 16, 25, 55n.29, 105
ephebe, 13, 17, 28n.4
Eriomin, Mikhail, 172n.4
Esenin, S., 42, 54n.13, 182
Eliot, S.T., 35, 54n.27, 95, 103, 112, 147, 156
Etkind, E., 29n.17
Evtushenko, E., 51, 178

Faraday, Michael, 38
Feuerbach, L., 38
Fisher, Roy, 173n.12
Flaubert, G., 29n.10, 98
Florensky, P., 54n.24
Flynn, Erroll, 38
Ford, John, 99
France, Peter, 29n.10, 98
Freud, Z., 38
Froelich, C., 111
Frost, R., 1
Froude, J.A., 110

Gasparov, M.L., 178, 192n.9
Genette, Gérard, 172n.1
Gibbon, L.G., 110
Girey, 41
Goethe, J.W., von, 83, 164
Gogol', N.V., 172n.3
Gorbachev, M.S., 140
Graham, A.C., 32n.37
Grigor'ev, V.P., 193n.18
Grigoryeva, A.D., 172n.1
Grupinsky, Rafal, 149n.10
Gumilev, N.S., 28n.10, 29n.10, 32n.42, 36, 50, 53n.6, 54n.26

Hannibal, 75
Harris, J.G., 27n.2
Hecht, Anthony, 70
Hegel, G.W.F., 26, 33n.49
Hermans, T., 28n.9, 29n.15, 31n.33, 32n.39
Hitler, A., 8
Hobbes, Th., 36
Hoffmann, E.T.A., 103
Horace, Gregory, 32n.38
Horace (Horatius), Quintus Flaccus, 84n.12
hyperbole, 42, 165

iamb, 18, 107–8, 178–9
idiolect, 54n.23
idiostyle, 16
irony, 45, 103, 112, 137, 140
Isaak, 110
Isenberg, C., 29n.10, n.16
Ivan the Terrible, 74
Ivanov, Vyacheslav, 106

Johnson, Samuel, 110
Jones, Chris, 97

Kafka, F., 142
Kalomirov, A., 75, 86n.29, 204n.3
Kant, I., 38
Karabchievsky, Yu., 197–8, 204n.4
Kepler, J., 38
Kerényi, 29n.15
Khlebnikov, V., 170, 183, 195, 197, 199
Khodasevich, V., 135, 140
Kline, G.L., 56, 72–3
Knox, Jane, 56
Knox, John, 111
Kreps, M., 29n.17, 78, 84n.10, 86n.28
Krivulin, V., 197, 204n.3
Krudener, Baroness, 102
Kushner, A., 95, 97n.5, 178
Kuzmina, N.A., 172n.9

Lapeza, David, 29n.10
Leander, Zarah, 111, 113
Lenin, V.I., 8, 126
Leontiev, K., 138
Lindberg, Ch.A., 37
Lipset, James, 204
Livshitz, B., 36
Lochhead, Liz, 112
Lomonosov, M., 35, 185
Loseff, L., 29n.17, 34, 62, 70–1, 74, 78, 84n.3, n.12, 172n.9, 173n.12, 192n.4, 173n.12, 192n.4, 193n.19, 204n.3
Lotman, Yu.M., 139, 149n.5
Lowell, Robert, 95

McDuff, David, 173n.12
McMillin, A.B., 29n.17
Malevich, Kazimir, 93, 96
Mallarmé, S., 31n.31
Mamardashvili, M., 173n.20
Mandelstam, N., 145, 149n.16
Mandelstam, O., 1, 9, 12–33, 45, 95–6, 103, 136–7, 149n.11, n.20, 170, 199–200
Manet, E., 100–101
Mao Tse-tung, 8

Marconi, G.M., 36–7
Mariotte, E., 38
Martial (Martialus) Marcus
    Valerius, 63–4, 84n.12, 90–1
Marvell, A., 105
Marxist political economy, 41
Mary Stuart (Mary Queen of
    Scots), 12, 28n.6, 30n.23, 59,
    71, 98–123
Mayakovsky, V.V., 35, 192n.3,
    197–9
Meares, B., 28n.3
Melville, H., 8
Mendel, G.J., 38
Messerer, B., 204n.1
metaphor, 17, 28n.6, 29n.10, 31–9,
    47, 50–2, 53n.9, 103, 128, 140,
    142, 156, 163, 165, 167, 170,
    173n.12, n.16
metaphysical poetry/poetics, 35
metaphysicals, 12, 25
metonymy, 19, 26, 42, 105, 130,
    140, 142, 156–8, 160, 165–6,
    169, 173n.12
meter, 103, 154, 173n.12, 178
Miller, Jane, 55, 149
Milosz, Czeslaw, 54n.27
Mineralov, Yu.I., 192n.8
Mints, Z.G., 149n.7
Montale, E., 6
Mozart, W.A., 99, 102
Musil, R.E. von, 8
Myers, Alan, 83, 113, 135, 173n.13

Nabokov, V., 98, 196, 204n.2
Naiman, A., 84n.5
Nalbantian, S., 31n.36
Napoleon, Bonaparte, 86n.29, 163
Nekrasova, E.A., 172n.9
neologism, 29n.18, 105
Newton, A., 38
Nikitin, Afanasy, 141
Nilsson, N.A., 32n.42
Nivat, Georges, 89
Novalis, 10

Okudzhava, B., 51
Ostolopov, N., 185–6
Ovid (Ovidius), Publius Naso, 23,
    25, 33n.50, 83, 84n.12, 90
oxymoron, 22, 165

Pasternak, B.L., 35, 78, 84n.6,
    95–6, 136, 199–200
Paul I, Tsar, 86n.28
Peter the Great, 138
Persephone, 13, 17, 20, 24, 29n.15,
    30n.25
personification, 129, 167, 171
Petrarch, F., 106–8
Piatigorsky, A., 173n.20
Plato, 76
Platonov, A., 53n.4
Pliny the Elder, 64
Pliny the Younger, 64
Plotinus, 10
Poe, E., 32n.39
poetics, 9, 89, 150
Polukhina, V., 29n.17, 53n.9, 113,
    150, 194
Pompey, 75
Pope, A., 98
Proffer, Carl, 172n.3
Propertius, Sextus, 93
Proust, M., 8
pun, 41, 49, 98, 113
Pushkin, A.S., 13, 23, 32n.39,
    54n.18, 101–2, 106, 112, 136,
    143, 164, 186, 192n.10,
    199–201, 203

Rabelais, F., 38, 84n.9
Racine, J., 103
Radishchev, A., 136
rhyme, 11, 18, 36, 41, 86n.26, 99,
    103, 106–7, 113–14, 140, 154,
    170, 176–93
    approximate, 178, 180–4, 191
    compound, 83, 181–2, 185
    dactylic, 81, 83, 184
    homonym, 183
    feminine, 81, 107, 180, 184, 191,
        193
    internal, 176
    masculine, 81, 107, 180–1,
        183–4, 190–1
    pre-tonic, 178, 180–1, 185
    triple, 81–3, 184

reification, 167, 171
Rilke, Rainer Maria, 3
Ronen, O., 36, 106–7
Ronsard, P. de, 108

Saadi, 54n.15
Saint-Exupéry, Antoine de, 47
Saint Francis, 38
Samoylov, D.S., 192n.11, 193n.15, n.16
Sappho, 102
Savel'eva, Judge, 87n.32
Savitsky, D., 204n.8
Scherr, B.P., 178
Shiller, F. von, 102, 109, 111–13
Shaftesbury, A.C., Earl of, 10
Shakespeare, W., 38, 106, 108
Shalamov, V., 52
Shelley, P.B., 150
Sheridan, Alan, 172n.1
simile, 25, 150–75
Siniavsky, A.D., 81, 83
Siva, 100
Skvorecky, J., 83
Slutsky, B., 178
Smith, Barbara, 31n.32, 193n.22
Smith, G.S., 124, 188, 193n.24
Socrates, 146
Solovyov, V., 41, 45, 50, 54n.11, n.25
Solzhenitsyn, A., 52, 83
Stalin, J., 8, 9, 39, 104
Stendhal, 7, 8
Stern, L., 8
Stevens, W. 172n.4
Strand, Mark, 9
subtext, 13, 25, 28n.6, 32n.39
Suslov, M.A., 138
Suvorov, A., General, 76, 86n.28
symbol, 39, 50, 91, 143
Symbolism, 29n.10, 96
Symbolists, 17, 25, 30n.20

Tamerlane, 138
Taranovsky, K., 27n.1, 30n.22, 32n.39, 33n.46, 186, 193n.23
Tarkovsky, A., 178
Terras, V., 27n.1

terza rima, 81
Tessera, 13–14, 20, 28n.6
Tiberius, 138
Tiutchev, F., 28n.6, 102
Tolstoy, L., 38
Toporov, V.N., 149n.14
Toropygin, V.V., 35
transformation, 22, 25, 128, 159, 167, 168, 173n.16
Trediakovsky, V.K., 35
Tsiolkovsky, 135
Tsvetaeva, M.I., 1, 33n.45, 35–6, 53n.4, 87n.31, 133, 173n.18, 176–7, 192n.4, 195, 197, 199
Turgenev, I.S., 30n.23, 31n.34, 172n.3, 196

Ulysses, 110

Vasmer, M., 32n.40
Veidle, V., 54n.26
Venclova, Tomas, 54n.12, 130, 135
Vinogradov, V.V., 154, 172n.5, n.6
Virgil (Vergilius) Publius Maro, 97, 145, 147
Vladi, Marina, 204n.2
Voznesensky, A., 51, 178
Vyazemsky, P.A., 149n.18
Vysotsky, V., 204n.2

Wesling, Donald, 192n.5
Wilbur, Richard, 76, 188–190
Wimsatt, W.K., 182, 193n.17

Yeats, W.B., 135–6, 193n.25

zastoi, 51
Zeman, Karel, 36
Zhirmunsky, V., 176, 186, 192n.1, 193n.21
Zholkovsky, A., 102, 104, 113n.3
Zhovtis, A.L., 192n.7
Zhukov, G., Marshal, 59, 71, 74–6, 86n.28
Zhukovsky, V.A., 31n.36, 78
Zoshchenko, M., 136